BHUTAN *TO* BLACKTOWN

OM DHUNGEL arrived in Australia as a student in 1998 before being granted a refugee visa in light of the Bhutanese government's persecution of the ethnic Nepali of southern Bhutan. As inaugural president of the Association of Bhutanese in Australia, Om played a critical role in the settlement of 5000 Bhutanese refugees in Australia. Before coming to Australia he was a senior civil servant in Bhutan's Department of Telecommunications, then, while a refugee in Nepal, general secretary of the Human Rights Organisation of Bhutan and co-editor of *The Bhutan Review*. In Australia he worked for ten years as a senior business analyst at Telstra, and today sits on the NSW Ministry of Health Advisory Committee, the NSW Police Multicultural Advisory Council and the Blacktown Multicultural Advisory Committee. He runs Om Dhungel Consulting.

JAMES BUTTON is a former journalist and Europe correspondent for *The Age* and *Sydney Morning Herald*. He is the author of *Speechless: A year in my father's business* and *Comeback: The fall and rise of Geelong*, and has won three Walkley awards and a Melbourne Press Club Quill for feature writing. He is a freelance writer and editor.

'Om Dhungel's journey of the heart and soul, from the fields of southern Bhutan to the streets of Blacktown, Sydney, is a journey from which we can all learn, regardless of our origins.'

Michael Hutt, Professor of Nepali and Himalayan Studies, School of Oriental and African Studies, University of London

'Bhutan to Blacktown is a riveting and deeply personal account of Om's journey, where he tells his readers "What I learnt as a refugee ... has shaped my life ever since". Om has utilised his astonishing experiences and considerable skills and attributes into becoming a power for good, elevating the strengths and resilience of individuals and communities. He has dedicated his time as an impactful leader for the Bhutanese and broader diverse communities in Western Sydney. He is inspirational and a change-maker.'

Violet Roumeliotis AM, CEO of Settlement Services International

'A beautifully written memoir, which integrates deeply moving personal reflections on Om's remarkable life and journey from Bhutan to Australia with practical suggestions on how Australia can best unlock the skills and energies of its refugee communities.'

Daniel Ghezelbash, Deputy Director, Kaldor Centre for International Refugee Law, UNSW

'Om's optimism and tenacity helped him travel the harrowing path of a stateless person to build a new life for himself and his community. By telling his inspirational story and shedding light on the resettlement experience of Bhutanese refugees in Australia, Om brings the issue of refugees and the conditions for their successful integration in their new countries to a wider audience.'

Bhim Subba, author of *Himalayan waters* and former Director General of the Department of Power in the Government of Bhutan

'Om has devoted his life to serving others – his old homeland Bhutan, his fellow refugees and other migrants, and his new homeland Australia. He has refused to be defined or embittered by Bhutan's tragic legacy of ethnic cleansing and has shown extraordinary resilience in the face of state violence and the global scattering of his family, friends and compatriots. He is a powerful and humane voice for innovative community-led resettlement and solidarity among all Australians.'

Ben Saul, Challis Chair of International Law, University of Sydney

'Om Dhungel's resilience, generosity and humanity shine through this powerful book. It is at once a remarkable story of individual achievement and a considered reflection on the broader policies and practices that shape refugees' experiences. Om's deep and abiding commitment to his community helped thousands of Bhutanese people find safety in Australia: in his words, "a home, a home for all of us".'

Jane McAdam, Director, Kaldor Centre for International Refugee Law, UNSW

BHUTAN *TO* BLACKTOWN

Losing everything and finding Australia

OM DHUNGEL *with* **JAMES BUTTON**

NEWSOUTH

A NewSouth book

Published by
NewSouth Publishing
University of New South Wales Press Ltd
University of New South Wales
Sydney NSW 2052
AUSTRALIA
https://unsw.press/

A catalogue record for this
book is available from the
National Library of Australia

ISBN   9781742237893 (paperback)
         9781742238692 (ebook)
         9781742239637 (ePDF)

Internal design Josephine Pajor-Markus
Cover design Mika Tabata
Cover images: Front cover photo by Mridula Amin; back cover
    photo shows Om Dhungel (rear centre), Smriti, in pink pullover
    being held by her aunt Padma, and Saroja (far left) and family in
    Lamidara, Bhutan, 1990
Printer Griffin Press

This book is printed on paper using fibre supplied from plantation or
sustainably managed forests.

FOREWORD

When I first met Om Dhungel, I was struck by his warmth, his positivity, his energy, and his generosity of spirit. And although he was still in his thirties, he came across as someone who had already amassed a few lifetimes of experience. As you read his extraordinary story, it will become clear why.

It's the story of one man who has come through adversity to make a difference. It's a story about possibility and new beginnings. Above all, it's a love story about family and community, and the power of the human spirit that holds everything together.

While there is nothing to celebrate about the circumstances under which Om had to leave his homeland, the one positive is that he chose us. Thanks to that choice, what you hold in your hands is a great Australian story.

The Hon Anthony Albanese MP
Prime Minister of Australia

CONTENTS

CHINA
(TIBET
AUTONOMOUS
REGION)

New Delhi

NEPAL

Kathmandu

INDIA

NEPAL

Beldangi

Pathri

Kakarbhitta

Maidhar

Surunga

Birtamod

Charpane

MORANG

JHAPA

INDIA

0   10
km

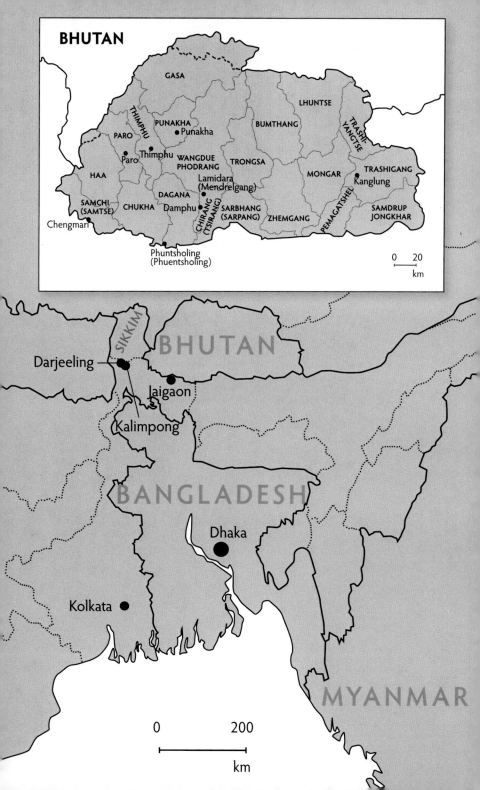

A NOTE ON
NEPALI NAMES

How people from Bhutan and Nepal address each other in the Nepali language presents a problem to anyone writing a book in English. At birth everyone in our culture is given a first and second name, but in the main we use these names only in formal settings, such as filling out a census or enrolling in school. In conversation we rarely use them.

Instead, we identify each other in two ways. We either use a term that denotes the order in which we were born – Jetho, Mailo, Sailo, Kancho (first, second, third, youngest and so on) for boys, and Jethi, Maili, Saili and Kanchi for girls – or through a term that indicates our relationship to the other person.

For example, my eldest sister is named Bhagiratha. But I would never call her that, it would sound rude. I call her Thul Didi, meaning eldest sister. If I talk to or about her by name, I always add the relational word at the end – Bhagiratha Didi – but even this form is rare when speaking to or about an older person.

Similarly, Dr Om Dhungyel, discussed often in this book, is technically my cousin since our fathers are brothers, but there is no word for cousin in Nepali, so I call him Daju, meaning older brother, and he calls me Bhai, meaning younger brother.

Some of these terms can get quite precise: for example, my niece Mona calls me Om Bada, meaning an uncle who is older than her father. Om Daju's wife, Pabitra, I call Bhauju, meaning sister-in-law married to an older brother. This custom emerges from a culture in which the relationships between people and the need to respect them are of utmost importance.

The problem is that use of these terms in this book would confuse English-speaking readers. Which Daju is that? Which Kaki (aunty), which Bhai? So, instead, we have mostly used people's given names.

The book contains a few exceptions to this rule. One is Om Daju, whom I consistently call Daju, to mark him out from me. Another is the use of Baba or Baa (Dad), and Ama (Mum) to denote both my parents and those of my wife, Saroja. In the writing we have tried to make clear at each point which Baba and Ama we are talking about.

It feels strange and even uncomfortable for me to use a given name to identify people such as my late sister, Yoga, when I always called her Saili, the third daughter born to my parents, but I have done so for clarity. I hope Nepali-speaking readers will understand and forgive.

AN AUSTRALIAN
BY ACCIDENT

I click on a link on my computer, and one by one, faces appear. 'Hi Nalika! ... Sarjoh, I think you're on mute.' Here's Haroun, here's Maryam. Lazarus doesn't have access to a laptop so he phones in, his line often dropping out. Others come a little late – either they are struggling to work out this new thing called Zoom, or it's Friday night at dinnertime, and people have to be fed.

Not just any Friday night, but 27 March 2020, a week after the Australian government has declared a 'human biosecurity emergency'. The COVID-19 virus is already killing people. The border is shut, pubs and restaurants too. Large gatherings are banned, city streets are empty as life moves indoors and online. On the Facebook page of our housing estate, we are trying to cheer up kids through a teddy bear hunt, with all bears placed on windows and balconies. Our neighbour's four-year-old son Ryan used to like coming into our house to chat with my wife Saroja and me, and enjoy a chocolate or two. Now he climbs the pole in his backyard and calls: 'Om Uncle, can you open the garage so I can come in? And where is Saroja? I can't see her.'

Earlier today, I had another Zoom call with elders from the Bhutanese community, to which I belong. Some are panicking about the virus, or how the new social distancing rules are stopping them from meeting. They are getting a torrent of information, much of it unhelpful. I say, 'Don't consult Dr Google. Don't automatically believe stuff on WhatsApp. Follow what the Australian chief medical officer is saying. Let's all stay calm.'

Yet while I'm not panicked, I feel on edge too. I'm reminded of my refugee days, of never knowing what tomorrow will bring.

Saroja, away in India visiting her mum, has been caught by the lockdown, and I won't see her until June. Luckily for me, my daughter Smriti and her husband Sudeep are staying here before they move to their new house around the corner. While they cook, I go upstairs to my study for my next online meeting.

The eight of us on the call know each other through our work as community advocates. Nalika Padmasena was born in Sri Lanka, Sarjoh Bah in Sierra Leone. Lazarus Okello and Haroun Abdelrahman are originally South Sudanese. Maryam Zahid, Prakriti Shrestha and Lisa Lewis are from the Afghan, Nepali and Indian communities respectively. But we're all Australians, pulled together by a need to respond to this pandemic, meeting online tonight to support our home, the Western Sydney area of Blacktown.

We plan online information sessions to tell people in our communities about the need to wash their hands, practise social distancing, stay active indoors. We agree to meet again the following Friday. We create a hashtag, #WhatCanWeDo? Then I go downstairs for a meal of delicious baked salmon and a glass of red wine.

Nearly four million migrants – almost one in six of the population – have come to Australia in the past 25 years. I am one of them. In Blacktown I live among people from 188 countries. It's one of the most multicultural communities in Australia, perhaps the world. Far from Sydney's settled inner suburbs, where most decision-makers live, we are 400 000 citizens squeezed onto the wide, flat and often hot plain between Parramatta and the hazy Blue Mountains. In our streets all cultures meet, and Australia is being made every day, as Blacktown's remarkable response to the pandemic – set out in this book – reveals.

When I worked in a skyscraper in the Sydney CBD, during our Monday morning team talks many of my colleagues would worry aloud that I lived in such a dangerous neighbourhood. They saw Blacktown as a place of football players, fibro houses and felons – a place to avoid. I have never seen it that way. I'm proud to call myself a Blacktown boy.

Yet I am an Australian by accident. As a young man, I had met only a few Australians, and one Australian cow. I knew almost nothing about the country, and never once did I consider living there, or anywhere other than the country in which I was born, Bhutan.

At the age of 29, I was appointed to run the Planning and Development Division of Bhutan's Department of Telecommunications, one of the youngest civil servants to hold such a senior role. I was a loyal, patriotic, ambitious bureaucrat, bent on developing a telecommunications system that would help to bring our tiny Himalayan kingdom into the modern world. I gave instructions; people obeyed. I travelled overseas representing the government. I was married, with a child, living in a fine house in Bhutan's capital, Thimphu. At night a government car and driver took me home.

Less than a year after I got that job, Saroja and I lay sleepless and terrified all night, whispering under the blanket, with our two-year old daughter Smriti asleep beside us. We could not talk for fear our house was bugged. Agents of the same government that had feted me now followed me in the street. A friend connected to senior police told me I was about to be arrested. In the south of the country, homes were being confiscated and burnt, men tortured, women raped. My father, a farmer and shopkeeper from a tiny village, a man with no interest in politics, had twice been arrested and tortured.

One morning in April 1992, I got into our car, left my wife and daughter, and fled my beloved Bhutan. I became a refugee. I was not the most oppressed – others had it much worse than me. Yet I was forced to make agonising decisions. Who would abandon his wife and child? I lived in a state of confusion, guilt and self-doubt, having to feel my way along a dark path towards a life I believed should be possible but had no map to find. I lost my possessions, my salary, my status, my career, my country. And in that fall, I gained everything.

If people know one thing about Bhutan, they know it as the land of gross national happiness. In 1998, the government announced at a United Nations forum that it was adopting gross national happiness as the indicator of national well-being ahead of gross domestic product, which the king said was far too narrow and money-minded a measure to capture the true meaning of human life. For more than two decades, this concept has helped to spawn a global happiness industry and warmed the hearts of many westerners, who look at Bhutan and naively imagine a Buddhist Shangri-la, fighting bravely to preserve its spiritual values against the gross materialism of the West. Alas, these people have not looked hard enough.

With the approval of the same king – a man I had met several times and had greatly admired – the government of the land of gross national happiness embarked on one of the most thorough ethnic cleansing campaigns of the late 20th century. In a population of about 700 000, more than 100 000 southern Bhutanese of Nepali ancestry were uprooted and expelled.

Most refugees, including my parents, six siblings and other family members, were forced into camps in eastern Nepal, where they remained for up to 20 years, sometimes more. Reunited with my wife and daughter, I lived in Nepal's capital, Kathmandu, joining a small number of refugee activists who lobbied foreign governments and international organisations to try to persuade or compel the Bhutanese government to allow us to return home.

We failed in our efforts, and for some the pain of that failure will never fade, yet I learnt lessons I will never forget. As a civil servant I had been able to say to an underling, 'The boss wants this', and the discussion was over. Now I was the underling, the supplicant tugging someone else's coat. I had to try to get what I wanted through persuasion, goodwill, the strength of my relationships and character.

As a refugee I lost the secure path to success, a path that, over time, might have made me complacent, even arrogant, a bureaucrat constantly comparing himself to others in the hierarchy, unable to speak his mind and always fearful of offending the king. But I don't regret or begrudge the loss of that path. For what I learnt as a refugee has shaped my life.

In Sydney, I was again separated from my wife and child. I faced wrenching loneliness, applied for 52 jobs and was rejected 52 times, before my luck turned and Australia opened its door and heart to me. Having finally found a safe home, in September 2008 I stood in the Sydney Airport arrivals hall, waiting to welcome 17 other refugees and to embark on what, apart from keeping my family together, has been the most important role of my life: helping to create a Bhutanese community in Sydney and across Australia. This book began as something of a practitioner's manual for refugee settlement. But as I researched it, I realised I couldn't write about the refugee experience without describing my own. This book is not a comprehensive history of the expulsion of the Bhutanese, the camps in Nepal, the democratic movement that sought repatriation of the refugees, or of the settlement of Bhutanese refugees in Australia and other countries. It is above all one person's story, an attempt to share what I saw and learnt during my struggle, shared by so many migrants, to bring my family together in one place; my search for belonging.

Nevertheless, in this book I do propose ways to improve our country's refugee and migrant programs, to the benefit of the wider community. About 850 000 refugees have come to Australia since the end of World War Two. Between 13 000 and 17 500 refugees, and ten or more times as many migrants, settle in this country nearly every year. Australia's old model of settlement seems unsuited to such diversity. We need new ways to unlock the skills, energies and stories of the newcomers inside our door. What is working well? What brings us together?

The refugees I know are just like other migrants: they want to better themselves and their families, and contribute to their new society. Yet in most conventional uses of the word, to be a 'refugee' is to be vulnerable, a victim. That idea has shaped recent Australian policy. But I don't believe most refugees are vulnerable.

No one who has not been a refugee can understand the

resilience that is born out of that life. I saw people in Nepal recover from awful sickness, live for a long time with almost no food, or divide one mango between two families. Of course, some people are damaged by their past experiences; yet those who have survived being expelled violently from their homes, who have been forced to wander and wait for years, are more likely to be strong than fragile when they emerge in the quiet streets of Australia. They don't need charity, they need inspiration.

This book tries to show how that inspiration might be found. It asks a vital question for any multicultural nation: how do we keep the best, and shed the worst, of our old and new worlds? I am not talking about the surface multiculturalism of tika, saris and topis, the narrow hats you see on Nepali men's heads, as bright and lovely as these things are. I am talking about the place of family and tradition, of the rights of women, of the rights and responsibilities of each person, of where the 'I' ends and the 'we' begins.

I have learnt that former refugees, often coming from communal cultures, have things to teach the more individualist Australian culture, but the lessons are by no means all one way. I have seen Bhutanese women in this country seize opportunities they never would have had in their birthplace. But in Australia, the Hindu caste system still causes social torture in the lives of the southern Bhutanese, including in my own family. How to deal with it is a question that has dogged me all my life.

I've learnt that we must resist the powerful forces in contemporary society that seek to define us on the basis of our ethnic or cultural identities rather than as Australians, as human beings, as the residents of a suburb or a street. I've learnt, too, that each one of us should see ourselves as neither dependent nor independent, but interdependent. It's a great paradox: we must solve our own problems, set our own course, yet we are nothing without other people.

I have learnt from every single person I have met along the way – even the king of Bhutan.

When I first came to Sydney, I would tell the story of how the king persecuted our people. Many Australians, including people who worked with refugees, encouraged me – they saw my story as a mark of my entitlement to a good life in this country. But after a while I realised that continually telling this story was nurturing my wound, my victimhood. I not only survived the king's cruelty, he gave me strength. Clinging to a sense of anger, injustice and loss, outsourcing my happiness to him, will only hurt me. What I can do is accept what has happened, forgive, and move on. It's not his life, it's mine.

I have learnt many things on the journey from Bhutan to Blacktown, from one of the poorest to one of the richest countries on Earth. It's been a journey of the feet and the heart, and it began when, as a six-year-old boy working on a rice terrace, I looked across the fields and saw something that would change the course of my life.

1

'OM PRAKASH HAS PASSED!'

As a boy I sometimes went with my parents to work in the fields. As I was pulling weeds from the rice terrace one afternoon, I heard some noise and looked up the slope to the next field. About 20 children were gathered under the trees. Some boys were climbing a tree to pick amala, Indian gooseberries, while others were playing soccer with a jyamir, a big lemon. Girls were playing gatti, a game that involves throwing five stones in the air and trying to catch as many as you can on the back of your hand. Teachers and older children were busy cooking in big pots on three fires, while others were collecting wood. Everyone was chatting and laughing and having fun.

I walked over and asked a boy what they were doing. He replied, using an English word: 'We're having a picnic.' 'What's a picnic?' I asked. That night I told my parents I wanted to go to the school where the children went on picnics.

Up until then, I had gone to the pathshala, a semi-formal school, run by the villagers, that taught the Nepali language and some religious books. There had been no admission process, I just started attending. If I stayed home, I was often asked to do small chores such as helping to look after the cows, feed the goats and so on. I didn't enjoy those chores. I liked the pathshala because we had to learn religious verses by heart and I was good at it. Within a year, I was able to recite large sections of the Bhagavad Gita. I loved reading these stories.

But the education was very limited, and I was already getting bored with it when I saw the picnic.

The next day I did not go back to the pathshala, but instead accompanied my eldest brother Bholanath to the government school. The head teacher, Mr Subba, was known for punishing students by pinching them or pulling their hair. He often bought groceries in our shop and I knew him well by sight. He called me in and said, 'So you are Dhungel Baa's youngest son?' He asked if I knew the alphabets. I went into action, reciting not only the alphabet in Nepali, my mother tongue, but the English alphabet, which some friends at the pathshala had taught me. I finished with slabs of the Bhagavad Gita, the Hindu holy text, word for word.

Mr Subba was impressed. 'You will go to UKG (upper kindergarten) for the next few months and into Year 1 next year.' I had only to tell him my name – no one in the village had birth certificates or identity documents – and my formal education began. I think it was my destiny that I saw those children having a picnic.

I was born in 1961, the sixth of 14 children, in the village of Lamidara in southern Bhutan, a tiny, reclusive monarchy 'wound into the rope of the Himalaya mountains', as the British historian of Bhutan Michael Hutt once wrote. In a country that even today is nearly two-thirds forested, the southern part is a land not of mountains but of green, rolling hills, warm and humid in summer, particularly along the Indian border, and in winter cold and sometimes frosty, but without snow.

Into this country, so good for farming but largely empty

of people, my great-grandparents migrated from their homes in Nepal and Sikkim, along with tens of thousands of others, near the end of the 19th century. They came at the invitation of local rulers, who wanted them to cut down trees, plant fields, raise cattle, pay taxes, and by populating the countryside, strengthen the southern border.

In this way the Nepali Bhutanese lived for generations, growing in number until, by the time I was born, they numbered nearly a third of the country's population. Known as Lhotshampas, or southerners, they were largely cut off from the northern Bhutanese, who are mostly of Tibetan origin and Buddhist, but they also lost their links to Nepal, which faded in their memory until it was nearly forgotten, and their only home became Bhutan. On the wall of my parents' home was a photo of the king – not the Nepali monarch but Jigme Dorji Wangchuck, the third and much-loved king of Bhutan.

My mother, Damanta, and my father, Durga Prasad, were born in Bhutan. Neither went to school. When they married he was 15 years old, she was 11. At 17, she had her first child, Bhagiratha, my eldest sister. After that she gave birth to a child almost every two years for the next 26; growing up, I rarely saw her without a baby on her hip.

My parents' ninth child, Rukmina, a cute little darling, fell ill at about two months old. There was no hospital or doctor in the district. A few dhamis, or witch doctors, were called in. These traditional healers, most of them men, shook a bundle of leaves known as a syauli to brush away evil spirits, then furiously shook their bodies, but Rukmina didn't recover. A similar fate met my eleventh and most adorable sibling, Rewati, whom everyone wanted to carry or play with or put in their lap. She fell ill when she was four years old and died shortly after, despite the efforts of the faith healers to cure her.

Many years later, Yoga Maya, my immediate younger sister and my dearest friend, was electrocuted in her bathroom due to faulty wiring. She left two young children, Uma and Prem, who are now grown up and live in Australia. More than 30 years later I still have not gotten over her death. But eleven of my parents' children survived, which I believe wasn't a bad outcome in Bhutan at that time. Today, when the siblings talk or argue about when we were born, our Mum doesn't remember the time on a clock but will say, 'I think we were getting the cows out', or 'The sun was halfway through the day.'

My father's side of the family had come to Bhutan via Sikkim, now part of India but in those days a small, independent kingdom separating Bhutan and Nepal. We were called the Sikkimey Dhungels to mark us out from other Dhungels who lived in and around Lamidara. My father was called Sikkimey Sailo, meaning he is the third son. The priest named me Umanath in the traditional naming ceremony held on the eleventh day after a baby's birth, but no one called me that. I was Kancho – youngest son – and when another son, Gopal, came along he was Sano Kancho, the little youngest son. But I didn't like my given name, so when I went to school my parents changed it to Om Prakash Dhungel.

Lamidara was a remote place, with no phones, no electricity, not even a road. A few years ago, I read A.B. Facey's wonderful memoir *A Fortunate Life*, about growing up in Victoria and Western Australia in the early 20th century. His life was full of hardship, yet when he wrote about streetlights I thought, 'We didn't have those in Lamidara.' I did not see a car until I left the village to go to high school. We had to go to the stream about ten or 15 minutes away to collect water and carry it home in containers on our backs.

About 3500 people, all of Nepali origin, lived in Lamidara. Houses were spread out, and the closest neighbour was a few minutes' walk away. It took two hours to walk to the district headquarters, Damphu, a bigger town. Lamidara had a primary school, a few shops, a small civil administration office, and a very basic health unit, set up when I was a child, that distributed painkillers but not much else. Mum would call in the witch doctor all the time. My dad was also well known for repairing broken legs and hands: 'Go to Dhungel Baa. He can fix it,' people would say. He would go to the jungle to collect herbs, mix them and apply them to the broken limb before holding it in place with a splint made of bamboo.

But mostly, Dad was a farmer. Everybody was a farmer. Our family had two cows, more in some years, and two oxen for ploughing the fields. We had terraced land for rice and wheat, and non-terraced land for maize and other vegetables. Dad milked the cows every morning and evening. We also had six to ten goats and sheep. My parents got up at around four or five o'clock in the morning. They would stay on the farm all day, and Mum would cook too. I don't know how she managed it without the equipment and utensils we have today. A few years ago, in Sydney, we started planning our daughter's wedding five months before the date. Mum just laughed: 'All this preparation, for one girl's wedding?'

As children our jobs were to collect grass to feed the animals and take them to the fields, to gather potatoes, chokos and other vegetables, to dig edible roots and get firewood from the nearby forest. My elder brother, Chandra Prasad, made a cart out of cardboard and pulled my sisters and me down the hill. To play soccer we used rubber balls, about twice the size of golf balls; sometimes we swapped them with our friends for peaches.

It was a democratic life, especially for boys. My parents didn't really force anybody to do anything – children naturally fitted into doing one thing or another, and had the freedom to choose. My younger sister, Chandra, was very interested in running the shop, which she could do by herself even when she was quite young. I tended to be focused on my studies, and I should thank my siblings and parents for allowing me to do that.

Neither my big sister, Bhagiratha, nor my second brother, Rudra Lal, went to school. My two other older brothers, Bholanath and Chandra Prasad, went only to the pathshala and briefly to the government school. Kaushila, who was two years older than me, missed out because someone had to help Mum look after the younger ones and do chores around the house. But things were changing in my childhood, and my younger sisters, Yoga, Punam, Tulasha and Padma, and my younger brother, Gopal, all went to school; the last three would eventually get university degrees. When my sisters got ready for school in the morning, I would help Mum plait their hair.

Our farm was small but my parents worked hard, and eventually we moved to a bigger house on a larger, more fertile block about half an hour's walk down the hill. I remember walking to the new house when I was quite little, carrying my slipper because the strap on it had just broken, and we never threw anything away.

We were among the most privileged in the village. Thanks to our grocery store, we had a very healthy diet. We had milk every morning, as well as butter, ghee and buttermilk, which we made out of yogurt. My father boiled the milk, allowed it to stand and become yoghurt in a wooden jar, then sat cross-legged on the floor and, by pulling on ropes that turned a paddle on a wooden spindle, churned the yoghurt into butter. He then took out the butter, leaving the buttermilk behind.

We ate vegetables and rice every day, and meat, usually goat, maybe three or four times a year. Once we children got older we started eating eggs, which most Brahmins – the Hindu caste of priests and teachers to which we belong – don't eat. Later some of us even ate chicken, though never at home. Chicken is banned for Brahmins, but my parents, although religious, were fairly open, and not fussy.

We ate on the floor, sitting on beautiful mats that my father had woven out of corn husks and stuffed with hay. We each had a plate for rice, with bowls for curry and vegetables. Our parents told us not to talk too much as we ate, but sometimes we would tussle over who had a bigger or better mat, or who got to sit close to the fireplace, especially during winter.

Mum and Kaushila cooked all our regular meals but Sunday dinner was special. As the sun began to go down, Dad would come in from the fields, take up a seat beside the main fireplace in our kitchen, and make kheer, a sweet rice pudding cooked in milk and eaten only on Sundays and special occasions like weddings or Dashain, the Hindu festival.

As a boy, I believed that as the youngest son it would be my life's responsibility, once my older siblings got married, to look after my parents. When I was 11 Gopal was born, and I was no longer the youngest boy, but that idea never left me. Even in my youth, I thought there was something special about older people. They were in this world before me, and like God they seemed to know everything; also, they gave me good things to eat. All of which explains why I liked walking to the house of my grandmother, Sabitra, and bringing her to our place on Sunday night for dinner.

I would go to get her while it was still light – otherwise she would find the walk difficult, and anyway, I was scared of the dark. 'Are you going to school and studying well?' she would ask on the walk down. I would answer her questions politely, or tell her how I came first in the running race, and she would say, 'Oh, that's nice.' As we neared home, I would run ahead and announce, 'Granny is here', and other siblings would run out to meet her.

While the family sat around the fireplace, Dad would stir the pot very slowly, now and then adding sugar and various spices, or stoking the fire. In the hour before dinner there was normally a lot of commotion – 'Mum, he pushed me!', 'Mum, *she* pushed *me!*' – but on Sundays, when Dad was cooking and Grandma was around, we were quieter. Dad was not especially strict but he had natural authority and we were all a little scared of him. With my mother it was always a two-way chat but conversations with Dad were mainly his requests and commands and our responses. When he asked me to do a chore I would sometimes venture that one of my siblings was not doing anything, but we would all end up doing what he wanted us to do.

I don't remember Mum ever hitting any of us, although it was common for parents to punish children that way. I think Dad hit me just once. One day I fought with Kaushila. I was quite naughty, and I had to get my way. I pulled out her earring and threw it as far as possible. It was made of gold, very valuable, and no one ever found it. When Dad heard the news he was furious, and he hit me hard with a stick. Mum got a few strokes too, trying to stop him.

Every night I slept in the bed beside him. I felt very safe. But when I was six, there was a terrifying flood. Our house was on a slope, and it rained so hard in the night that it felt as if rivers were rushing down both sides of the house and the water would carry everything away. When the flood subsided, much of our paddy land had become a sand pit, which took years to clear. Later, when houses and government buildings were constructed in the village, my brothers and sisters and I would dig out the sand, put it in sacks and carry it to the building sites about 20 minutes away. That was the first time I earnt money.

Before I was born, my parents started selling groceries from our home. They wanted their children to be educated and I think they felt the business would help financially. We kept the groceries in a big cupboard, and on Tuesdays, market day, we had a shop at the market. At first, we carried the groceries in bags to the market and brought back what remained unsold. Later, my father built a shopfront that could be locked down, so that we didn't have to carry the groceries from home anymore; in time, he opened the shop all week. We sold sugar, salt, spices, flour and sweets – but never beer. Liquor could not be sold in a grocery store and, as a Brahmin, my father wouldn't sell it anyway.

To get his groceries, my father would walk for a day or even a day and a half to Sarbhang, an administrative centre about 30 kilometres away, near the Indian border, where Indian traders sold goods wholesale. Then he would carry the goods home on his back.

My parents had a knack for customer service. Most people paid cash but some asked for credit or bartered. Mangoes and jackfruit were quite rare, and when they were in season people would come to the shop and exchange them for things like sugar or salt. My mother could not read at that time, or do sums, but she and Dad calculated amounts of sugar or flour without having to weigh them, and added up bills on their fingers or in their heads. They remembered every transaction, sometimes asking each other, 'Does this fellow owe us seven rupees and 50 paisa, or is it 75 paisa?' At the end of Tuesday, we'd sit around the fireplace, and Dad would open the bag of money, and we'd start organising and counting the notes and coins. That was a fun thing to do.

My parents also made money just by lending money. After the shop closed on market day, one or two people would hang around, asking to borrow 100 or 200 rupees for the next few months. If they could not afford to pay back the money, my parents would allow them to pay it back with rice or other goods. Everyone paid it back.

In Canada some years ago, an elderly gentleman from my village told me how he wanted to buy a goat or a cow but never had the money. 'So I would go outside your shop on a Tuesday evening, wait for your dad to close, and ask him if I could borrow 200 rupees.' As I was leaving his house, the man called me back. 'I forgot to tell you – I always repaid everything I borrowed from him. Please ask your dad to confirm', and we laughed. Another time, when I was in Norway, somebody said, 'Who are you?' and I said I was Sikkimey Dhungel's son from Lamidara. He said, 'Oh, I bought a cow from your dad. It was a dark colour, and it gave me so much milk.' He hugged me, and I cried because he was so emotional.

Cows were how I first heard about Australia. An aid program donated Australian jersey cows, and one was given to our village to be auctioned. The local subdistrict officer was close to my father and told him to bid for the cow, because Australian jerseys were the best cows in the world, they gave so much milk. My father paid 310 rupees, an unthinkable amount in those days, especially for a calf, not even yet a milking cow. But you wouldn't believe it – when my dad started milking the cow, he had to ask for another bucket because this cow gave not two but three buckets of milk. Because cow in Nepali is gai, we called her Gothu, our go-to guy. Gothu gave us not only milk but a few generations of fine cows. We were deeply attached to her for her whole life.

From the age of nine or ten I was keen to work in the shop, and I would sit next to my parents and help when it was busy. The Hindu festivals were the busiest times, and the biggest was Dashain – known as Dussehra in India – which runs for five days and celebrates the victory of good over evil. Dashain was generally the only time of year we would get new clothes. Our parents would buy pieces of cloth for each of us, and we would take it to the local tailor to get it turned into clothes that we wore for the rest of the year: trousers and shirts for boys, blouses and skirts for girls. All children looked forward to Dashain. We liked the clothes, but we loved the fact that close relatives, particularly elders, would bless us by daubing our foreheads with tika – rice grains mixed with curd and barley sprouts – then give us money.

Next to the pathshala was a shivalaya, a temple dedicated to Shiva. Nearly all Nepali Bhutanese are Hindu, but some are Buddhist, and so in the 1970s the government built temples in some villages in which people could worship both faiths.

One was built in Lamidara. People could go in one side and worship the Hindu gods, and on the other side, the Buddhist deities. That was a good, inclusive thing the government did.

Five or six times in my childhood my father disappeared for a month or so. The government required all men, as part of their national service, to help build roads and other infrastructure that would develop the nation. The men were given rations but not paid. My father helped to build the road between the national capital, Thimphu, and the southern commercial centre of Phuntsholing, on the Indian border. He also worked on the Chukha dam and power station, Bhutan's biggest hydropower project, launched in the 1970s and financed by the Indian government.

When I was about ten, a road was built that came within an hour's walk of our village. When I reached that road I saw a motor vehicle for the first time, a truck lumbering slowly along a narrow road, far away. But the world was coming closer. Now my father no longer had to walk all day to Sarbhang: he could get there in about three hours on the BGTS (Bhutan Government Transport Service) truck, put his goods on a truck coming back, then lug them down the hill for an hour to get them home.

Other people in Lamidara also saw new possibilities in that road. After it was built, there was a town meeting. 'We can grow wheat now, make some money,' someone said. 'We don't just have to rear cows and goats and grow rice.' More enterprising people began to enlarge their orange orchards and expand their crops of cardamom into colder and more remote areas. Others could buy pipes in Sarbhang and transport them by truck to carry water from the creek to their farms and homes.

Muktinath Baral, an entrepreneurial farmer who married

my sister Kaushila, began using the road to expand his trade into oranges, pears and other fruits, and hired porters to carry his produce to the road for trucks to pick up. He started a small tea shop and went to Sarbhang to learn how to make sweets. Others who went to Sarbhang saw electricity for the first time and wondered if they could have that too. Exposure to the outside world changes everything.

But the change that most affected my life was education. In 1961, the year I was born, the government announced its first five-year plan for national development. At that time the country had just 59 state primary schools and not one high school, although a few children went to high school in India. Boys from Buddhist families could be educated in Buddhist monasteries, and Hindu children at the pathshala.

But King Jigme Dorji Wangchuck wanted to bring Bhutan, cautiously, into the modern world. Education and building new schools were central to his government's five-year plan. The third king of the Wangchuck dynasty had been heavily influenced by Indian independence in 1947, and Bhutan's prime minister, Jigmi Palden Dorji, cultivated close relationships with senior Indian bureaucrats. India, official protector of Bhutan, helped to set up the schools. Jesuit fathers from Darjeeling and Kalimpong, just across Bhutan's southern border, were invited to run them. Most teachers were Indian men, and many came from Kerala, a southern state with high levels of education. They contributed immensely to the quality of education in Bhutan.

In my state primary school all classes were in English, a legacy of Bhutan's proximity to the hill station Darjeeling, where English was favoured in the schools that emerged out of the British colonial period. In those days fewer than a third of Bhutanese people spoke Dzongkha, the national language, and nearly all of them were Ngalongs, who lived in western Bhutan. In the east the Sharchops, a Tibetan-Burmese people, spoke Tshangla, and in the south we spoke Nepali. So the government decided that the language of education and government would be English.

The new schools were free and open to everyone. Girls made up at least a third of students in the lower classes. In terms of treatment of girls and women, Bhutan is less rigid than its neighbours, India and Nepal. It is still a male-dominated society but neither northern nor southern Bhutanese practise the dowry system that is so oppressive to women in India. The sexes are not kept apart but are free to mix. The rural areas, though, were conservative: at my school the number of girls dwindled in the higher classes as parents took them out to look after younger children or work around the house, or to marry them off. By year 5, only two of the twelve students in the class were girls.

Children of so-called lower castes and Dalits – the caste formerly and cruelly known as untouchables – could attend our school. The caste system in southern Bhutan was looser than it was in India and Nepal. Migration had relaxed some of Hinduism's rigid traditions – whoever was able to clear more land had more land, for example. Also, Bhutanese society, being Buddhist, did not recognise Brahmins as having more right to school education than others. It gave equal opportunity to all castes, and we grew up together.

And yet, the cast-iron rules of caste are so hard to eradicate. One of my primary school friends, Kul Bahadur Darjee, was the son of a tailor, and tailors, like street sweepers, drain cleaners and garbage collectors, are considered to work in a dirty, untouchable profession – I don't know why. Kul Bahadur and I could sit next to each other in class, but I couldn't eat food in his house, nor could he come inside mine. In year 3 or 4, I brought my friend to my place and then realised he could not come in. I could give him a glass of water, but the glass had to be washed outside before I could take it inside. That really hurt me.

It was the same with my younger sister Yoga, whose best friend was Indira Darjee, Kul Bahadur's sister and perhaps the most beautiful girl in the village. She could not mingle with us at home.

Although I was only ten years old, these events had a huge impact on me. I was quite a religious child. Since I could read Nepali, illiterate neighbours would come to our house and ask me to read them religious books, particularly during the month-long fast of *swasthani barta*, when women forgo food during the day to enhance the well-being of their husbands. I enjoyed these sessions because everyone would praise me for my fluency.

But now I started questioning myself: what did it mean to be an upper-caste Brahmin? How was I superior to my untouchable friend? The way he was treated was shameful, inhuman. My attitude to formal religion was never quite the same after that.

My parents accepted this state of affairs, the caste system, as natural and timeless. I don't remember discussing it with them, but I was a stubborn, single-minded boy and perhaps they divined my opinions. When I was in high school, a particular sect of Hinduism – Vaishnav, meaning followers of Vishnu – came to the south of Bhutan. My parents and other Brahmins from the village went to a town inside the Indian border to get baptised by a Vaishnav high priest and have their arms stamped with a hot iron rod. When people returned to the village, they introduced new discriminations within our own caste – between converts to Vaishnav and the rest. Some converted ones wouldn't eat food cooked by the non-converted, even within the same family. Yet the scriptures that I knew so well said we had to respect all humanity.

My parents did not discriminate in this way at home. Nevertheless, they prevailed on all their children to convert to Vaishnav and be stamped with the hot iron – all except me. They never mentioned their conversion to me, and we never discussed the issue again.

When I was in year 3, government schools started teaching Dzongkha as a second language, after English. In the morning we had Buddhist prayers in Dzongkha. Because I was good at learning by heart and loved those prayer books, I was asked to be a prayer leader, along with my cousin, also known as Om, and another boy. We had to sit at the front, bang on the desk and begin: 'Ohm aha hun baja guru padma sidhi hun …' It was the famous mantra of Guru Rinpoche, or Padmasambhava, an 8th-century Indian sage who is said to have brought Buddhism to Bhutan by flying into the land on the back of a tigress.

The school's headmaster, Mr R.D. Nair, who was from Kerala, was one of the finest gentlemen I have ever met. He was a teacher, a father, everything a student could ask for. Once, when I had a high fever, he took me to his room and made me sleep there all day. But he was very strict. He tolerated no indiscipline and always had a bunch of canes handy. It amazes me to this day how neat and tidy he was, in his impeccable white shirt and blue or black trousers.

Mr Nair had a huge influence on me; I still remember him in my prayers. One day he said to me, 'If you are good in maths and science, you become an engineer.' Because I was good in maths and science, not so good at literature, from then on I would say, 'My ambition is to be an engineer.' Neither I nor my parents knew what an engineer was, but Mr Nair said I would be one, so I believed it.

At the start of year 5, the most senior class, Mr Nair told us the government had decided to introduce the All Bhutan Common Examinations. Questions would be set by the Department of Education and examinations conducted centrally from Thimphu.

In 1972 there were 12 students in year 5 at my school. Mr Nair had been headmaster for about four years and was required to show significant improvement. Since this was the first national examination, he worked hard and helped our class in every way possible. Worried that we didn't have enough teachers to cover the necessary content, he mobilised all the staff to help teach additional subjects.

We sat the exams in November. Questions came packed and sealed from Thimphu and were opened in class each day by an external examiner. It made us all very nervous. I normally came in the top three in class. But as the exams progressed, I wasn't confident that I had done as well as I normally did, and I was worried about being assessed by an external examiner.

A week after school reopened the following February, the headmaster came in to announce the results. The class was silent. My palms were sweating. Mr Nair spoke for a while and then said, 'We have only one student who passed.' His eyes moved across the ten or so students present, then he looked at me and said, 'Om Prakash has passed!' Two of my close friends, Shah Bahadur Khadka and Kala Maya Baral, were the best students and I couldn't believe they hadn't made it through. I had tears in my eyes and didn't know what to say to them, but I believe they understood.

The headmaster then said the Department had recommended that I go to Sarbhang High School in the nearby district for year 6. The headmaster sat with my father the next day and explained the situation. My parents were in two minds. Sarbhang was 60 kilometres away. I would have to leave home.

On Wednesday 14 March 1973, I awoke to a lot of noise. Everyone was out of bed, and as usual I was the last to get up. Dad entered the house with the milk bucket in one hand and a sickle in the other. Mum was busy cooking while trying to keep the children under control. Kaushila was stoking firewood in the fireplace and bringing food to the kitchen. My younger sisters, Yoga Maya and Punam, were deep in conversation; Chandra Kala was almost crying, trying to get her older sisters' attention, while the youngest, Rewati, was happily on her own.

When I walked into the kitchen, Yoga told me to get ready – it was nearly time to leave. The night before, everyone had helped me pack my small tin trunk, and they were all very excited. We ate, and everyone gathered to see me off. My mother, Kaushila and Yoga ran out to slip money into my hand. Although I was the only one to have gone to year 5 and on to middle school, my success felt like a collective thing, as if everyone in the family was getting educated. It must have been a hard moment for my parents, though. They could have easily made me stay home and look after the cows, but they were sending me far away so that I could go to school. They were amazing people. They had foresight.

My father and I walked for an hour with our luggage up the hill to Dhupidara, from where we could catch the transport to Sarbhang. A few years earlier, I had walked all day with my father to Sarbhang to pick up his groceries. By the time we got there my legs were swollen, and Dad massaged them for a long time. But this time I was riding on the back of a truck.

When it arrived it was almost full, with passengers sitting on the floor and two next to the driver. My dad climbed onto the back and pulled me in. As we drove, the wind on our faces got very chilly, and I was almost freezing when we finally arrived in Sarbhang at around 5 pm. We stayed in the back of the shop of our wholesalers, who were like family to us.

The next morning we walked to the school and Dad presented a letter from Mr Nair, my headmaster. The principal went through the letter and asked for proof of citizenship. Since the government didn't issue citizenship cards or certificates, we had to go to the nearby district office and apply for one. Sarbhang is lower and much hotter than Lamidara and we stood there for half a day in the scorching heat, my fingers hanging by my sides for so long they were swollen.

Finally, we got the papers. I was very hungry by the time we walked back to the school and I was admitted. I was to report to the warden of my new hostel. My father didn't wait. He patted me on the shoulder, said goodbye, and turned for home.

2

AT HIS MAJESTY'S PLEASURE

It was early 1978 and Jigme Singye Wangchuck had been king for just over five years when we met him in his palace in Thimphu. I was very nervous, with no idea how to behave. To my parents' generation the king was like Vishnu or Bhagwan, a god.

The aide-de-camp gave us a short lecture before we went in: 'If you have thoughts don't express them unless you are asked to. Do not say anything on your own; reply only if he speaks to you. Keep your eyes down at all times. You cannot look at the king's face.'

Ten year 10 boys filed into the room in the palace. We stood in front of our seats, eyes down. My heart was beating, my palms sweating. In a few minutes I saw a pair of high Bhutanese boots, coloured yellow in their lower half, as the king traditionally wears, approaching our seats. He sat on the sofa facing us, told us to sit down and started asking questions: 'What is your name? What do you want to do?'

He asked in Dzongkha, the national language. Because he didn't know our names we had to squint, look out the corner of our eye, and guess which boy he was talking to. I guessed he was talking to me.

'My name is Om Dhungel, Your Majesty, and I want to be an engineer,' I replied.

'That's good,' the king said. The government was building highways, phone systems, the massive Chukha power station and other hydroelectricity projects. 'We have many expatriates working in our country so we need our own engineers,' he said.

In turn, each student stated what he hoped to study: engineering, medicine, teaching, agriculture and nuclear physics. All these professions were needed to develop the country, the king said.

Then, out of the blue, he said: 'I hear you Gaupey boys steal apples.'

It was a tradition that year 10 boys from Paro Central School would go out and steal apples and peaches from the nearby orchards in Gaupey. We would do it at night, particularly in the rain, so that no one would notice, but the king's main security officer happened to have a big apple orchard and he must have reported the thefts. I thought, 'Are we in trouble?'

But the king was chuckling. Suddenly I felt relaxed and comfortable: 'Oh, he's joking with us like a friend.' I lifted my face very slightly, and I still remember his little smile.

After we left, the king's aide-de-camp took me aside and said in a stern voice, 'You were almost looking at the king's face.'

That day Jigme Singye Wangchuck talked to us about the nation he wanted to create, with our help. He was 22 years old, energetic, a moderniser seemingly focused on improving the lives of all the Bhutanese. Over the next decade I met him several times, and until I fled the country I never lost the admiration I felt at that first meeting. Why, then, he would betray his southern subjects is something I cannot explain.

He took charge in 1972, after the death of his father, Jigme Dorji Wangchuck, who had taken the first tentative steps towards creating a multi-ethnic society in Bhutan. King Jigme Dorji had established a National Assembly – with MPs and ministers hand-picked by the government, not democratically elected, but nevertheless representing the whole country, including the Nepali southerners, the Lhotshampas. The 1958 *Citizenship Act* formally recognised the Lhotshampas as Bhutanese. High schools and civil service jobs began to open to us. When King Jigme Dorji visited southern Bhutan he said, 'I do not discriminate against you.' He loved both his northern and southern people. 'I see them both. I have two eyes. If I favoured one over the other it would be as if I had gone blind.'

His son, Jigme Singye Wangchuck, took the throne seemingly bent on continuing his father's policies. While I was away at high school he came to Lamidara, and there is a photo of my sister Yoga hanging a garland of flowers around his neck. He even introduced payments to encourage Lhotshampas and other Bhutanese to intermarry. Integration through education continued apace. I directly benefited from these policies. I see now that I went to high school and university during a golden period in the history of the nation, when it was opening gently to the world, its people were getting a little richer, and the dream of a multicultural and even democratic Bhutan had not yet been snuffed out.

*

My high school years began not in Paro, in the Himalaya ranges of north-west Bhutan, but in Sarbhang in the south, where my father left me that day in 1973. I was quite scared of living in a new place, but luckily my older brother, also Om, was at Sarbhang High School too.

Although I call him older brother – Daju – it is actually our fathers who are brothers, but we don't say 'cousin' in Nepali. Om Daju and I had been friends in Lamidara, but never as close as we were about to become. From that night in Sarbhang onwards, at just about every testing moment in my life, Om Daju has been there, looking out for me.

He helped me carry my luggage to the school hostel, a big, single-storey house with four large rooms. Each room had bunk beds, with steel frames and a wooden underlay to hold the mattress. I had never seen anything like those beds and felt quite excited about sleeping in one.

Word spread quickly about a new boy, and a lot of boys gathered in the room, asking who I was, where I came from and what class I would be in. Since Om and I had the same name, boys immediately started calling me Sanu (little) Om, while he was Thulo (big) Om. Family and friends still use these terms for us today.

Having my brother around gave me a lot of comfort. He was already well known and respected, and seemed older, more formal and serious, than most boys. Perhaps it was because he was already married, to Pabitra, a girl from our village, and had been since he was 13 years old and she was 11. Arranged marriages of this kind were still common in Nepali society, and my uncle, Bhanu Bhakta, was quite a conservative Brahmin. In the first years after their marriage, Om Daju and Pabitra – whom I have always called Bhauju, older brother's wife – lived with their families, but when Om Daju moved to Sarbhang, Pabitra moved in with his family to help keep the house.

I was allocated an upper bunk next to Om Daju in room No. 1, overlooking a police camp across the road. He helped me make my bed, told me what rules I had to follow, then handed me a mug and went to the kitchen to get tea. Soon after, we had to go back to the school for an hour and a half of evening study. I didn't have any books, so Om Daju gave me one to read and introduced me to my classmates, who were happy to share theirs. The bell rang and it was time for dinner.

I was given a plate and lined up behind my brother outside the kitchen. When he was served – rice and vegetables and lentil soup in the mug – he introduced me proudly to the cook, saying, 'This is my Bhai', meaning younger brother. There were a lot of jokes, boys talking noisily over the top of each other. I had come from a much quieter life, but I was enjoying the attention and the opportunity to meet such a variety of people.

Until that night I had never in my life slept alone, always with my dad. When he travelled from home to get groceries I would sneak in and sleep with Mum, making my younger sisters move over. So I was dreading that night in the hostel. But my brother said, 'Come and sleep with me.' After a few days, he made my bed and said, 'You sleep in your own bed now.' I tried, but I never managed it. Since he went to bed early, I would sneak in later, and for the next three years I slept with him.

But one night in my first year, I opened my eyes to find Om Daju's uncle, Hari Prasad Adhikari, leaning over our bed: 'Bhanja (Nephew), get ready. Mum is not well, we need to go home.' As my brother left in a truck for Lamidara, I lay miserably in the dark. I did not learn till later that his mother, Chandra Kala, had already died. He did not come back for 13 days, after all the mourning rituals were finished.

Sarbhang High School was big, with close to 400 students, nearly all Lhotshampas, studying from kindergarten to year 10. About one in five was a girl. My maths teacher, Mr Varghese, an old gentleman from Kerala in southern India, was a serious disciplinarian. But the language teacher, Lopen Ugen Geytay, would crack jokes with us, then say, 'Don't make fun of me.' He was such a lovely fellow. I played sport, made friends quickly, and was happy. I loved going home for two months over winter, spending time with Yoga as we ate green chillies from the garden sprinkled with salt, or walking with Mum to the stream to collect water and pouring out stories of my new life.

One thing I didn't like about Sarbhang was having to fetch firewood in the forest – I was scared of leeches. We tagged along with older boys, who would help us find firewood and sometimes carry it halfway back for us. In return, we were expected to pass on love letters to girls they admired. A friend taught me how to pick up a big piece of wood and drop it with a thump outside the hostel. The captain in charge would hear the sound and I could go inside and report that I had brought my share. I did it once but felt very guilty and never did it again.

Food at the school could be bad. Once, there was a supply shortage in the town just across the Indian border, and we were served smelly and very grim parboiled rice. I didn't eat dinner for 17 nights in a row and only managed because of snacks that Om Daju gave me. I was also sick a lot with boils, and was once admitted to a nearby hospital.

I studied quite hard, but we also did naughty things, like sneaking out of the hostel to watch Indian movies at the movie hall in town. We had to watch out for my brother, though. He was very well behaved, never drank or smoked, as we did from time to time, and he would reprimand us if he caught us. Although he was only in year 7, even boys in year 10 were a bit scared of him.

When I was in Year 8, there was a scandal that had big consequences for my schooling. Our school went to play in a football tournament in Chirang, my home district. On the way home, some of the boys had a few drinks in the back of the truck. The games teacher also had a few drinks, but he sat in the cabin while we sat in the freezing cold. The boys, swearing a lot, said he hadn't talked to them during the game and wouldn't provide water and drinks, and so on.

As the truck stopped at a roadside tea stall, the teacher took a cup of tea, then came back to the truck and accused the boys of stealing his whisky. 'How dare you call us thieves?' the boys shouted back.

That night the players got us all together in the hostel and said they were preparing to bash the teacher. He would be walking back to the office through the courtyard after lunch, the boys said. One guy was designated to go and accuse him of calling us thieves, two others would come from other classrooms, and a fourth would hit him. I was the smallest. They said, 'You'd better keep quiet about all this.'

That night I couldn't sleep, and I couldn't tell anybody. I felt as if the boys were trying to copy the violent scenes in the Indian movies we watched. Otherwise, how could anyone think of assaulting an elderly person, let alone a teacher? Couldn't we settle our grievance through talk? But there was no time to reason – the boys spoke with one voice.

The next day it happened just like in one of those movies. The first boy started an argument with the teacher, two other boys came in, and the fourth punched him. He fell to the ground and struggled to get up. I watched horrified from the window with the two girls in my class, Chandra and Shanti.

The principal, Mr Kurup, was big and very strong; everyone was afraid of him. He called a school assembly, then he lined up the boys and beat them with sticks until blood dripped from their hands. The police and education authorities were called in and the investigation went on for months. Everybody was interviewed many times. A guy would put a finger in my face and say, 'Make sure you tell the truth.' I would be shivering, not sure if I had remembered correctly. Would they put me in jail? On winter break in Lamidara, I stayed very close to Mum, telling the story over and over, walking with her as she fetched water from the stream.

All students involved in the attack were suspended. All the teachers boycotted our class. How were we ever going to pass the All Bhutan Common Examination for year 8? Most teachers lived in school quarters, and a few let Shanti, Chandra and me sneak into their houses to study. We thought our classmates wouldn't like us doing that, so we didn't tell them.

Having had no classes for months, we sat the exams. All through the winter break I worried about my performance. The letter came to Dad at our grocery shop. I was very nervous opening it. I had passed and was promoted to year 9. Shanti, an Indian national whose father worked in Bhutan, was my only other classmate to pass.

Then I read the letter further. I was to go to Paro Central School in western Bhutan. Because of the assault on the teacher, the government had ceased years 9 and 10 at our school.

It would take me at least three days to get to Paro. I had never in my life travelled beyond Sarbhang and the southern areas where ethnic Nepalis lived. I was anxious but as it turned out, I made the journey in an unusual, elated state of mind. Even today, I remember nearly everything about it. Although I was only 14, I realised I was an adult, able to take care of myself and travel the world.

I had to go from Lamidara back to Sarbhang, then take a bus six hours west to Phuntsholing, the second largest town in Bhutan. There was no direct route within Bhutan so the bus had to travel via the Indian states of Assam and West Bengal before reaching Jaigaon, an Indian border town next door to Phuntsholing. I spent that evening with my cousin, Dilli Ram Kafley, the first graduate in our family and a civil servant. One of his departmental vehicles was going to Thimphu the next day and could take me.

For the first time I left the warm south and travelled to the chilly, mountainous north. I had never travelled in a small jeep. It took eight hours to get to Thimphu, up mountains and winding roads, and I vomited a few times on the way. Although Lhotshampas were now supposedly fully Bhutanese, when our jeep passed a police checkpoint I still had to produce a permit saying I was allowed to enter the north of the country. I didn't think twice about it at the time.

Thimphu was very cold. That night the driver and his family put me up in their home. Next morning, he took me to the bus to Paro, and three and half hours later I was there.

By then I was very hungry. I found a shop that seemed to serve food; an elderly Tibetan woman was stoking a fire in the kitchen. I asked her in Nepali what was available, since I spoke very little Dzongkha. It turned out she spoke some Nepali, as many Tibetan refugees do. The rice and vegetables she served me tasted good, and since the room was poorly lit I didn't realise until halfway through the meal that the rice was red. I asked the woman what was wrong with it. Nothing, she said; it was a variety grown in this part of the country. She asked why I had come to Paro and was impressed that I had come all this way, alone, to study.

I took a taxi to the Central School, and as we drove along the Paro River and up the hill to Gaupey, I felt thrilled to be travelling for the first time in a taxi, paying the driver like a grown-up. By the time I got to the school I was very thirsty. In the hostel kitchen I approached a mature-looking male who was nevertheless wearing the school uniform. 'Chu thungni na?' he asked. I knew enough Dzongkha to know it meant water. He took a big ladle off the wall, filled it with water from a large pot and handed it to me. I held the heavy ladle on both sides and drank. These otherwise insignificant moments remain vivid in my memory, so alert was I to everything.

The boy who gave me water was Ganesh Thapa, an ethnic Nepali, and I met him properly that evening, when I went to my first class. Half of the ten students were Nepalis, the rest were Ngalongs and Sarchops, the main peoples of northern Bhutan. My class was unusual: out of 300 or 400 students at the school, just 15 to 20 were from Nepali backgrounds. There were also fewer girls than in Sarbhang, since most left school at the age of 15 or 16 to marry. At Paro there was only one girl in my class. Although we often used Nepali or Dzongkha, depending on who we were speaking to, our common language was English.

Paro is a stunningly beautiful place. Paro Taktsang monastery is perched so precariously on sheer cliffs that people say it clings to the side of the mountain like a gecko. It is called the tiger's nest because it was here, according to legend, that the great teacher Padmasambhava flew on the back of a tigress to bring Buddhism to Bhutan. The path along the cliff face to the monastery is very narrow, and several tourists have fallen to their deaths trying to reach it. I made the climb soon after arriving in Paro. As the ground fell away hundreds of feet, I began to feel giddy. 'Look straight ahead or up at the monastery,' my friend advised.

Not everything about the school was beautiful. The toilets were usually blocked and we often used the bushes outside. The bathrooms had hardly any water so we bathed once a week in the Paro River. And we were always hungry. If the cooks in the hostel didn't like you they would shake the ladle before pouring the stew onto your plate and a rare chunk of meat would drop off. I learnt that the cooks were from Nepal, and were often lonely. I would smile at them, discover that our mothers had the same name, and they would often give my friends and me some extra butter.

Paro, one of only five Central Schools in Bhutan that taught up to year 10, was well known for producing good exam results. Many teachers were from Kerala. The government paid for high school students' education: food, board, books and uniforms, including the national dress – or gho – a knee-length robe tied at the waist with a cloth belt known as the kera. In the south we didn't wear the national dress much, preferring a shirt and pants.

The school facilities were much better than at Sarbhang, and to my excitement an outdoor basketball court was installed during my first year. The school didn't have a soccer field since it was on a slope, so we normally played at the airport down in the valley. It wasn't used much, since Bhutan didn't have an airline at that time.

In year 9, a year before I met him in the palace in Thimphu, I saw the king in person for the first time. He had another palace next to Paro township and our school soccer team was invited to play the king's team. Since I wasn't on the team and was standing with friends outside the field, we could look at him. He was goalkeeper and one of my friends scored a goal while accidentally knocking the cap off his head.

Although I had a privileged schooling in Paro, I was homesick and lonely sometimes. The school was so far away that I had to wait until winter break at the end of the year to go home. I almost never had a visitor, but one day I got a letter from Om Daju saying that his year 10 class from Samchi High School, where he had been sent after the closure of Sarbhang, was coming to Paro on an excursion. After three years together in Sarbhang I missed him a lot. For a long month I counted the days, and I was waiting outside the school office when the bus arrived. He got off, took out a piece of betel nut from his mouth, and gave it to me. I looked around to make sure no other students were watching, and put it in my mouth. We hugged, and the next two days seemed to pass in an hour.

In year 10 I had another visitor. My second eldest brother, Rudra Lal, had joined the army during the year I left home to study in Sarbhang. As part of the drive to open the country's institutions, the Bhutanese army was recruiting among southerners, and both my brother and my uncle, Rup Narayan Kafley, had run away from home and enrolled without telling their parents. I was astonished to see my brother in an army uniform. We chatted for an hour. Before he left, he took out his wallet, counted out 15 new Indian 20-rupee notes and handed them to me, excited to help me, and to show me that for the first time he had earned money. As he was about to put the wallet in his pocket, he opened it again and gave me another five. I was already thinking about taking my friends to town and spending the cash.

At the beginning of 1978, all students in our class except two passed the year 10 Indian Certificate of Secondary Education. The eight of us were sent to Sherubtse College in Kanglung in eastern Bhutan. Kanglung is set deep in the Himalayas, on a ridge 2000 metres high, looking down on river valleys, rice paddies and villages far below. The school, the first in the country to teach up to year 12, was a town in its own right, with extensive facilities, shops and three restaurants. Students came from all over the country, and all lived in the college hostels.

The school was an example of the smart way Bhutan built a national education system. It adopted the Indian curriculum rather than going to the huge trouble of writing its own, and year 12 students studied for the Indian School Certificate. Indian teachers came to Bhutan in large numbers, and many spent years in remote villages, helping the first generations of children going to school to learn to read and write. Indian aid also built many school buildings, including those at Sherubtse College, which was affiliated with a university in Delhi that conducted all senior exams.

Jesuits from western countries also came to teach in Bhutan. In Kanglung our principal was Father Gerard LeClaire, a Canadian. He was strict, but he gave us a lot of freedom too. He would let us drink. Until I got to Paro I had never drunk, except for some homemade rice wine in Sarbhang at a friend's place, and there it was a secret pleasure. My parents never drank. But Father LeClaire encouraged us to be grown-ups. If he caught you drunk, he would kick your arse; if he caught you trying to bring bottles of drink into the hostel he would confiscate them for the teachers' mess. But if you came back in the evening after a few drinks in town he didn't care. At Paro boys and girls had not mixed, except in class. Having a girlfriend meant peeping from a window and smiling, exchanging autographs, and being teased about it by other boys. I remember girls and boys swapping geometry boxes with love letters inside. But you couldn't take a walk together. Father LeClaire, by contrast, encouraged boys and girls to be friends. 'It doesn't mean you're boyfriend and girlfriend,' he said.

He was a huge man, with a great girth and a sense of humour to match. He would let us drag him to the scales to weigh him. One time he challenged us to a game of basketball. But he was too big to run, so he insisted we play half court. One day he nearly threw me out of my chair for not eating enough. I never ate well: I picked through my meal to throw out any rice husks, letting it get cold. When he learnt that I wasn't eating the hostel food, he ordered me a special supplementary diet, including biscuits and Horlicks. When I got acute gastritis, he sent me to a nearby hospital. After three days I was in so much pain I wrote him a letter: 'Father I am dying – either send me home or to a bigger hospital where I can be cured.' At 5 am the next morning the college driver arrived to take me to the nearest big hospital, a day and a half's drive away in the Indian state of Assam. Even then, I insisted that my best friend, Deepak Kulung, come with me or I would not go. Father LeClaire allowed him to do that.

The king visited us at Kanglung. Standing with him in the main hall, Father LeClaire explained that most of us would go on to take university courses and some would become doctors, engineers and so on. The king asked, 'What about those who don't pass year 12?' The principal said, 'Oh, they will become teachers.' The king asked, 'What kind of students do you think we will get if they are taught by failed students?' Teaching at that time was not as well paid as other professions. The king said that from now on teachers should be better paid, and the government later enacted his wish.

In 1980, 75 year 12 students from Kanglung passed the exams for the Indian School Certificate. One classmate and a good friend, Dorji Choden, would become Bhutan's first female engineer and, in 2013, the country's first female cabinet minister.

Since Bhutan had no universities, students who wanted to study further were generally sent to India under an Indian government scholarship program. A few went to other countries. But Bhutan and Bangladesh had just opened diplomatic missions in each other's capitals; the new Bangladeshi Embassy in Thimphu was only the second diplomatic mission in Bhutan. To thank Bhutan for extending diplomatic recognition after its war of independence against Pakistan, Bangladesh offered Bhutanese students scholarships to study engineering, medicine and agriculture. I would go to the capital, Dacca (now Dhaka), to study at the highly respected Bangladeshi University of Engineering and Technology.

Before I went, I met the king another time. I was doing my national service, a requirement for all students on completion of year 12, by helping to collect the national census in the far east of the country.

Five of us from Kanglung were in the remote village of Nanglam when the king and his party walked past. They were hunting in the deep forest nearby. The king saw our college uniforms, asked his assistant who we were, and said, 'Invite them for lunch.' In the hunting lodge where he was having lunch with army officers and his bodyguards, he said to us, 'So you three are from Paro?' And he said to me, 'I remember, you want to be an engineer, right?'

We sat together for over an hour. The king had a gift for telling a story. He said to us, 'See, we are trying to develop this power station, build this hospital. We need engineers, doctors. We need you all to study and come and help us build the nation.' As he spoke I felt full of energy, and devotion to him.

Before we left, he told an assistant to give us each 500 rupees – almost a month's starting salary for a new graduate. The people in the village started thinking, 'These guys must be somebody big because the king is spending so much time with them.' They even started bowing down when we walked past.

Back in Lamidara, relatives, neighbours and friends dropped by, full of questions about my trip to Dacca. Hardly anyone in our extended family had ever travelled outside Bhutan or India, or flown in a plane. Since the only thing anyone heard about Bangladesh and Dacca was about floods on the radio, people were worried about my safety. My parents and siblings felt sorrow, but also pride that someone from our family was the first from the village to not only go to another country outside of India to study but to become an electrical and electronic engineer. Sobbing and crying, everyone wished me good luck. Dad gave me some pocket money, Mum pulled me aside and handed me a few more rupees, Kaushila put some more money in my pocket, and my younger sisters Yoga and Punam gave me whatever they had. Once again, I had a grand send-off.

*

I had never seen anything like the streets of Dacca. People moving in all directions, cars banked up, rickshaws squeezing through the traffic, drivers shouting for rides. Noise, dust, humidity, relentless heat. Bhutan seemed so small and calm by comparison.

I arrived with Bola Gyeltshen, a Sharchop from the east of Bhutan, a fellow engineering student who became a great friend. Six medical students had also gone to Dacca. At schools in Bhutan I had nearly always got the highest marks, but at university the Bengali guys were the cream of the cream; I was nowhere near the top.

It was a volatile time in Bangladesh. A few months after we arrived, in 1981, President Ziaur Rahman was assassinated, and in 1982 the army took over in a coup. Crowds of 10 000 people were often in the streets, protesting. We had never seen a demonstration and we were scared. I saw water hoses turned on protestors, army trucks running over a crowd, hitting bodies, killing people. That night I could not sleep.

Because students were among the most active demonstrators, the army would target the student hostels. Several times Bola and I took refuge in the Bhutanese Embassy. We often wanted to go home; Bola was even more frightened than I was. Whenever there was a little noise outside, he would start panicking.

Gradually, we got used to life in Dacca, and what was frightening became fascinating and wonderful. I loved the warmth of the people: when you said you were from Bhutan they would give you food, everything they had. The Bengali language is quite close to Nepali, and I picked it up quickly.

I travelled a lot, stayed with Bengali friends all over the country, and saw two sides of the society. Some friends at the university lived like kings, taking holidays in the UK or somewhere like that. At the other extreme, so many people lived on daily wages, and others, often with disabilities, begged on the streets.

Bola and I were like brothers, together all the time. We were social animals, and organised many parties and gatherings. Several students and friends were from the Bangladeshi army, and some were high-ranking officers who would take me to their barracks. Foreigners are not allowed to go there but I could easily pass for a Bengali. When people asked why I didn't speak the language well, I said that my parents were diplomats and I had lived most of my life overseas. I also spent a lot of time at the American Marines Club, which was open only to foreigners, and one of the few places you could get a beer in this Muslim country. They had great parties there.

We also celebrated the Muslim, Christian and Hindu holy days with Bengali students from those religions. I began to learn about other religions and cultures – there is nothing like going to a mosque and standing next to your Muslim friends as they pray. My friends also taught me much about activism, democracy and the country's struggle for independence. But I also saw people dying over a protest and I thought, 'It doesn't make sense.' A lot of leaders would pull their people onto the streets but were nowhere to be seen when the violence began. They spoke so well, they could mould their followers in any way, and some misused that, driving people to their deaths, and for what? For the cycle of anger and hatred to continue.

Student demonstrations were almost a way of life, and

the university shut down so often that my four-year course took five years. In those times we had to stay in the Bhutanese Embassy or go home. Students were protesting against the loss of that first hope of a democratic, secular Bangladesh, born when the country declared independence from Pakistan in 1971. Most protestors were anti-military and left-wing, but some were Islamists who were locked into conflict with the state. Bangladesh in those days was a much more moderate Muslim country than it is today. A medical student at my friend's university came to classes in a burka and a teacher would not allow her into class. There was political pressure to make him change his mind but he refused to budge.

My interests in those years were social, not political. In my first year we set up a Bhutanese Students Association, and I was elected president, serving in the position until I graduated. I put a lot of time into the role. I edited the association's student magazine and travelled around the country meeting Bhutanese students, often at the request of the Embassy, for which I became an unofficial liaison officer.

Because the Embassy would ask me to go to the airport to greet high-ups from Bhutan and show them around, I became close to a number of dignitaries, including the foreign minister, Dawa Tsering, and the secretary of the Royal Civil Service Commission, Dasho Jigme Thinley, who later would become prime minister. I was lucky to be making these relationships. I spent a lot of time in the ambassador's house. One of the three ambassadors who were there in my time was Dago Tshering, whose half-brother had been my classmate in Paro. Dago Tshering's wife, Aum Tshokey, would send the car to my hostel to pick me up on weekends and I would go swimming with their children. Less than a decade later, this man would become home minister and mastermind the policy of expelling the ethnic Nepali population, including my family.

Every year the Bhutanese government gave the association funds to celebrate the birthday of King Jigme Singye Wangchuck. We would hire a big hall and invite university teachers, vice-chancellors, people from the Embassy and our friends, both Bengali and international students. Bhutan's national day – 17 December – marks the day in 1907 that the first king of the Wangchuck dynasty was crowned, but we also took three days holiday to celebrate the king's birthday – 11 November.

He visited Dacca twice while I was there – a state visit in 1984, and to attend the South Asian Association of Regional Cooperation Summit a year later. On the first visit, I and some other students stood at the airport with Embassy staff, other diplomats and dignitaries from the Bangladeshi government, all bowing down to meet him. I think he felt awkward, because as he walked past he said to us, 'Don't bend down too much.' In another surreal VIP moment, I was in the seventh car in the convoy, travelling on roads that were normally packed with people but had been emptied today and were lined with fluttering flags. I attended the state banquet hosted by the president of Bangladesh, Hussain Muhammad Ershad. Each table setting had ten or eleven pieces of cutlery, and we students looked at each other trying to figure out which knife or fork to use for which dish. One of my friends could not eat the dessert since he had no spoon left and he couldn't gather the courage to ask for one.

In case the royal entourage needed someone with local knowledge, I stayed at the state guesthouse with another

Bhutanese student. He was Bhampa Rai, a medical doctor, more than ten years older than me, who was studying for his master's in surgery. Bhampa Rai – whom I called Bhampa Daju – would play a crucial role in our refugee crisis in the years to come. He had such a big heart: one night, we didn't have mosquito nets at the Embassy quarters and while my friend Bola Gyeltshen and I slumbered away, Bhampa Daju sat beside our beds all night, fanning the air and keeping the swarming mosquitoes at bay.

I was charged with looking after the golden butter lamps the king used during his daily prayers. About ten students were invited to the ambassador's residence to meet him. Once again, he showed the political gifts I had seen in Thimphu and Kanglung. I remember the ambassador's wife getting so excited because the king remembered her name.

During his second visit to Dacca, he met the students again and told us he had heard that our stipend from the Bangladeshi government was too low. It was, but we could not tell the king that, so we protested that the allowance was fine. But the king told the ambassador to give us the equivalent of US$10 extra a month. He said to us, 'I want you to enjoy yourselves. You are international students – have fun. But don't forget you have to study too, so that when you finish you can come home and serve the country.' Again, I took those words to heart.

Despite my busy social life I knew I wanted to be a good engineer and to serve Bhutan. I would come back from the Marines Club at 2 am and study. I never deviated from my goal.

I kept in touch with my brother Om Daju, who had finished his veterinary science degree in Kerala and was now working in the Bhutanese Department of Animal Husbandry. He had heard that some friends were pulling money together to buy a plot of land in Gelephu, a southern Bhutanese town that was becoming a commercial centre. 'If we tell our parents they will say it's a crazy idea and squash it,' we agreed. I spoke quietly to my brother-in-law, Muktinath Baral, Kaushila's husband and an entrepreneur who traded goats, oranges, betel nuts and other things. He gave me a loan. The southern Bhutanese, increasingly exposed to the world, were starting to see a future beyond raising cows and goats. The increasing affluence of the south, however modest, was beginning to be noticed in the north, and not favourably. But I did not realise this for some years to come.

In 1985, during another university shutdown, the Bhutan government allowed us to go home. On my return to Bangladesh, I had to travel from Lamidara to Sarbhang, to Phuntsoling and then Bagdogra in northern India, where I would fly to Calcutta (now Kolkata) before taking another flight to Dacca. I walked for an hour with my luggage to take the bus to Sarbhang. While I was waiting, Muktinath Baral came by with his truck and said that after it had been loaded with oranges in Lamidara, his driver could give me a lift straight to Phuntsholing, via Assam and West Bengal in India. This lift would save me a day's journey.

It was dark by the time we finally loaded the truck, and after midnight when the five of us – my brother-in-law's business partner (whom I called Kharka Daju, meaning older brother), the driver and his assistant, a boy going to school who had hitched a lift, and me – crossed the border into India. It was pitch black, with forest on both sides, and everyone apart from the driver and me was asleep. Suddenly the truck in front of us started slowing down. 'Trouble, trouble, trouble,' muttered the driver.

Soon our truck was also shuddering and coming to a halt. There were spikes on the road, and both trucks had punctured tyres. The driver and his assistant got out to change the tyre, and Kharka Daju and I followed. As we talked with the driver and his assistant under the truck, out of the darkness loomed a man with a big knife, then another with a huge stick. They swung their weapons and I saw two men fall to the ground, moaning. Next moment, another man with a huge stick hit Kharka Daju on his head. As I cried for help, I felt a bang on my head, then on my knees and hands. I was now flat on the road, in extreme pain.

They pulled the boy from the truck and demanded, 'Who is the owner?' The boy pointed to Kharka Daju. They went back to him, hit him again and demanded in broken Hindi that he give them his money. I was bleeding hard from the top of my head; if it continued I knew I would die. I thought of my father, my mother, my sisters. Until Gopal was born, I had been the youngest son. In the scriptures, the youngest son looks after his parents. I believe these thoughts of love and duty and longing for life kept me alive. I pressed my hands to my head; the blood kept coming. Then I fell unconscious.

I don't know how long I lay on the road. I could feel the wind from trucks rushing by. The robbers had taken my jacket and it was very cold. I could hear a little noise here or there, perhaps from wild animals. The driver was hiding under the truck, another guy was moaning, then falling quiet. I rolled away from the road so I wouldn't be killed. Slowly, pulling with one hand then another, I dragged myself into the back of the truck, and got under a tarpaulin.

As darkness gave way to daylight, I heard voices, saw people in uniform – Indian police. They took us to the police station and took our statement. They said our assailants might have been members of the Bodo Movement – an ethnic insurgency in Assam seeking statehood for the Bodo tribe and known for highway robberies – or simply a gang of thieves. I was still in pain but very hungry – a good sign. The police were kind and brought us to a roadside café and gave us milk and roti. After about two hours, with tyres repaired, we got back on the road to Phuntsholing, where my sister Yoga was working at the Food Corporation of Bhutan. She and her husband, Puspa Acharya, drove me to the hospital. Through Om Daju I knew the doctor there, Dorji Wangchuck, and he was surprised to see me caked in dried blood. He started stitching my head even as I lay on a bench in the corridor. It was so painful I scratched his hand.

Three days later, with a white bandage covering my head, I was on a plane. In Dacca, my friend Bhampa Daju took the stitches out of my head. His kindness only reinforced my overwhelming sense of the preciousness of life.

In May 1986, I graduated and became an engineer. The ambassador, D.K. Chhetri, suggested I stay in his Dacca residence while he took his wife to Bangkok for some medical treatment. He said, 'Use the chauffeur-driven car, but take the flag off it.' I rode around Dacca with the chauffeur. I stayed two or three months, and had a ball.

One day, Om Daju wrote to me from Thimphu. 'It's time to start your career,' he said. 'Students who were junior to you have already started working in the government. They're bypassing you. You'd better hurry home.'

3

LOVE AND WORK
IN THIMPHU

It was early afternoon when I knocked on the door of the white, two-storey house in Thimphu. Saroja let me in, and ushered me into a living room, where I sat on the couch. 'I'll go and get Mum,' she said. I nodded but said nothing. I was so nervous I was sweating.

Saroja and I had been dating for more than a year. We had met when her older sister, Jyotsna, and her brother-in-law, Bhim Subba, director of Bhutan's Department of Power, had invited me for dinner. Saroja was a shy young woman sitting in the corner, and we said little to each other that night. Now I was the shy one.

I had heard that her mother, Kamala Gurung, was a proud, tough woman. She had grown up in a palatial home, with 52 doors and 52 windows and 11 servants, in Samchi district in the south of Bhutan. The house belonged to her grandfather, Garjaman Gurung, an almost mythic figure in our culture. The Gurung caste, who make up many of the Gurkhas, are famous warriors.

In 1887 the then ruler of western Bhutan issued a decree authorising Dalchan Gurung and his son Garjaman to settle and govern Nepalis in the vast southern foothills that eventually became Samchi district. It was said that Garjaman became such a powerful administrator that when he went to Paro to hand over the taxes he had collected, the ruler of the south had him poisoned and killed. Garjaman's mystique certainly added to my nerves as I waited for his granddaughter on the couch.

She walked in, immaculately dressed in a blue floral sari, a woman in her early fifties, aristocratic, beautiful. I stood up and bowed, hands in prayer position on my chest: 'Namaste, Ama.' She acknowledged my greeting without smiling and called for tea. We sat facing each other, but this was no conversation between equals – it was an interview.

'Are you aware of the difficulties of this marriage?' she asked me. 'Will Saroja not face problems with your family and your community? You had better consider these factors before you decide.'

I was inarticulate in my reply but somehow I got the words out. I said I understood the challenges. It was my responsibility to take care of Saroja and protect her. And I didn't believe in the caste system, though I didn't say that. The conversation was cool, and ended in less than half an hour after she summoned others into the room. Yet I left it with a faint sense that she had liked me.

At home that night I felt agitated. Why had she asked so many questions? Why did I have to justify myself? But as time passed, I felt ever more respect for Ama and the way she fought for her daughter. I feel it even more today.

In my world, Brahmins married Brahmins; marrying someone from a lower caste – how I hate that term – was not done. Some Brahmins, even in Australia, still hold those views. At different times they have caused both Saroja and me pain. But the way we have negotiated these difficulties has made our marriage strong, and taught me a lesson that has shaped my life: we cannot control how people treat us, but we can control our response.

*

Two years before meeting Kamala Gurung, I arrived in Thimphu from Dacca, a 24-year-old graduate, keen to serve my country and start my career. Over the next six years, I gained a wife and a daughter. I lost a beloved sister. I helped Bhutan acquire a proper national and international phone system. At the age of 29 I became head of Planning and Development in the Telecommunications Department. I represented the government at UN conferences overseas, then was thrown out of my country by that same government with nearly all of my family, probably never to return. Perhaps, apart from my early days in Australia, no period in my life has been as tumultuous as the time I spent in Thimphu as a Bhutanese civil servant.

If I wasn't such a stubborn fellow, I never would have joined the Telecommunications Department. After returning from Dacca in 1986, I got all sorts of advice. I stayed with my cousin, Dilli Ram Kafley, then a deputy director in the Ministry of Trade and Industry, and his wife, Rup Meena, a teacher and an unfailingly generous woman who never let me leave the house without eating. Dilli Ram was very proud of me as the first engineer in the extended family and had big plans for me. He urged me to join the Department of Power, which needed hundreds of engineers to design the big hydroelectric dams and power stations that the country was planning. Other people suggested I join the Foreign Ministry, since I had done so much diplomatic work in Bangladesh and had developed a relationship with the foreign minister, Dawa Tsering. But when I raised telecommunications, everyone said, 'That's the worst thing you could do. It's a terrible department.'

Yet I thought, 'If it's so crappy, I have an opportunity to do something about it.' To complete my national service, I worked for six months in the department in 1986, going out with technicians repairing the Thimphu phone lines. I had seen how the system worked, and didn't. I was sure that telecommunications, especially digital technology, which I had studied a little in my engineering course, were going to change the world. In my last interview, I expressed my wish to the country's top civil servant, Dasho Jigme Thinley, secretary of the Royal Civil Service Commission. He granted it, and I started work on 1 January 1987. Overnight, I was the third most senior telecommunications engineer in Bhutan.

Thimphu is a beautiful city of winding roads and white-walled buildings set among forested hills and, behind them, white-capped mountains. By royal decree, all buildings must be in the traditional, western Bhutanese architectural style: multi-coloured wood frontages, small arched windows, sloping red roofs and, in most cases, no nails or iron bars used in construction. Thimphu was a small town, with 29 000 residents (100 000 today). It had so few cars I could tell you who owned many of them.

Phone numbers were just four digits, and television was banned – to prevent outside influences, the government said. There was one movie hall, showing only Indian films. Every morning the finance minister, Lyonpo Chogyal, was reputed to walk or drive around the city and check it for cleanliness.

If you threw a piece of paper or spat betel nut on the street you would be locked up for three hours; if you peed on the street, three days. On Thimphu's first day of snow every year, the government would declare a public holiday for the capital.

In this tiny place, where everybody knew everybody else and mixed every day, the plum jobs were in the civil service. It had 13 000 employees across the country and, with the business sector very undeveloped, was by far the largest employer. After the king and his ministers, leading civil servants pretty much ran the country, and had much more power than members of parliament, who were often uneducated and had been plucked out of their villages to ensure the National Assembly looked representative. Ministers also sat in the National Assembly, but were hand-picked by the king. One home minister, Tamji Jagar, had previously looked after the third king's horses, and was illiterate. In those days, even a low-level civil servant could boss MPs around. Like me, most of the southern MPs stayed at Dilli Ram Kafley's house when they came to Thimphu for sessions of parliament.

Bhutan had no independent parliament or judiciary, no freedom of thought or expression. The only mass media were the Bhutan Broadcasting Service and the weekly newspaper, *Kuensel*, both owned and tightly controlled by the government. Mail was censored, demonstrations were forbidden, and to say anything against the king was an offence that carried severe legal punishments. Rights, as westerners know the term, did not exist, only privileges bestowed on citizens by the king and his coterie.

The society sounds harsh, but to me, a fresh civil servant, it did not feel that way at all. I was part of a generation of educated southern Bhutanese who, freed of the segregation of the past, had enthusiastically joined the government. Apart from my cousin Dilli Ram and Bhim Subba, Saroja's brother-in-law, there was Sangpa Tamang, another engineer, who ran the Public Works Department. Dr Bhampa Rai, my fellow student in Dacca, now worked as a surgeon in Thimphu hospital. One of Saroja's uncles, R.B. (Ran Bahadur) Basnet, was managing director of the State Trading Corporation of Bhutan, and the king's regular tennis partner. The king himself would phone some of these civil servants, often at home, to discuss power generation or economic management.

Beneath this group was a much larger one, typically around ten years younger, of civil servants, doctors, engineers and teachers. We were young, upcoming, idealistic, ready to work hard, and keen to mingle with the northern and eastern Bhutanese. Looking back, I can see that our increasing visibility was making some people uneasy, even envious, but there were no obvious signs of that at the time. Our diversity simply wasn't an issue; we thought we were all committed – though we never used this phrase – to our multicultural future.

I was paid 1150 Indian rupees a month, a big salary. The department also paid my rent of 2500 rupees a month. My house was so big you could almost play tennis inside it. I lived with a friend, Nar Bahadur Dhital, a mining engineer. We knew nearly all the westerners in Thimphu, who mostly worked in jobs funded by the United Nations Development Program (UNDP) or the World Bank. A Norwegian entomologist whom we met over a beer stayed with us for a while. He would go out at 10 pm to collect insects from the forest, returning at 3 am and often waking us up with his excitement at what he had found. Our house was full of boxes of butterflies and other insects.

In the department, my two great mentors were its director, Bap Yeshey Dorji, and one of his deputies, Thinley Dorji. (They were not related – Dorji is a common name in Bhutan.) Bap Yeshey, a mechanical engineer and ex-army captain whom everyone called 'Captain', was a leader ahead of his time. He would unfailingly take the blame when things went wrong, but he was happy to credit his subordinates for successes: 'It was your idea, you deserve the recognition,' he would say. With his support I took two or three trips overseas for training and meetings every year.

Thinley, who became my direct boss when I moved to the projects division in 1988, was about ten years older than me, but was youthful, excitable and kind. As an engineer I was more theory than practice, but he was both. He had big plans for Bhutan and was the main brain behind early developments in telecommunications. But he also avoided the limelight and would often push me forward instead.

My first role was to run the Thimphu phone network. It had 900 lines, and about half were not working at any one time. Some expatriates would turn up at the exchange late at night to follow up on their 'booking' and end up arguing fiercely with the operators, who would call me around midnight saying, 'There is a lady banging on the door.' I would rush to the exchange to hear the lady say she had been waiting since morning to put through a call. I would try to soothe her, to no avail. It was a big problem. The expatriates we needed to develop the country would not come if they could not phone home.

Our most important client, however, lived in Samteling Palace. The king had foregone Thimphu's far grander palace at Dechencholing to live in a simple, wooden log house with a separate sunroom which he reportedly used as an office. Bhutan's terrible phone system was non-discriminatory – I once got a call from the palace saying the line was not working and sent some technicians to fix it. When Bap Yeshey heard the news he was shocked: 'Om, how could you do this? You must go yourself.' I had to quickly learn practical skills for fixing phone lines. Another time, the palace called asking us to fix a washing machine. I had never even seen a washing machine. I was nervous, but Thinley came to the rescue. A practical man who had trained as an engineer at the Western Australian Institute of Technology in Perth, he pulled out his tools and said, 'Let's go.' He fixed the machine himself.

Another time Thinley and I were fixing the palace phones when one of the king's four queens, Ashi Dorji Wangmo, dropped by and offered us a cup of tea. It wasn't the most exciting tea of my life but I was thrilled to be in the palace. After we left, Thinley said, 'Why did you say yes to tea? If you say no, she will give you a present.' Sure enough, next time she offered us tea I said no, and she gave me a bottle of high-quality whisky. Later, when fixing the phone in the palace of Ashi Dechen, the king's older sister, I said no to tea, and was given a shiny gold Citizen watch, which I wore for the next ten years. I collected quite a few gifts by refusing to have tea.

I was acquiring practical skills but was hungry to learn bigger things. I came across a course in the US that offered scholarships. Bap Yeshey told me to apply and I got in. The UNDP would pay for the six-week course, plus travel expenses and a stipend of $150 to $200 a day. In those days the UNDP was far too generous. For three nights I stayed in a vast suite in Washington, DC that must have cost a small fortune.

The training comprised one course on analogue systems,

and another on the new world of digital technology. Six students, from Guyana, Egypt, Honduras and Bhutan, took the first course, which was run by COMPRO, a telecommunications manufacturing company based in Memphis. Every morning I ate donuts – a new delicacy for me – and nearly every night I went out to watch rock-and-roll bands in the local pubs. I visited Graceland – I was a big Elvis fan – but just as extraordinary was our invitation to the Memphis mansion of COMPRO president James Fri. It had an indoor swimming pool and a flowing waterfall, and it took almost an hour to show us around. In the living room there was a picture of James and his wife with Ronald Reagan, then president, and Nancy.

After two weeks we flew to Raleigh, North Carolina, for the second course, which was run by Northern Telecom, a Canadian company. Students from Chile, Mexico, South Korea and India joined us, making twelve in total. Finally, we flew to Dallas, Texas, to learn about private branch exchanges. In Dacca I had been an avid watcher of the TV soap opera *Dallas*, and was excited to see the real thing. After checking into the hotel in the late afternoon, I went downstairs to the bar and asked for a beer. A huge barman pulled out a huge mug, filled it from the tap and handed it over – but then looked at me more closely, grabbed the beer back, and said, 'Sorry, we don't serve alcohol to kids. Can you show me your ID?' I was 25 years old and here for training, I protested. 'Sorry, man, I need to see your ID.' Determined, I went back to my room, got my passport – and got the beer. As I went to pay, the barman said, 'It's free for you, man. Sorry I didn't trust you.' My age was challenged in many bars in Texas.

Everything about this trip, the might and glittering

power of the US, was intoxicating to me, a minor civil servant from one of the smallest and poorest countries on Earth. But however glamorous it was, I never wanted to leave my country for the US or any place like it. At the end of the six-week training we all had to stand up and give a little speech. In mine I said so many good things about the king and what he was trying to achieve that afterwards some Americans came up to me: 'Why are you embracing this king? Are we living in the same century?' We joked, but my speech had been entirely serious.

About six months before travelling to the US, I had to undertake three months of cultural orientation in Driglam Namzha, the code of etiquette for Bhutanese citizens, especially government employees. The king's Zimpon, or chamberlain, taught the course himself, instructing 70 new civil servants in such matters as how to avoid looking into the eyes of high officials, how far we had to bow down when we met a minister, and how much further down we bowed before the king.

We learnt how to put on our gho, traditional dress for men, and how to wear the kabney, the silk scarf that comes in several colours, each denoting a place in the Bhutanese hierarchy: white for ordinary civil servants, red for higher officials, orange for ministers, and saffron for the king. Today I see the Driglam Namzha course as a lesson in servitude, but at the time I had no such thought. I accepted Bhutan's feudal power structure. And perhaps one day, I thought, I would rise so far in the civil service that I would wear the red kabney. Then I would be known as Dasho, or Excellent One.

In Thimphu, our slumbering department was stirring, largely thanks to Thinley Dorji. Not long after my return from the US, he and I were sitting around a table, drinking tea from the flask Thinley always carried, drawing satellites on paper. Our department was seen as a backwater, so we had time to think up crazy things.

Bhutan had just 2000 phone lines in a country of around 750 000 people. The system was run mainly by Indians on secondment from their government; we depended on India for everything. But Thinley loved to daydream and I was his zealous apprentice. Why couldn't we have an international phone system, with a satellite Earth station and switching system that would allow our people to call any country? Why couldn't we have a national phone system that would allow Bhutanese people to call each other? We said, 'Let's build an internal and external telecommunication system that is one of the most modern in the world.'

We pulled together a one-page plan. Thinley was friends with Ugen Tshering, director of the National Planning Commission and a well-connected man in Bhutan. He ran a sceptical eye over our page. 'I'll talk to the boss,' he said. The boss was the king, who, as head of state, chaired the Planning Commission.

A month or so later, the director got back in touch: the king wanted us to work up a more detailed proposal. Thinley started working with his contacts, and we reached out to the International Telecommunications Union, a branch of the UN, through the Thimphu office of the UNDP. After six weeks' work we sent our document to the director. Two weeks later, he called Thinley and asked him to drop by for a chat. 'The king is excited,' he said. 'He wants to spend three and a half million (US) dollars on this, four and a half – whatever it takes.'

It was a huge commitment – to my knowledge, Bhutan's

total foreign currency reserves at that time amounted to just US$45 million. But there was common sense behind the king's command. Developing a proper telephone service was crucial if Bhutan was going to become a modern nation.

Around that time, I heard that Saroja was back from India. She had studied for a postgraduate diploma in medical laboratory technology in Pune, near Mumbai. After we had met, a year earlier, I began to go often to her sister Jyotsna's place, where Saroja also lived. It helped my cause that if I didn't visit for a few days, her adorable little nieces Yesha and Nisha would start asking for me – perhaps because I often brought them chocolate!

I found Saroja special in so many ways. She was quiet, genuine, kind, but also a leader in her field, one of Bhutan's first public health analysts. She was also very pretty. She was the fifth of six daughters, followed by a son, Nilakash, then another boy, Sarad, to her father's second wife, Hari Maya. Her parents had decided that every child would get a university education, and all six girls had seized their chances. Deepa worked in the Department of Revenue and Customs, Jyotsna worked in tourism for the government. Usha was a senior official in the Royal Monetary Authority, Anupa was a high school teacher, and Rebecca would become Bhutan's first female architect.

Saroja and I started meeting at the Chorten, the Buddhist stupa near the centre of Thimphu that was built to honour Bhutan's third king. The Gurungs are Buddhists as well as Hindus, and Buddhism is also important in our Brahmin culture. We would walk three times around the shrine alongside shaven-headed monks in red robes and crowds of visitors, then find a quieter place to talk.

At the time, I was living with my younger brother Gopal, who had come to Thimphu to go to school, and a boy from our village, Santabir, who cooked and cleaned for us, because we were hopeless. Saroja looked in our cupboards and said, 'Where are your spices?' Because I suffered from gastritis I took no chilli and ate boiled food only. Saroja wasn't having that. She got me eating well again. Before long I was thinking she was someone I could spend my life with. Could she help me look after my parents and younger siblings? I was sure she could.

I didn't propose – that's a western notion – but I brought up the idea of marriage. We talked about it carefully for months. My sister Yoga came several times to Thimphu and soon she and Saroja were fast friends. Saroja said Yoga told her I had become so happy since meeting her; Yoga also said: 'My brother's a very nice man. You should marry him.'

Saroja and I went for a few days to Punakha, about two hours from Thimphu, and stayed with her sister Anupa, who taught at the high school. Punakha, the old capital, stands at the confluence of Bhutan's two main rivers, the Pho Chhu and the Mo Chhu. We sat together by the Dzong, the old Buddhist fortress built to repel invaders from Tibet, and watched the rivers flowing on both sides before they met. She and I still talk about going back there one day.

Weeks after that trip, Saroja said to me, 'Baba (Dad) would like to see you.' Ganga Prasad Gurung was coming to Thimphu to visit his daughters. A highly respected teacher, he was known to all as Guru Babu. As soon as we talked, my nerves vanished and I admired him very much. I thought, 'I would love to be part of this family.'

Guru Babu was like my father in many ways. Both were

simple, humble men, who always spoke to others as human beings, never thinking that one was higher than another. When Saroja told him I would be visiting, he said, 'Let me go and shave.' It was a mark of respect from him that I have never forgotten.

I learnt that Guru Babu regularly had lower-caste people, including Dalits, at his home in Chengmari. The family had one of the two or three TVs in the village, and he would invite kids from all castes to come and watch, then stay for a meal. If he had done this in our part of Bhutan he would have been an outcast but in Chengmari he was Guru Babu, and people did not dare challenge him. Saroja's district, Samchi, was also less conservative than ours. It was close to the Indian border – if you threw a stone from Saroja's house it would almost land in India. Traders moved across the border, children like Saroja and her sisters went to good schools in Darjeeling and Kalimpong. Samchi people were exposed to a more modern world.

A month or so after meeting Guru Babu, I met Ama, Saroja's mother. Later, I learnt to my great relief that she had approved the marriage, no doubt influenced by her daughters Jyotsna and Usha, who were behind it. Saroja moved into my house on 4 August 1988 – the day we mark as our marriage anniversary. She did so on blind faith: she had not met my parents and knew very little about my family. After growing up in a fairly liberal family, and very ignorant about the caste issue, she was now entering a conservative one.

From the day she moved in, our house of three boys – Gopal, Santabir and me – became a home. On day two, as the new man of the house, I took her to and from work on my Yamaha motorcycle. A week later, as we left the house, the bike slipped on some sand and Saroja nearly fell. She got off and politely declined to get back on. Much later, she said she never felt confident on the bike with me in the first place.

She took over most of the cooking. One time she was sick, and I cooked her some noodles. She told me they were good, but 30 years later she says she could hardly eat them. As she lay there with a fever I sat on her bed, half talking to her, half focused on the mass of work papers I had spread out on the quilt. She still rightly chides me about that.

Two weeks after she moved in, we travelled to Yoga's home in the southern city of Phuntsholing to be formally married in a temple. Yoga helped Saroja buy a sari and a potey, a necklace of green beads that signals that a woman is married. The wedding party was just Yoga, her husband Puspa, and their two young children, Uma and Prem. In western language, we had eloped.

But my parents still did not know. I am not one for starting revolutions – what if they opposed my decision? I could not deal with that.

Once again, Om Daju was my saviour. Like his father, he is a fairly conservative man, yet we have an understanding that often does not need words. For instance, he never drinks, whereas I do. On one of his visits to Thimphu, I poured a drink for myself at a gathering, in his presence. He said nothing, but I knew he understood and accepted my action.

I told Om Daju about my marriage. He listened, then said, 'I will talk to your parents.' He told them, 'There is no point arguing with him; he will not change his mind. You have to accept his decision.'

They did, but I knew they would not be present when I publicly married Saroja early the following year. It wasn't ideal. But if I was determined to marry the girl I loved, I had to accept that not everything would happen the way I wanted. Saroja and I made sure to focus on what we had, not what we lacked. And what we had was so much.

In November 1988, we attended another wedding celebration – a luncheon for a thousand people at Dechencholing Palace to mark the king's marriage to four sisters, whom he had formally married a few days before. In fact, the king had married the women nine years earlier, in a private ceremony, and already had eight children with them. News of the marriages had gradually reached the ears of the people, but until the ceremony in 1988 no one was allowed, by law, to discuss them. The king, it seems, decided to make the marriages public to ensure the succession to the throne of his eldest son, Jigme Khesar Namgyel Wangchuck. Bhutan is an unusual place!

After lunch, we left the palace late in the afternoon. When we got home, we heard that my brother-in-law Puspa had called many times from Phuntsholing, where he and Yoga lived. I dialled their number, thinking they were calling about the fresh fruit and vegetables they regularly sent us by bus. Normally my sister would pick up the phone, but this time it was Puspa. He took a very long time to speak. Yoga had gone into the bathroom to have a shower, and stepped into water that had been electrified by faulty wiring. My sister was gone.

Not only my sister, my closest friend. Yoga was kind, friendly, warm – beautiful in every way. Saroja and I immediately got in the car. We spoke little on the five-hour drive through the night. I felt numb; grief would only come later. By 11 pm we were in Phuntsholing. To see Puspa was hard enough, but looking at the two young children, Uma and Prem, was almost unbearable.

The next day, we took Yoga's body to Puspa's ancestral home in Salami, in Chirang district. After six days, we returned to Thimphu. Two months later, I learnt that Saroja was pregnant.

*

Our public wedding day was 3 February 1989. Om Daju was first up, as usual, and he went around waking the janti, or groom's party, including my older brother Chandra. We drove so slowly that it took us an hour to get to Ama and Guru Babu's house in Chengmari. A large crowd was waiting, and as I walked towards the house wearing my light brown suit, Saroja's relatives and other guests showered us with rice, from which the janti shielded me with umbrellas, to bring luck. As the groom's party sat down to a feast of goat meat, chicken and other delicacies, I was taken to the mandap, or wedding altar. A pandit, or Hindu priest, was already seated and performing rituals. After a while he announced, 'Bring in the bride.'

I looked up and saw Saroja in a light blue floral sari, accompanied by her sisters, Ama and Aunty (Saroja's father's second wife). She looked stunning and my heart leapt. We sat together in the mandap and exchanged rings; I placed a tilhari, a wedding necklace made out of gold I had bought specially on a trip to Bangkok, around her neck. As the ceremony progressed, she was required to change her dress, and she was brought back in a little floral red sari! In the same ceremony, Saroja's sister Anupa married Junga Thapa, a classmate of mine from Kanglung.

In the days afterwards, I took Saroja to Lamidara. My

parents put tika on our foreheads and blessed us. Nothing more, we had to be happy with that. Yet my father, especially, was very warm to Saroja. In time, she became like a daughter to my parents, for which I still thank them, especially Mum, who could be very strict on these things. I know that because they loved me, they were prepared to live with the consequences. Perhaps, too, they sensed that their world was changing. All my older siblings' marriages were arranged. After I married Saroja, my younger brother Gopal made an arranged marriage, but my four younger sisters, Punam, Chandra, Tulasha and Padma, all chose the men they married.

It took time for Saroja to understand the caste system but she was so patient about it all. I still thank her for her acceptance and love. And I thank Om Daju. A year after our wedding, he left for Australia to take up a Food and Agriculture Organisation scholarship to study for a master's degree in animal breeding and genetics at Sydney University. Through this move to Australia, Om Daju would again shape the course of my life.

In that strange time of marriage, death and an imminent birth, our work was all-consuming. In hindsight, I see that absorption in my work was my way of dealing with sorrow. Saroja was working alongside Irish and Japanese volunteers and other expatriates to set up a public health laboratory at Thimphu General Hospital, then travelling to other districts to set up similar facilities. I was recruiting from a list of global experts to coordinate our phone systems master plan and to provide technical expertise.

The buzzing project office we set up on the first floor of the telephone exchange felt like the United Nations. Thinley and I worked alongside experts from many countries – all under the sharp eye of project co-ordinator Ismet Hamiti, a former refugee from Kosovo in the former Yugoslavia. We were working ten or 12 hours a day, and on weekends, but it was exciting. The seeds we had sown a year earlier were bearing fruit.

One team member, Ross Dannecker, was an engineer from Telecom Australia. I had met many Australians working for international agencies and had a lot of regard for them. In telecommunications, they were more open than people from other countries to sharing their ideas and methods. Quite a few Bhutanese officials had studied in Australia, some under the Colombo Plan, a postwar initiative of the British Commonwealth to develop Asia-Pacific countries by training their promising students.

Finally, we liked Australians' warmth, their straight, can-do attitude. Ross, for example, was astonished to hear I had an official driver who dropped me home. When I told him that I did not know how to drive, he said, 'Tomorrow, after work, I'll start teaching you.' I thought we would get straight into a car but on day one he made drawings and explained how cars worked. Only on day three did he allow me to touch a car. Ross taught me how to drive.

The master plan established the number of towers, telephone exchanges and phone lines Bhutan would have. Our tender led to offers from France, Sweden and Japan. A partnership between Japanese trading conglomerate Mitsui & Co. and equipment manufacturer NEC quoted an extraordinary US$3.9 million to supply and install both the satellite Earth station and the international switching system. The next offer came in at $11 million. Years later, when I was a refugee in Nepal, I told a senior manager of Nepal's Telecommunications

Corporation, a man I had known through my job in Bhutan, what we had got for $3.9 million. He was incredulous: 'Nowhere in the world can you get it for this price.' But the Japanese, always strategic, knew that if we took their system we would go with their products for a long time. We negotiated to include training for a group of our engineers and technicians. In June 1989, Thinley and I went to Japan to sign the contracts, so proud of what we had achieved for Bhutan.

In August, I returned to Japan with a group of six engineers for nearly three months of training in transmissions and switching systems. On 26 August I got a telegram – I had a daughter. Because of the training, I did not see Smriti until she was two months old. In those days it was not unusual for men to be away working for long periods.

At Tokyo airport my colleagues and I were carrying so much Japanese gadgetry – TVs, VCRs, CDs, keyboards, often bought at a discount when our hosts took us on tours of factories – that we were charged the equivalent of US$1200 in excess baggage. The airline official was very interested in Bhutan, though, and he and I chatted for a while, until he said, 'How much can you pay?' I asked the guys to empty their pockets – we had about $175. The Japanese official said, 'Fine.'

As the Drukair plane manoeuvred through the gorges into Bhutan to land at Paro airport, I thought of the little girl I was about to meet. I quickly cleared customs and collected my luggage, which was stuffed with a baby blanket, dresses and a pram, and almost ran towards our babysitter, Ongmit, and Saroja, who was holding a little bundle. I wrapped my arms around Saroja and the baby, who was wrapped in a red and white floral blanket. It was cold and she was fully covered, except for a round face with eyes closed. As I kissed her she woke and opened her eyes. I carried her in my lap all the way back to Thimpu, two and a half hours' drive. On the spot I called her Bhukuli, which in Nepali means something like 'round one', a name I still sometimes use today. I also called her Kuchu, a word that appears in no language but my own.

Our house became a busy, happy place, holding not just our small family but my brother Gopal and sister Punam, our cousins Ram and Kavita, and Ongmit. Saroja went back to work and would slip home often to breastfeed, and we all ate dinner together before I returned to the office. One night 17 Japan Overseas Cooperation Volunteers, many of whom worked with Saroja, came to our house for dinner. One ate an extremely fiery chilli from a jar, thinking it was a cherry, and nearly fainted.

In 1991, I became head of my department's Planning and Development Division. That job made me a member of the Policy and Planning Division, a body of representatives from every ministry, with oversight of planning across government. Ten to 15 people attended meetings, and discussions were exciting since many of us were young and focused on developing the country in a sustainable way. The king himself would chair meetings of the National Planning Commission, the ministers and senior officials to whom the Policy and Planning Division reported. He wanted to have his eye on everything.

I felt I was part of a strong bureaucracy. Many senior civil servants had trained overseas, and were open to the outside world. To my knowledge, there was no corruption. A few years later, when I arrived in Nepal, my counterpart in telecommunications, the same man who had expressed astonishment at the price we had obtained from the Japanese, said to me, 'I assume you've come here with at least half a million dollars?' I had come with nothing.

Bhutan seemed to be a country on the move, led by a king who was like a forward-thinking CEO. We were starting to sell hydropower to India. In the south, villagers were replacing thatched roofs with corrugated tin. My parents had a good income from the shop and land from which they could get cash crops, and they had just built a new house. After India began to allow direct exports to Bangladesh from Bhutan through a narrow corridor in West Bengal, southerners could export cardamom, oranges, timber and betel nut, and get paid in US dollars, not Indian rupees. Saroja and I, and her sister and husband, bought a few acres of land in Phuntsholing, the commercial hub of the south-west, because we knew it was going to grow.

But these changes had impacts. People in the north started to look jealously at the south, with its growing population and wealth. Moreover, political events around the world and close to home might have begun to worry the king and the powerful people around him.

In neighbouring Sikkim in 1975, the monarch, Palden Thondup Namgyal, a relative of the Bhutanese king, was deposed and the country became a state of India after a referendum voted overwhelmingly to abolish the monarchy. Ethnic Nepalis, who form a majority in Sikkim, played an important role in that movement.

In the 1980s, in the neighbouring Indian district of Darjeeling, a movement of ethnic Nepalis arose seeking to create a Gorkhaland state, part of India but independent of West Bengal. That insurgency, which continues in a flickering way even today, has claimed more than a thousand lives.

And in Nepal itself, in 1990, a coalition comprising the Nepali Congress, a pro-democracy party, and a range of parties that combined to form the United Left Front, overthrew the country's absolute monarchy and replaced it with a constitutional monarchy and a multi-party democratic system.

The Bhutanese elite watched these events – not to mention the fall of the Berlin Wall and the emergence of democracy movements across the former Soviet bloc – with alarm. They began to point to the four million ethnic Nepalis in the Indian state of Assam, another million in West Bengal, and 18 million in Nepal itself – compared to 500 000 ethnic Bhutanese. People in the government started to say: we in the north are the true Bhutanese, and then we have these southern Bhutanese. Bhutan might become a Nepali state; the southerners might 'dismember the Kingdom', one leader said. The Lhotshampas who were entering the civil service in growing numbers might be a Nepali fifth column, bringing demands for democracy.

It was a dark fantasy. Yes, many of us were democrats, but before that we were Bhutanese, at times even more so than the ethnic Bhutanese themselves. I always wore the national dress at official occasions overseas. When my northern Bhutanese colleagues asked why I bothered, since it was not required, I said I was proud to represent my country, and my king. As for the vast bulk of the southerners, they were simple, pious farmers, interested not in politics but in their crops.

In those years, my head was so full of work challenges, my daughter's birth and sister's death, that I did not see the looming threat. I was not alone.

In 1981, the government had introduced national citizenship identity cards for all Bhutanese, but forced only Lhotshampas to carry them. In 1985, a new Citizenship Act required both parents to be Bhutanese citizens. Those who could not provide proof to satisfy this requirement were retroactively declared illegal immigrants. The king had begun to undo the work of his father.

In 1987 and 1988 the government conducted a one-off census, this time for southern Bhutan only. It justified this act by claiming that it had detected the presence of 100 000 illegal Nepalis who had flooded into southern Bhutan to take advantage of its economic prosperity and development programs. It may be no coincidence that 100 000 was exactly the number that would later be expelled. The government produced no evidence for its assertions, because there was none. No one could enter Bhutan from India without a permit and the border was well policed. If a few Nepali workers overstayed in Bhutan, they would have been a minuscule fraction of the number the government claimed.

The new census collectors were not local officials but, for the first time, home ministry officials sent down from Thimphu. Many conducted the census harshly and arbitrarily. Nepali Bhutanese had to prove their citizenship by producing a receipt for land tax they had paid in 1958, the year of the Nationality Law that had made them citizens for the first time. No other year would do. Without this piece of paper, they were deemed to be non-citizens. People who had moved into an area after 1958 had to produce a Certificate of Origin, which often required them to return to their birthplaces to obtain the documents. Luckily, because more than two-thirds of Bhutanese were illiterate, they would keep any document given to them by the government, and 30 years later most people were able to produce this receipt.

The government used this census to create seven categories of citizens. Only the first – a person born and raised in Bhutan, whose family could produce the 1958 tax receipt – would come to be accepted as fully Bhutanese. The seventh category – so-called migrants and illegal settlers – was the most dangerous to be in. Some of these people would in time lose their citizenship and be branded as 'non-nationals', sometimes divided from citizens within their own family.

A year after the census, the government announced it would create a kilometre-wide green belt of forested land along the southern border with India. The initiative would have displaced many thousands of families, including Saroja's. My father-in-law got a letter saying his family had three weeks to leave their home, after which the government would level it. Guru Babu appealed to the local authorities, to no avail. That initiative lapsed when donor countries such as Austria, Denmark and Japan, which Bhutan had asked to fund the initiative as an environmental measure, declined the request when they realised it was designed to uproot southern Bhutanese.

People I knew were astonished: why would anyone want to evict such a decent, respected person as Guru Babu? But we were also very naïve. In Thimphu, far from the areas of conflict, many southerners had close relationships with ethnic Northern and Eastern Bhutanese. Not only was there no discrimination, we never thought about our differences. One of Saroja's cousins had married the king's younger sister. The marriage would not last, in large part because of the conflict that was about to erupt, but it was a sign of how we viewed ourselves as one and the same. The government even gave 5000 rupees, a lot of money, for intermarriages between ethnic Nepalis and other groups. Our next-door neighbour in Thimphu, a southerner, married a woman from Eastern Bhutan. They used their incentive payment to buy a sound system for dancing and parties in their house.

In 1988, I was required for the first time, as a southerner, to complete the census by reporting to officials in my hometown. I watched my father dust off some papers nicely wrapped in a dark piece of cloth torn off an old shirt. He carefully pulled out each paper and asked me to find the receipt for 1958. I found one for 1949, for 1952, and for almost every year since then. The million-dollar 1958 tax receipt was there too! We were all so happy. We thought we were safe.

4

DARKNESS FALLS
ON BHUTAN

I looked again at my watch. It was almost 4 am. Saroja and I had hardly slept, and had spent the night in the darkness, whispering to each other under the blanket. We could not talk aloud for fear someone was listening. I was sure our phone was bugged, maybe our house, too. Beside Saroja lay our daughter Smriti, two and a half years old, in deep, blissful sleep.

That Sunday morning of 19 April 1992 was unlike any other. There would be no visits to a friend or relative, no shopping for vegetables at the Sunday market near our home in Thimphu. For almost a year, the government's special security forces had kept me under surveillance. My movements were restricted. If I wanted to leave Thimphu, even to visit my home town of Lamidara, six hours' drive away, I had to get a permit.

A few days earlier, a friend with connections to senior police officials told me, 'Om, you're going to be arrested any day.' The security forces were indiscriminately arresting and torturing people in the south. Knowing their fate, I feared for my life.

Nearly nine months earlier, as he lay in bed on a night in July, my father heard his oldest son, Bholanath, calling to him from outside the house: 'Baa, I need you to take care of my children.' Five or six soldiers stood around Bholanath. One shouted, 'Hey, old man, you come down too. You need to go with us.'

In minutes, my father ran downstairs, with my mother close behind, trying to wrap a bed sheet around himself, since he had not had time to put on clothes. My sisters Tulasha and Padma, aged 14 and ten, ran outside crying, clinging to my father, my other sister Chandra and my sister-in-law Parbata begged the soldiers not to take him. The men pulled the girls away, and ordered Dad and Bholanath to start walking with a group of five or six people from the village who had also been arrested. As he walked, my father heard a wailing behind him that gradually faded into the darkness.

A military van drove them for about half an hour to Damphu, the district headquarters, then to the high school. All schools in southern Bhutan had been closed; most had been converted to temporary prisons and detention centres. It was past midnight when my father and Bholanath were herded into a classroom with a tin roof and cement floor. There was no light inside but when the door was opened, they glimpsed the movement of a large crowd of people sitting and lying on the floor. The soldiers pushed the prisoners into the room and locked the door. The school is on top of a windy hill, and that night was very cold. Huddled under his bedsheet on the cement floor, my father could hardly sleep.

The next day soldiers came back and began interrogations. The officer in charge, Lieutenant Chimmi Dorji, was a sadist. He would turn up around midnight and with his army boots start kicking any prisoner who did not stand to attention as soon as he entered the room. My father was accused of supporting the organisers of protests a year earlier, when southern Bhutanese had for the first time taken to the streets, demanding their human rights. Dad had taken no part in the demonstrations but he was beaten and kicked, and accused of providing food to the dissidents. Because most youths in our village were avoiding their homes for fear of arrest, they would sometimes come hungry to the home of my parents, who simply honoured the village tradition of giving any visitor food.

For this, the soldiers put a metal clamp on my father's thighs and tightened it so hard that he fainted. Although 62 years old, he was made to carry stones to a nearby construction site nearly every day. He was released after three months – on condition that he leave the country.

The deep causes of these events had been building for a decade, but the immediate cause lay in the national census the government had taken three years before. Citing the results of the census, the government announced that nearly 30 per cent of the population was of Nepali origin. It had long been an open secret that Bhutan inflated its population numbers to qualify for more UN aid. But in 1990 the king admitted to the lie, telling an Indian magazine that the population was about 600 000, not more than a million and growing, as had been stated officially for nearly 20 years. He put the new number, however, at least 100 000 too low – to show that the Nepali population was a larger proportion of the total than it actually was.

The government's constant references to Nepali heritage bewildered the southern Bhutanese. We were indeed ethnic Nepalis, with a distinct cultural identity. But we did not identify in any way with the nation of Nepal, let alone have any separatist desires. We were Bhutanese, loyal to king and country, and we had been loyal for a hundred years.

My own grandfather had migrated to Bhutan 80 years earlier. His son, my father, had made a few short visits to Nepal, and sometimes crossed the Indian border to buy groceries, but otherwise he had never left Bhutan. The government now deemed him, and many thousands of other southern Bhutanese, to be a ngolop – an anti-national. Yet he revered the king. When the soldiers said he had to leave the country, he stayed in Lamidara. He had nowhere else to go.

In Thimphu, a few southerners began to speak up, and one of the first was a man from my village. Tek Nath Rizal, who was about 15 years older than me, lived with his family in a modest place not far from our farm. I remember my father helping his parents by giving them loans from time to time. Rizal's mother was a lovely woman whom my father called Didi – sister. Rizal drove a bulldozer but he was eloquent and ambitious, and in 1975 he was elected as a National Assembly member for Chirang. The king liked him. In 1980 the government even sent him to Australia for ten months to learn English.

In 1985 Rizal was appointed as one of two southern representatives on the Royal Advisory Council. When the implementation of the 1988 census began to create uncertainty and fear in the south, Rizal went to the king, who told him to put his case in writing. Lacking writing skills, Rizal asked a group of senior southern Bhutanese civil servants – including Saroja's relatives, R.B. and D.P. Basnet and Bhim Subba – to help him.

Some of these bureaucrats, worried about events in the south, had already begun to meet. To do that was risky but, they reasoned, if the king had asked Rizal to write up his concerns, how dangerous could it be?

The petition they drafted was signed by Rizal and Bidya Pati Bhandari, another councillor from Southern Bhutan, and handed to the king in April 1988. It alleged that census teams, by harshly interrogating people and classifying them into various categories, had produced 'panic and confusion' and 'disturbed the peace and tranquillity that has reigned in the hearts of Your Majesty's loyal subjects'. Addressing the government's claim about a tide of illegal Nepali immigrants, the petitioners said Lhotshampas would also be concerned if any entered Bhutan. To blame people 'for allegedly colluding with immigrants to secrete them into the country is unfair and unjust.' The petition ended with an expression of 'deepest gratitude to Your Majesty that we have never had an occasion to even feel the slightest disappointment in our lives from the wisdom of Your Majesty's decisions'.

This forthright but highly respectful document caused consternation within the cabinet and other close advisors of the king. I believe that these officials, and especially Dago Tshering, later to become home minister, put fear into the king's mind by telling him he faced serious opposition from the southern Bhutanese, and in particular from the civil servants who had drafted the petition.

In June that year, the cabinet pronounced the petition seditious, and recommended capital punishment for Rizal. He was removed from his public post, arrested and tortured. After three days behind bars, he was released, but not before being forced to sign a so-called confession. Under surveillance, afraid of being re-arrested and killed, Rizal fled the country. In 1989 he and two other activists, Jogen Gazmere and

Sushil Pokhrel, were arrested by police in Nepal, which at that time was still ruled by an absolute monarchy allied to the Bhutanese king. Extradited to Bhutan, Rizal was kept in solitary confinement for three years before the High Court sentenced him to life imprisonment.

In the same year the government recaptured Rizal, a royal proclamation introduced the One Nation, One People policy. The king issued a kasho, or decree, requiring anyone going out in public to wear national dress: for men the gho; for women the kira, a rectangular piece of cloth wrapped around the body from neck to ankle and fastened with brooches; and for both sexes the shawl draped across one shoulder, the kabney.

The Tibetan-style garments are heavy, and suited for the northern cold, not for farmers working in the southern heat. Older women in particular struggled with the complexities of putting on the kira. Anyone who went out, even to buy salt, had to wear the garments or incur an on-the-spot fine or even imprisonment. My father was fined several times for opening his shop when he was not in national dress, although he planned to put it on before he went behind the counter. Women were also told to cut their hair short, in the Bhutanese way. Hindu priests could no longer wear traditional white religious dress while presiding over worship in the temples. Others were fined, assaulted or even imprisoned for wearing traditional Nepali costume at weddings and funerals, as we had always done in the past.

Even harsher restrictions followed. That same year, the government decreed that people in several of its new census categories – including anyone married to a non-Bhutanese citizen – could no longer send their children to school. Nepali was no longer to be taught in primary schools in the south. Many teachers of the Nepali language, and some southern officials of Nepali heritage, were fired from their jobs.

Some southerners decided they had had enough. In June 1990, activists formed the Bhutan People's Party and set up camp in the forests of Assam and West Bengal, just beyond the Bhutan border. Without doubt, some of these activists reacted violently at some points, targeting both Bhutanese officials and Lhotshampas who did not support the protesters. That violence was unacceptable, but if people are put under pressure they will react, and some are likely to go to extremes.

Far away in Thimphu, we southern civil servants struggled to read the situation. The bureaucracy was functioning well, engrossed in its nation-building work. I had many close colleagues and friends among the northern Bhutanese. What I did not know was that high-ranking southerners like R.B. Basnet, managing director of the State Trading Corporation of Bhutan and Saroja's uncle, were being watched for signs they were talking to dissidents. R.B. Basnet was a no-nonsense man. He had been a tough soccer player in the national competition; he was the king's tennis partner. Perhaps his bluntness, his refusal to be submissive, angered some northern Bhutanese.

One day we got news that southern Bhutanese demonstrators were marching to the capital. We were thrown into confusion. Should we give them food, shelter? We were told that the march would arrive on 26 August, the day of Smriti's first birthday celebrations.

The rally turned out to be a rumour, but between September and October big rallies were held across the south. The biggest, in my home district of Chirang, reportedly brought about 40000 people onto the streets.

Bhutan had never known such political opposition, and it shook the government to the core. It imposed an economic embargo on southern Bhutan. All shops, including my parents' grocery, were ordered to shut. The flow of salt, sugar, cooking oil and other essential items was restricted. The government stopped paying for cash crops and instead confiscated them, a clear attempt to starve people. Then it sent in the army, and the violence began.

Schools were shut and turned into prisons. Nepali textbooks were burnt in public. Women and girls were raped. In Samchi, soldiers fired on one crowd then charged it with bayonets, killing several people and injuring many more. Just above our house in Lamidara, security forces shot dead four people, including our neighbour, Deo Narayan Adhikari, after a crowd tried to stop soldiers from closing the local health unit and taking away medical supplies.

People were often held for months without trial, then released under one condition: they had to leave the country or be arrested and tortured again. And so, first as a trickle and then as a flood, people began to leave the only country they had ever known.

They first set up camps across the border in India. But Indian security forces captured some and handed them back to Bhutan, where they faced imprisonment and torture. Worried for their safety, confused, humiliated, most began making the five- to ten-hour journey to Nepal. They fled in cramped truckloads, before lugging their remaining belongings in gunny sacks across the Nepalese border.

The Bhutanese government helped them on their way by introducing what it called voluntary migration forms. People would be summoned to the district office and told,

'You're leaving, sign this form and you'll be compensated for your house and land.' The forms were written in Dzongkha, so few southerners understood that their compensation was usually worth about a tenth of the value of their property. If a landowner or a family member had been jailed during the protests, 2000 rupees would be deducted for every month of imprisonment. The money lay in piles of 50- and 100-rupee notes in the district office, and people had to take it on the spot, then smile in front of a video camera, saying, 'I am selling my property and leaving the country willingly and migrating to Nepal.' Many did so, certain they had no choice.

In May 1991, the conflict entered a new phase when six senior civil servants, all southern Bhutanese, fled the country. Two of them were Saroja's sister, Usha Tamang, a senior foreign currency officer in the Royal Monetary Authority, and her husband, Mandhoj Tamang, deputy director of the Planning Commission. Then there were R.B. Basnet and his cousin D.P. Basnet, who was joint director of the Department of Industries; and Bhim Subba, director-general of the Power Department and married to Saroja's sister Jyotsna. The one civil servant in the group not related to Saroja was Rakesh Chettri, deputy director of the State Trading Corporation.

The six planned to leave the country to protest against government policies in the south. Driving their own cars, taking their immediate families, they travelled to India and stayed for three days in Kalimpong with my mother-in-law Kamala Gurung, who had built a house there many years ago to be with her children while they studied in the town. I think the civil servants believed they would be gone from Bhutan for a few months, until the trouble passed. Not one would ever return.

Bhutanese security forces, which the Indian government allowed to operate with impunity in the border areas inside India, sent commandos to capture them. The soldiers arrived at my mother-in-law's house just hours after the group had left, after being tipped off about the imminent raid. Had they stayed they would have been kidnapped, and either killed or imprisoned for life.

The six made the 15-hour drive to Kathmandu, Nepal's capital. Their timing was good: attitudes in Nepal had changed since the overthrow of the monarchy the previous year. The new democratically elected government supported the dissidents and would allow Bhutanese refugees to enter the country. The civil servants met Girija Prasad Koirala, Nepal's first prime minister since the change of government, and held a press conference denouncing Bhutan's policies. These events drew significant international attention, finally putting the persecution of the Lhotshampas on the map. They also infuriated the Bhutanese government.

In Thimphu we could feel the change in mood. Two weeks after the civil servants left, Kipchu Namgyel, chief of intelligence of the Royal Bhutan Police and a man I knew, called me. 'You are related to Bhim Subba. We are taking possession of his house. Can you accompany us?' They wanted a family member to witness their house search. Two days later Namgyel called again: 'You are related to Mandhoj Tamang. We need you to come while we take possession of his house.'

I went along. In those bewildering days I had no idea what to do. I hadn't heard about the violence in the south until some time after it had begun. There was no independent press, no telephone service in Lamidara, and letters were not safe. Even after my father's first arrest, in July 1991, when I visited him he told me it was best to wait and see how things panned out; maybe the worst was over. Yet when I learnt about his torture, I spoke to the minister for communications, Dr T. Tobgyel, and the secretary of his department, Dasho Nado Rinchen. I spoke to the chief justice, Dasho Sonam Tobgye, and to the head of the Royal Civil Service Commission, Dasho Khandu Wangchuk, who would later become prime minister. I even met Colonel V. Namgyel, deputy chief of the Royal Bodyguards and aide-de-camp to the king.

All these discussions with high-ranking officials, whom I knew personally and held in high regard, were strictly informal and off-the-record. Any formal representation over the situation in the south, especially by a civil servant in my position, would lead to arrest and imprisonment.

All these men either feigned ignorance of the situation or told me they were not in a position to do anything. They insisted it was 'not government policy to harass the people'. Colonel Namgyel said, 'I will try to find out which officers are ordering these actions.' I think he tried to comfort me with these words, but later I learned that the Royal Bodyguard effectively administered the state of martial law in Southern Bhutan.

I continued to believe, or at least hope, that things would improve. I kept working on my part of the government's seventh five-year plan. In September 1991, I organised the 12th South Asian Association of Regional Cooperation meeting on telecommunications in Thimphu.

Saroja and I tried to lead a normal life. Smriti slept in our bed and on weekend mornings she would slowly open my eyes with her little fingers and pull me out of bed to go for a morning walk. She never did this on weekdays and we never understood how she knew it was a weekend, being not yet two years old.

But a net was closing around us. I had organised a group of seven engineers to go to Australia for five months training with Telecom Australia. Not long before their departure date, my boss and friend, Tshering Dorji, looked down the list and said to me, 'You need to drop these two.' I protested that these men were the most qualified in the group. Both were southern Bhutanese and one was my close friend Rabilal Pokhrel, who had studied with me in Dacca. The two replacements were northern Bhutanese with lower qualifications. Tshering said he had instructions from the secretary of the Royal Civil Service Commission. He tried to reassure me: 'Don't take it personally, I'm sure things will settle down.'

They did not. Saroja had planned to go to the UK to undertake a master's degree, and Smriti and I were going with her; I had applied to do postgraduate studies in tele-communications at Essex University. But the government withdrew her approval to travel. My 16-year-old brother, Gopal, had to halt his studies after I was unable to get him a No Objection Certificate, a police pass designed predomin-antly to monitor the movements of southerners. My youngest siblings, Tulasha and Padma, could not study since all schools were closed in Southern Bhutan.

In December 1991, as parts of the international media focused for the first time on the violence, the king sent his home minister, Dago Tshering, to the south to investigate complaints of arbitrary arrest, torture and forced deportation. The problem was that Tshering was the architect of these policies. He held a meeting in the district centre of Damphu, near Lamidara. When asked, my father stood up in the meeting and said he had been tortured. I knew Tshering well from when he had been ambassador to Bangladesh. When Dad replied to a question about his family by saying he had a son working in Thimphu, Tshering said, 'Oh, you are Om's father.' He said he would look into his case. But when I met Tshering by chance in Thimphu a week later, he was friendly but did not mention meeting my father. At that moment I realised that my connections in government counted for nothing.

In December 1991, five months after their first visit, Lieutenant Dorji and his soldiers came again to my father's door. 'Why are you still here?' they demanded. My terrified mother and sisters promised the soldiers they would leave the country immediately if my father was not arrested. Their crying and pleading got no response; my father was driven back to the school in Damphu.

In the middle of the night, he and others were herded into a classroom. When the soldiers opened the door, some older inmates could not stand to attention immediately. Dorji kicked them and told them to be quicker. The soldiers warned my father that he would be detained for years. He was then beaten till he collapsed.

The next day, the soldiers gave the inmates two options: leave the country immediately or face regular beatings and torture in prison for years. My father said he would leave. He was released later that day, but again, having nowhere to go, he stayed.

Two and a half months passed. The fear in my family subsided a little. But in March 1992, the soldiers came a third time. Luckily, my father had gone to the farm. When he returned, my mother, who believed he would not survive the beating and torture if he were arrested again, urged him to leave at once. It was late in the afternoon and a neighbour, Rabilal Khanal, who was also sought by the soldiers, came in to discuss how to escape their impending arrests.

The two men decided to leave together. They walked the whole night, hid the following day, and crossed the Indian border that evening. The next day they met some other refugees from Bhutan, who told them it was not safe to stay in the area. People were hungry and getting sick with malaria. Bhutanese agents and soldiers were moving through the region and abducting democracy activists with the connivance of local authorities. No Indian border town was safe.

They decided to go to Nepal. After changing buses three times, travelling for a day through fields, forests and tea plantations, they reached Kakarvitta and crossed the border, pretending to be Indians, who can travel to Nepal with no restrictions. My father then took another bus and travelled to Charpane, in Jhapa district, where my oldest sister, Bhagiratha, lived with her husband and their six children after migrating to Nepal in 1979. Next day, my father went to Maidhar, a short trip by bus. There he saw lines of temporary huts, housing thousands of Bhutanese, strung along the banks of the Mai River.

Dorji's soldiers also came regularly to my older sister Kaushila's house. They said they would pay 2000 rupees for her best cow – it was worth at least 30 000 rupees. Kaushila shouted at them, 'Don't insult me. Just take it.' She is very tough and mouthy. But she was alone: her husband, Muktinath Baral, had fled a year earlier after the government accused him of collecting funds for dissidents. I heard that news on national radio in Thimphu.

Fearing she would be arrested and tortured, probably

raped, we urged Kaushila to go as well. I went to her place, to bring her back to Thimphu so that we could get her out of the country. But when the family talked, we decided that it was better if she took the shorter route south to India, via Sarbhang. My brother Gopal would accompany her and the children.

What money she and Muktinath had left was hidden around their property. Kaushila and I went cash-hunting. We found piles of notes at the back of the house next to the gutter, in the goat shed, stashed inside bamboo sticks holding up plants – about 70000 rupees in all, nearly an annual salary for me. I later smuggled the money out of Bhutan, and Muktinath used it to trade profitably in oranges and betel nut in Nepal. After Kaushila left with her seven children and joined him in a refugee camp, the army demolished their home, which they had just built.

As people left, the government used the videos they had made of their departure to show international organisations that they were leaving by choice. Too many of these agencies, I believe, were gullible, and accepted this clearly cooked-up story. Others kept quiet. Australia had an assistance program but its diplomats, like officials from all governments that gave aid to Bhutan, would have been very reluctant to raise any concerns for fear their programs would be stopped. Ismet Hamiti, the engineer from Kosovo who was co-ordinator of the International Telecommunication Union and who had been a refugee himself, told me many years later that he could see what was going on, but you kept your mouth shut or lost your job; that was the deal.

Amnesty International fought hard for us, but its requests to investigate the situation were repeatedly blocked. The government finally allowed a visit, in January 1992, but it organised the whole tour, and banned any individual from talking with the Amnesty delegation. The US State Department also played a very honourable role. Its 1993 human rights report found that abuses committed by police and soldiers in southern Bhutan 'were a consequence of government policies intended to reduce the presence of ethnic Nepalese. These policies created a climate in which intimidation of ethnic Nepalese was encouraged and physical abuse tacitly condoned.'

But the overall international response was shameful. Bhutan's heavy reliance on aid from India, western nations and non-government organisations gives the global community huge leverage, but it has never used it, not even when the Bhutanese government choked funds to the south for ten years after the expulsions. Bhutan not only interpreted the uninterrupted flow of donor funding as tacit support for its policies in the south, it used that funding to divert its own internal resources in order to pursue those policies.

UN agencies and international NGOs had reasons for their silence. They saw Bhutan as a perfect place in which to execute their programs: its bureaucracy was not corrupt, money did not simply disappear. It was an environmental paradise; in February 1992, United Nations Development Programme head William Draper lauded Bhutan as a leader in 'sustainable development'. In that year, as the refugee exodus reached its peak, Bhutan received its largest aid package ever. Even foreign minister Dawa Tsering was surprised, saying, 'We did not expect so much pledging.' The lesson he must have drawn was that, whatever happened, Bhutan's image remained untarnished.

The king and his ministers were shrewd: they knew how to cater to western prejudices. They told the Swiss, Danish and Dutch governments that Bhutan was just like them, a small country at risk of being overpowered by surrounding giants. As the historian of Bhutan Michael Hutt writes, the policies the government enacted to preserve Bhutan's distinctive Drukpa culture were carefully presented 'in a way which reflected Western constructions of "indigenous" cultures, and spoke to Western anxieties about the deleterious effects of "modernisation" on such cultures.' Bhutanese leaders often described their people as an 'endangered species', with nothing to protect them but their national identity. That line played well with internationals, especially journalists. It helps to explain why Bhutan's ethnic cleansing never attracted the attention that such violence attracted in the former Yugoslavia, Africa, and other parts of the world.

*

In early February 1992, I was sent to Spain to represent Bhutan at the World Administrative Radio Conference. The secretary for communications had to pull out at the last minute and I took his place in the huge plenary sessions. I raised a 'Yes' or 'No' card on behalf of Bhutan, looking across the room beforehand to make sure I voted with the Indians, as Bhutanese officials always did.

Back in Thimphu, Saroja and I agonised about what to do. Since my father had been classified as an 'anti-national' and all family members were registered under his name, none of us could obtain a police No Objection Certificate. Without that document we could not travel, send children to school, run a business, use government services or stay in a job.

My boss, Tshering Dorji, had told me earlier that the

civil service secretary said I must not leave Thimphu. But my sister Tulasha, then 13 years old, had been at a student rally in Damphu. It was no longer safe for her at home; soldiers were raping girls her age. In 1990 we had bought our first car, a red Maruti Suzuki van. Saroja and her driver took it to Lamidara, and brought Tulasha to Thimphu, a brave act that brought Saroja much closer to my parents. From there, a relative drove Tulasha to Saroja's mother's house in Kalimpong. Saroja, at some risk to herself, also managed to smuggle food to tortured southern Bhutanese prisoners in Thimphu Hospital.

She and I were both being watched. No one would talk to us when we walked down the street. I was often aware of a man following me as I left home. I was sure my office phone was bugged. Through my job I knew the government had imported bugging equipment from the US in 1990, and the man responsible for phone security was head of operations in my department. But although it was directly opposite my office, I had no access to the room where phone tapping took place.

It was painful to see my friends and colleagues, people for whom I still have the highest respect, vanish from my life. If I tried to approach them, they avoided me or didn't respond. I understood: they had to save their skins and positions in the government. Because Bhutan is small, people don't take stands. In Australia, if I'm in the prime minister's bad books, who cares? If you're in the bad books of the king of Bhutan, you're finished.

For a long time, King Jigme Singye Wangchuck had continued his father's inclusive policies. The southerners are true citizens, he had said during the National Day celebrations in 1978. But in the 1980s he was coming under increasing pressure from his close advisers, who saw their power as being challenged in a more democratic, multi-ethnic country.

In 1992, foreign minister Dawa Tsering told the *Calcutta Statesman* that if the 'influx' of illegal immigrants continued, Bhutan would become another 'Sikkim and Darjeeling'. Echoing Tsering's words, the king told Reuters that Bhutan was facing 'the greatest threat to its survival since the 7th century ... In the next 10, 15 or 20 years, Bhutan will no longer be a Bhutanese nation. It will be a Nepali state, just like Sikkim.'

In saying these things, the king showed that he now identified as a king only of the northern Bhutanese. 'The main problem is that the aspirations of the northern and southern Bhutanese are different,' he told his cabinet in January 1990. How so, he did not say.

He made many contradictory statements. I believe he was genuinely conflicted. He granted more than 1500 amnesties to convicted ngolops, the so-called anti-nationals. He exempted southern Bhutanese from rural taxes for a year and called for development to be resumed in the south. He once even offered to abdicate if he could not solve the problem.

'Short of literally going down on my knees with folded hands, I have tried everything possible to resolve the serious problem we have today,' he said in an address in southern Bhutan. 'I have come here from Thimphu to ask you all not to migrate and leave your country. Although I do not know all of you, I know some of you here personally ... I can now only hope that you will stay back so that we can all live together like members of one household and make our country strong and secure.'

I'm not sure he knew all that was going on in the south,

the atrocities his home minister and zealous officials had set in train. But he knew enough; the rest he chose not to know. All power in Bhutan ultimately resided with him. If he had said, 'These are my people, this stops with me', he could have ended the violence at once. Instead, he presided over the expulsion of 100 000 of his citizens, a seventh of the population, one of the greatest acts of ethnic cleansing, per capita, that the world has seen.

To this day I cannot but feel that a part of him regrets his actions. In 1992 Michael Hutt interviewed him for his book on the flight of the southern Bhutanese. At the end of their conversation the king said to Hutt, 'You can go and talk to the boys now.' It was an oddly friendly reference to the civil servants who had worked for him so loyally and were now languishing in Nepal. Yet he could have sought their advice. Instead, he totally cut himself off from them.

He saw himself as a nationalist, a patriot. But once a leader takes on a particular identity on behalf of one group, protecting that identity becomes paramount. Even atrocities, inhuman suffering, can be justified to achieve that goal. King Jigme Singye Wangchuck, who is still alive today, although not on the throne, chose to identify himself as ruler of the Northern and Eastern Bhutanese, not of all Bhutanese. By helping to destroy his own people, he fatally diminished his nation and himself. That is his place in history.

In my last year in Bhutan, Saroja and I made the 170-kilometre journey to Lamidara three times. It was the only way we could find out what was going on. Each time I had to get a permit from the Ministry of Home Affairs. Soldiers stopped us, circled the car with guns and usually searched it, waking and frightening our little daughter.

When we visited after Dad left, Mum went outside with a torch and a small spade. When she came back, Saroja and I and other family members were sitting on the floor in a circle. The room was dimly lit so as not to attract soldiers patrolling the village. Mum sat next to Padma, my youngest sister, and opened an aluminium jar she had hidden in a hole behind the house. In it were all her savings. Bhutan had very few banks, the nearest was too far from our home to use. Besides, if you put money in the banks during this time, the government would take it. If you hid money inside the house, the army would come and take it.

Mum put her hand into the container and her face went pale. Water had seeped in; all the notes were ruined, and they stank. I told her we would try to dry the notes on our heater in Thimphu. On the drive back Saroja and I hid bundles of them under the car carpet. Saroja managed to salvage most of them and remove the smell by drying them on an iron firewood box that was connected to the chimney and spraying them with a perfume I had bought her in Japan.

On my last visit, Saroja, Smriti and I drove to Lamidara to pick up my mother and ten-year-old sister Padma. I boarded up my parents' shop and hammered nails into the boards. At the farm, Gopal and I released our two cows and a calf into open land. My mother cried as she got ready to leave. Then the five of us drove back to Thimpu. A few days later we sent Mum and Padma to Phuntsholing. From there they crossed the border into India, and thence to Nepal.

As late as a month before I left, I went on a national tour to inspect sites for telephone exchanges and towers. I think I believed even then that life could return to normal. Saroja also went about her work, setting up public health laboratories. But I was afraid. It pained me to think about the scars on my father's body. Where was he now? And Mum and my three youngest siblings? Saroja and I had to care for them, but I had no idea how they were faring and I could be convicted of treachery if I called Nepal to find out.

As a son and older brother, I longed to leave. But as a husband and father, I was bound to stay. The thought of little Smriti haunted me. What if the government found out I had absconded, and arrested my wife? Would I ever see them again?

In urgent whispers, Saroja and I debated our choices. We decided I had to leave. She and Smriti would follow a few days later. We could not go together – the government would know we were trying to leave the country and arrest us at once.

I arranged a work trip to Phuntsholing, on the Indian border. My sister Chandra, her infant son Jeewan, and Uma and Prem, the children of my sister Yoga, were all living with us in Thimphu, for their safety. After Yoga's death in 1988, her husband, Puspa, had married Chandra, and was now in India, waiting for his wife and children. I decided to take them with me.

The morning of Sunday, 19 April, was cold, clear and beautiful. The world was quiet. To leave behind the people I loved most was the hardest decision I have ever made. Afraid of being apprehended, sad that I could not say goodbye to dear friends like Rabilal Pokhrel and Thinley Dorji, nor even to my own sister Punam, who lived just ten minutes away, I made the five-hour drive to Phuntsholing with Chandra, as the children chattered happily in the back of the car.

We spent the night at my cousin Tara Kafley's place. Early

the next morning I told Chandra and the kids to walk across the border, which was an open crossing on foot, and meet Puspa at a designated place. I went to the nearby Telecom Central Stores and met with Tenzin Dorji, the official in charge of the Phuntsholing telephone system. I told him I needed to repair my car across the border in India, a common practice. 'I'll come with you. I know all the local workshops,' he insisted.

Once across the border, I had to find an excuse to get rid of Tenzin, a thorough gentlemen whom I deeply respected. Time was running out. 'You go back to the office. I have a bit of shopping to do for the kids,' I said. As soon as he left, I asked the mechanic to finish up, and I drove away.

In my mother-in-law's house in Kalimpong, I waited four long days for Saroja and Smriti. Even in India I could be arrested at any time. At midnight on 23 April, a jeep that I had organised to pick them up from the border town of Jaigaon finally arrived. I held my little daughter again.

It was not safe for us to stay, so at about 3.30 am we left for Nepal in our own car. Bad roads forced us to make a long detour and the journey to the border took ten hours, another nightmare. I was too nervous to drive, so one of my wife's cousins, Hemraj Gurung, took the wheel. As we drove through Darjeeling some of the most beautiful country on Earth, I thought only of being apprehended by Indian security forces, who might have noticed our red van with Bhutanese number plates, and taken back to Bhutan.

Early that afternoon we crossed the Nepali border. At last we were in a country where the Bhutanese government could not touch us. I breathed. We were homeless, stateless, but alive. My second life had begun.

5

A BROKEN HOUSE, NEW FOUNDATIONS

It was late afternoon by the time we got to the Mai River, and the wind was blowing hard, with a storm building. As it grew dark, rain began to fall in heavy sheets. People were carrying bags of food on their backs, hoping to find somewhere dry to store them, or trying to get hold of blue tarpaulins flapping madly in the wind and reattach them to trees. I tried to help but I'm no handyman, and gusts of wind kept pulling away the tarpaulins. Everyone was soaked. This was one of the makeshift refugee camps I had heard so much about; these plastic sheets were people's walls and roofs.

After about an hour the rain stopped, and I was able to move around and meet some people from my hometown. It was one of the most painful experiences of my life. I saw elderly people struggling to keep piles of belongings dry and in order, children who should have been at school sitting in a kind of daze. I learnt that people were getting sick, and some were dying. I left with my young nephew, Tika Ram, and a few of his neighbours who had come along with us, and headed back to the solid house of my eldest sister Bhagiratha. In bed that night Saroja kept telling me to get some sleep, but I lay awake until early morning. I couldn't stop thinking, 'Why?'

Saroja, Smriti and I had arrived in Nepal that day, Friday 24 April. We had met my parents and my siblings Gopal and Padma, who were staying at Bhagiratha's house at Charpane, near the town of Birtamod, in Jhapa District, 45 minutes drive from the Indian border. I will never forget the look of relief on my parents' faces when they saw us. I was also seeing my sister and brother-in-law Jiwa Nath and their children for only the second time since they moved to Nepal when I was a boy.

The next day I went to Surunga, a town near the Mai River, and met Dr Bhampa Rai, my old friend from student days in Dacca. Bhampa Daju (out of respect I addressed him as Daju, older brother) had been a senior surgeon in Thimphu and had treated the royal family, but the expulsions of the southerners had so appalled him that he had left in protest with his family. We talked for hours, and he gave me the devastating news.

More than 10 000 people were coming to the camps every month. Indian military police were simply herding them onto trucks and dumping them at the Nepali border. People were trying to put up whatever shelter they could along the river. Staff from the United Nations High Commissioner for Refugees (UNHCR) had begun to arrive in Jhapa to organise permanent camps, and were negotiating locations with Nepali officials, but until now the refugees had done nearly everything themselves. Local Nepalis were helping with great kindness, but still there was a desperate need for food, shelter, medicines. Some people had taken sacks to nearby villages to ask for food, then handed it around in tobacco tins. With no toilets, people had to relieve themselves in bushes or along the river, further risking the general health. Bhampa Daju and a few other doctors were treating not only malaria but cholera, beriberi, tuberculosis, scurvy and measles. There had been an outbreak of meningitis, and some people were starving; I was told that 48 children had died on one day.

But the emergency would pass, Bhampa Daju told me. Then the refugees would have another need: to tell the world about the atrocities committed by the Bhutanese government, and to obtain international support for our campaign to go home. A group of exiled civil servants, including Bhampa Daju, had set up the Human Rights Organisation of Bhutan (HUROB) to work towards these goals. Bhampa Daju, always blunt, got straight to the point: 'Om, you should go to Kathmandu and work with our leadership team. We need you there.'

I said little in reply. I was overwhelmed. But I thought about his words. Three of the six civil servants who had fled Bhutan in protest in 1991 – Bhim Subba, D.P. Basnet and Mandhoj Tamang – were part of the HUROB leadership team. Through Saroja I was related to all three. My skills in the civil service had been in advocacy, planning, people management – in building relationships, not the practical skills that would be needed to build refugee camps.

I took the advice of Bhampa Daju and others. For the next six years I lived in Kathmandu, becoming a general secretary of HUROB, responsible for press and publicity. I flew overseas with colleagues to lobby foreign governments and organisations. I went to human rights conferences across Asia and Europe, and was interviewed live on BBC television.

But even as doors were opened to us, even as we persuaded some powerful people to acknowledge the justice of our claim, I saw our hopes dwindle and shrink. In the heaving, dangerous ocean of South Asian politics, with its religious tides, separatist movements, violent insurgencies and great power rivalries, with the whale of India patrolling the water, 100 000 southern Bhutanese refugees were small fish indeed. And as nothing changed, as the road back to Bhutan remained firmly shut, some of us began to ask whether home might have to mean something new.

The question of home was most raw in the burgeoning refugee camps of south-east Nepal. Faced with the wearying inactivity and uncertainty of camp life, people found an answer by taking charge of their lives as best as they could. They set up committees to run the camps. Inspired by Bhampa Daju, doctors tended the sick for little or no pay. Teachers set up schools to educate the children; adults took steps to educate themselves. This commitment to education would prove vital when the refugees finally got a chance, many years later, to build a new home on the other side of the world.

Three days after arriving in Nepal, Saroja and I drove the 12 hours to Kathmandu, a long and tiring journey on a pot-holed road. With us were Usha and Saroja's cousin Dipshika, both of whom had been in Jhapa helping newly arrived refugees. While the women slept in the back of our van, Smriti sat in the front as I drove, asking me questions, chatting happily. How wonderful, I thought, to be a child of two-and-a-half and not know the horrors of the world.

We rented a ground-floor apartment in Lagankhel, about half an hour's drive from the centre of Kathmandu. Our landlords, the couple upstairs, were very friendly, and soon we became part of their family. Smriti adored them. If she did not like the dinner Saroja had cooked for us she would march up the stairs, sometimes with a thump on the ground as she left, and eat with them.

Initially, only a handful of refugees lived in Kathmandu – those with enough money not to have to rely on UN-donated food in the camps. Yet Saroja and I had very little. As civil servants in Bhutan we had enjoyed many privileges. We could afford domestic help, buy imported cars, fridges and washing machines tax-free. I travelled overseas with a lavish allowance funded by international aid programs, and as a result I had saved the equivalent of US$3000 dollars from my last trip, to Spain.

These were our last funds, and we gave them to Saroja's uncle Devendra Gurung, who ran a high-end trekking business for tourists. Devendra invested them at a generous rate of return, and found a consulting firm who would hire our red Maruti van. For a time, we lived on these income sources – the bare minimum to survive. My sister Tulasha, who visited us from Kalimpong in India, where she was studying, later told us she saw how determined we were to stay cheerful, despite our poverty. Compared to refugees in the camps, we had so much.

I found Kathmandu very crowded. In Bhutan the air is pure, but the Nepali capital is set in a high valley that traps the air and makes it even dirtier than New Delhi's, as swarms of three-wheeler tempo taxis pump out noise and fumes around the clock. I suffered from asthma nearly every day.

I loved the Nepali people – they were so friendly to us, often emotional in their welcome. The newly democratic government embraced us as allies against an autocratic monarchy. But I worried that Nepal, as it urbanised and modernised, was losing its culture to India. All the music was Indian, all movies came from Bollywood. Unlike Bhutanese weddings, many Nepali weddings were pale imitations of Indian ones, dominated by Hindi songs and music. I was reminded, once again, that while we were ethnic Nepali, we were first of all Bhutanese.

I had a similar thought when, a few days after getting to Kathmandu, the HUROB leadership asked me to go on prime-time Nepali TV to discuss the plight of the refugees. *Chintan Manan* – meaning 'intellectual talk' – was live to air and moderated by TV personality Durga Nath Sharma. Guests included human rights advocates, journalists and Rishikesh Shah, a former Nepali foreign minister. The discussion was sympathetic to our position, but it was my first time on TV. I sweated under the cameras and struggled to articulate my views in fluent Nepali. Although it is my mother tongue, I studied it only in primary school and did not have a good enough grasp of the language to be able to speak in formal settings. In Bhutan, our Nepali contains lots of English words, and because I had been to school in the north, I spoke with a Dzongkha accent.

On 11 May, I sent my resignation letter to the chairman of the Bhutanese Royal Civil Service Commission. I began, 'Excellency, I have the honour of expressing my gratitude to the Royal Government for providing me with the opportunity to serve Bhutan and contribute towards the development of the nation. I served the Royal Government with devotion and diligence. With deep regret I take this opportunity to express my inability to continue my career in view of the policies and actions of the Royal Government with regard to southern Bhutanese.'

After listing these actions in all their brutality, I concluded, 'I believe that I have borne the humiliation meted out to me personally, to my family, and to the southern Bhutanese in general to the extent possible. However, I no longer believe that justice will ever prevail under the present circumstances. I have decided, therefore, to tender my resignation and join the struggle for human rights and justice in Bhutan.' I ended with a 'faint hope that a few nationalists at the higher echelons of the Government will take the risks, and make the necessary sacrifices, to challenge the destructive forces that are working to ruin the nation for personal gains.'

It was a very polite resignation letter. All those written by former senior civil servants were polite. The letters from Bhim Subba and R.B. Basnet were both conciliatory, full of ideas for how to move forward together. We spent so much time on every word because we were sure the king would change his mind, that we would soon be able to go home.

In my own mind, I was always back in Bhutan, travelling the countryside, looking at sites for new telecommunications facilities, walking into my boss's office to suggest a change to the five-year plan. Or I was in Lamidara, pulling the nails out of the boards in front of Dad and Mum's shop, and unlocking the door.

Every time we thought and talked about what had happened to us, we would get angry. The anger would subside, then a statement by the king saying we were not Bhutanese would enrage us again. Government officials said that some senior civil servants had left taking millions of Bhutanese ngultrums; in some cases the alleged amounts were more than their respective departmental budgets. We were all nearly broke, but at press conferences we had to respond to these lies.

These sad days also had their consolations. Soon after we arrived in Kathmandu, my brother Om Daju's wife Pabitra fled Bhutan with their three children, Sita, Geeta and Ramesh, and joined us in the Nepali capital. They rented an apartment five minutes' walk from ours, and Om Daju, worried about their safety, flew from Sydney, where he was studying, to see them for a few weeks. Our families' lives were entwined, and I finally got the chance to repay Om Daju for all the kindness he had shown me.

Ramesh spent a lot of time with us. He was the youngest child and Smriti, four years younger than him, was an only child. They were both spoilt, and they argued sometimes. But although Ramesh was very rough, he never hit Smriti, no matter how much she taunted him. He was also protective of her and, in time, they became very close. Whenever I left Kathmandu, Ramesh, aged seven or eight, would announce he was coming over to stay, since Saroja and Smriti needed a man around the house. Saroja, teasing him, said he only came over because he loved her fried potatoes and puris.

My days were spent on HUROB business, mostly working from a room in the home of Bhim Subba, who played a central but unofficial role within HUROB, and his wife Jyotsna, Saroja's sister. Leadership of our movement would be furnished from among the few hundred civil servants who had fled Bhutan. The standing of men like Bhim Subba and R.B. Basnet provided us with remarkable contacts inside the Nepali government – right up to the prime minister – and in international organisations. Without those relationships we would have had to bribe Nepali officials to get meetings, which Bhim Subba said we would never do.

HUROB was aligned with the Bhutan National Democratic Party (BNDP), one of the two Bhutanese political parties in Nepal. The other human rights organisation, the People's Forum for Human Rights, was linked to the Bhutan

People's Party (BPP). Both human rights bodies left their chair position vacant out of respect for Tek Nath Rizal, whose petition to the king in 1988 had put him in a prison cell in Bhutan. But the two organisations did not work well together in those early days because the political parties they were connected to were ideologically split.

The BNDP was led by R.B. Basnet and other senior civil servants, and its ideology was 'mutually beneficial capitalism'. The BPP was led by junior civil servants and was democratic socialist. Senior or junior, we were all novices at politics, bringing to it the rigid ways of the civil service.

In Bhutan the BPP leader, R.K. Budathoki, had worked in the same department as R.B. Basnet, but because he had been a long way down the hierarchy, the two leaders would not sit across the table as equals. We hung on to old power relations, forgetting that we were equal in our powerlessness. When I met former Telecommunications Department staff in Jhapa, they still bowed down before me to show respect.

A crucial difference between the parties was over how adversarial they should be. The BPP people liked to talk about fighting 'the despotic regime in Bhutan' or 'the aggressor in Thimphu'. Such language was encouraged by the Marxists and Maoists who ran many Nepali human rights groups and who were always telling us that armed struggle was the only way back to Bhutan. But I did not believe this approach would get us far with foreign governments, the only powers likely to put effective pressure on the king and his ministers.

The Nepali press also liked to print inflammatory rhetoric, to our cost. When two other HUROB activists and I took part in a press conference in Kathmandu, some newspapers quoted us using aggressive language that we hadn't used.

Furious, I contacted one of the editors. He said, 'Your name is in the newspaper. Why do you care?'

In those early days we demonstrated often outside the Indian Embassy, working closely with the Students Union of Bhutan. Students would come to our apartment after class and we would sit on the floor making placards, which usually said the same thing, in English, for the world to see: 'We want to go back to Bhutan'. When we got children to hold placards that read 'We want to go back to school in Bhutan', it made headlines as far away as the *Nation* in Bangkok and the *New York Times*.

But our rallies, while they had a place, quickly became a theatre piece. We would shout and wave our placards, the Kathmandu police would charge and pretend to beat us but say, quite kindly, as they pushed us into their vans, 'Just get in the vehicle.' With Nepali activists they were far less gentle, often beating them fiercely, while always trying to avoid getting caught on camera.

In south-east Nepal the tide of refugees continued to rise. In July 1991, a little over 200 were registered; a year later it was 68 000. The UNHCR, supported by agencies such as the Lutheran World Federation and the Nepal Red Cross Society, set up seven permanent camps that would eventually house more than 100 000 people. My parents, unwilling to be a burden to my sister Bhagiratha and her family, who had been so generous, moved to the largest camp, Beldangi II. Using materials provided by the UNHCR, my father built a hut out of bamboo, with a tarpaulin roof and dirt floor.

The camp huts, which often contained two families divided by a wall, ran in long, tight rows, separated by banana plants. They could be oppressively hot in summer, and during the monsoon rains many leaked and water pooled on the floor. But apart from the constant risk of fires and snakes, the camps were mostly safe. Beldangi II quickly became a town of 20 000 people. On a visit from Kathmandu, I looked at the huts rising on all sides and had a grim thought: 'When will they come down?'

But people's spirits were not broken. Helped by Nepali and international agencies, they built roads, health centres, meeting halls and toilets. In dusty squares, children played soccer and older people played cards. Although the Nepali government did not allow refugees to work outside the camps, on many days hundreds of men would ride their bicycles out to the fields to do labouring jobs for cash.

Dr Bhampa Rai began operating from a medical centre in Damak, a town near Beldangi, providing free care not just to refugees in the camps but also to poor Nepalis, including many rickshaw drivers. Nepali medical centres would offer Bhampa Daju attractive jobs but he turned them all down to work with his own people.

Each camp had a central management committee and subcommittees for each sector, all elected and run by refugees. Other committees registered births and deaths, handed out food rations, oversaw health treatment and responded to problems such as disputes between neighbours. The work of running the camps built an army of leaders, some of whom would have a big role when people reached Australia many years later.

What inspired me most were our schools. As the south of Bhutan had become better off, people had seen the opportunities that schooling brought: their children might even get to work in the government. So strong was this attitude that at

111

the height of the repression, some Lhotshampas chose to leave Bhutan because the government had closed the schools. In the camps, no sooner had a family cleared some forest and put up a hut than parents wanted their children to go to school.

Since every third refugee was a student, the camps had nearly a thousand teachers. Some of them said, 'I will start a school under that tree.' Under leafy shade that protected people from the furious summer heat, one teacher, sometimes two, would take classes of 60, sharing out limited supplies of books and stationery. Many teachers turned down better-paid offers from local Nepali schools in order to teach in the 'tree schools' and the huts that eventually replaced them. Schools taught an adapted version of the Bhutanese curriculum, in English. Dzongkha was also taught: we wanted to prepare the children for their return to Bhutan. At the start of each school day, perhaps at the very moment that soldiers were storming through southern villages, herding people into vans and levelling homes, our children in refugee camps stood up and sang Bhutan's national anthem.

Australia was an early supporter of our schools. The then foreign affairs minister Gareth Evans gave $100 000 through the Catholic aid organisation Caritas Nepal. The grant had a far-reaching impact, not only for the investment in education but because it enabled us to go to the German government, for example, and say, 'The Australians have given us this much – can you add to it?'

But our students faced many problems. Under Nepali law, no Bhutanese refugee could study at government-funded tertiary institutions. With Caritas and other international agencies, HUROB and the student union began lobbying for a change of policy. A group of us – Bhim Subba, D.P. Basnet and Mandhoj Tamang, plus student union activists Bishwa Nath Chettri and Kamal Dhital – knocked on doors right up to the prime minister, Girija Prasad Koirala.

While not changing its rule, Nepal eventually allowed Bhutanese students to sit local exams and thereby to qualify for secondary and tertiary colleges. Other students went to India to study. Aid agencies provided scholarships, some families sold rice and dahl to raise money, and after many years of lobbying, nearly all young people who wanted to pursue their studies were able to do so. It was a great victory for our activism, but we still hoped to open places, even a few, in universities in Nepal. Our early efforts centred around 18-year-old Prakash Subedi.

Prakash, who had done brilliantly in his year 12 exams in Sikkim in India, came to a meeting of refugee leaders in Kathmandu. 'I want to be a doctor, can you help me?' he asked. Someone whispered to me, 'How does this young fellow expect to be a doctor? He's a refugee. People are struggling to eat.' That really hurt me. I thought this young boy had guts and drive. In Bhutan I had known his father, a school inspector in the Department of Education. I said, 'Come to my place this evening. Bring your marks from school.'

Several of us lobbied for Prakash at high levels. We made one very modest request: enrol one Bhutanese student a year in each of three faculties – medicine, engineering and agricultural science. Our claim had to go right to cabinet but it was accepted, and on 13 December 1993, my birthday, I was elated to get a letter from the dean of the Medical College: Prakash had a place.

Today Prakash lives in the UK with his wife and two children and works as a doctor of emergency medicine.

He trains doctors in both the UK and Nepal. The second student, Lakshmi Prasad Dhakal, trained in Nepal, then in the Netherlands, and now lives and works as a doctor in the Australian town of Wangaratta. His Punya Foundation is dedicated to educating young people. Four young people went to medical college and became doctors through our program.

Camp life affected people in different ways. Some sought to reassert traditional power structures; some husbands tried to dominate their wives. But camp life also broke down traditions. The allocation of huts was random, and people from different castes lived side by side. Illiterate villagers were recognised for their skills in building houses or repairing leaks, whereas privileged former civil servants like me did not have those skills. Fixed ideas, the natural order of things, began to change. Again, the big driver was education.

In the mid-1990s, Oxfam started an adult education program for women – as soon as it began, domestic violence rates went through the roof. Many men who spent their time drinking or sitting at home doing nothing didn't like it when their women started talking about politics and other classroom topics. In time the classes were expanded to include men, and many joined in. Elderly people, including my mum, also attended. Just a few years ago I was in Atlanta, Georgia, in the US, visiting a 91-year-old relative. She came out of her room and showed me a notebook in which she had written her name, Chandra Kala Baral, in lovely script. When I asked why, she replied, 'I have to pass my test and get my citizenship.' I had tears in my eyes. That was the culture of learning we built in the camps.

But some saw that culture as a dangerous distraction from the main game: getting back to Bhutan. In a crowded meeting in a hall in Beldangi II camp, I got talking with ten or 15 young people, most of them men. When I raised the issue of education, some got angry and shouted at me, 'We need arms to go back to Bhutan to fight. Who are you to tell us to go to school?' Very timidly, I tried to engage them. How would they get across the 175 kilometres between Nepal and Bhutan without being arrested by Indian police? What level of study had they reached in Bhutan? Did they not want to continue? I told them about Prakash: they could follow him, or spend their lives carrying bags for other people. Some did not want to hear and stormed out, but others, still angry, talked with me for a long time. Some of these young men did indeed go back to school.

The young men's difficulty belonged to us all. We were invisible. In September 1992, I had a letter about Bhutan's ethnic cleansing published in *Asiaweek*, the news magazine published in Hong Kong. 'Had this occurred in Europe it would be another Bosnia-Herzogovina,' I wrote. 'World leaders would have met and discussed ways to help the victims. But alas, we are far away.'

I learnt that lesson sharply in June 1993, when Bhim Subba, activists Ratan Gajmere, Jogen Gazmere, Shiva Pradhan and I attended the World Conference on Human Rights in Vienna. I gave a speech setting out our troubles and our goals. After me, a refugee from Rwanda came to the podium. His story shocked me. I thought, 'Compared to the Rwandans, we don't have a problem.' That conference was held nearly a year before the mass killings of more than half a million Tutsis.

At the same conference I spotted Paljor Dorji, Bhutan's ambassador to the United Nations and a cousin of the king, relaxing in a corner with the foreign minister Dawa Tsering. Emboldened in this neutral territory, I walked up to the two men, said hello, bowed a little to show respect, and tried to hand them a HUROB document on human rights in Bhutan. Dawa Tsering refused to take it, politely telling me to hand it to Yeshey Dorji, another member of the delegation and a friend of mine from Dacca days. Later that day, Tsering made a statement to the conference that was full of falsehoods about the human rights situation. Bhim Subba and I quickly prepared and distributed a press release refuting his claims, but the episode exposed our problem. Bhutan claimed to be vulnerable and under threat, but in global forums no one was prepared to challenge the official story.

Getting media coverage was also a struggle. Using our contacts in embassies and other places, HUROB and other organisations arranged visits to the camps by the *New York Times* and the ABC and SBS from Australia. *The Nation* in Bangkok and *Himal* in Kathmandu reported reliably on the situation. But Bhutan's western sympathisers included some senior correspondents from British newspapers. Western journalists loved to go to Bhutan because their tours usually included a meal at the palace, but they knew that if their reports were too independent, they would not be invited back.

Another sympathiser was Tim Fischer, Australia's deputy prime minister from 1996 to 1999. When I got to Australia, I heard he was a decent fellow, but as a friend of the Bhutanese king, he played a very dirty role, repeating the lie that the refugees had left of their own free will, or had been tricked by activists wanting a greater Nepal. On one visit to Bhutan, in 1997, he accused the refugees of coming to the camps from parts of Nepal and India, attracted by the free food.

His book *Bold Bhutan Beckons* pumps up the country's image, completely ignoring its human rights violations. We had to work very hard to undo the damage Tim Fischer did.

In 1993, our family life in Kathmandu improved. My youngest sibling, Padma, aged 12, moved from Beldangi II camp to live with us and study at the same school as Ramesh and his sisters Sita and Geeta. Om Daju began to spend at least a month in Nepal every year with his family. His senior Australian colleague, Professor John Egerton of Sydney University, had found him a role on a research project in Nepal to study footrot in sheep and goats. It was a life-changing opportunity for Om Daju: the vaccine he eventually developed from that project would significantly reduce footrot in Nepal and be patented all over the world.

That same year, Saroja started work as a science teacher at an English language private school, while I was invited to work as a consultant to the Kathmandu office of Japanese trading firm Mitsui & Co. In Bhutan I had worked long hours in my office and travelled often. Now, with Saroja teaching and me at home, I would often take Smriti to meetings and rallies. I carried her in a pouch on my back, until she objected that she couldn't see my face and I had to carry her on my chest, from where she would tug my glasses or even scratch my cheek if I didn't pay attention to her. It was a magic time for me as a father. One day I was late for a meeting and rushed her dressing. As she came down the stairs, she thumped her foot and asked, 'Papa, does this dress go with these shoes?' I quietly changed her shoes.

Our new jobs took the financial pressure off our little household and enabled me to begin an unexpected line of work. Soon after my arrival in Kathmandu, the student union had asked me to write for its newspaper, *Bhutan Focus*. I thought journalism was the last thing I could do. At school I was weak at writing. But I was so upset about the refugee situation that my articles came from the heart, and the editor liked them. I even began writing for the *Kathmandu Post*, Nepal's main paper. One article I wrote earnt enough to pay our rent for two weeks. Even at the age of four, Smriti loved eating in restaurants – her great pleasure was studying the menu – so whenever she began lobbying to eat out, Saroja would say it was time I wrote an article for the *Kathmandu Post*.

Around that time, the HUROB leaders decided the movement needed a newspaper. Bhim Subba was a very good writer, and one of the few refugees with a computer, having brought his from Bhutan. The first issue of *The Bhutan Review* was published in January 1993, and it came out monthly for the next four-and-a-half years, mostly funded by our own money.

Bhim Subba and I would type articles into his computer and, with D.P. Basnet and Mandhoj Tamang, take them on a disk to a Kathmandu printing services business. Student activists, as well as my brother Gopal and cousin Bishnu, helped to fold and address copies at night, and the next day take them to embassies and NGO offices. We would post another lot to contacts overseas, and courier 500 copies by bus to Jhapa, where acting HUROB chairman S.B. Subba and general secretary Kishore Rai would send them to the camps, and arrange for clandestine distribution within Bhutan.

The Bhutan Review did a lot to draw attention to life in the camps. About once a month, a group of HUROB activists took the overnight bus from Kathmandu to the south-east. I would be introduced to newly arrived refugees, collect their stories, and write them up. To highlight the refugees' grit and resourcefulness, we reported on a remarkable technology invented in the camps. Kitchen waste scattered everywhere was attracting flies and animals, creating hygiene concerns in the crowded camps. To prevent that, people dug a big pit near their huts, then built a mud bowl over which to wash rice, with a bamboo pipe to carry the water and discarded grains into the pit, which had a piece of concrete over the top. Once a pit was filled, people dug another. Soon the camps became so clean that not a grain of rice could be found on the ground.

Foreign governments, agencies and media respected our determination to be truthful about the conflict. For example, if there was a shooting in Bhutan, *The Bhutan Review* would say that people were reportedly killed but that we could not verify the number. The authors of the 1993 US State Department annual human rights report, a highly credible source, quoted our survey of 1781 refugee families, in which 204 respondents said they left Bhutan because a family member had been beaten or tortured, and 21 said they had been raped.

The Bhutan Review marked a shift in HUROB's strategy from what I call adversarial advocacy to diplomatic advocacy. We had come to realise that shouting at the Bhutanese government was like throwing jelly at a wall. However hard you threw, the result was the same. Worse, it annoyed potential allies. So we changed tack. For example, the Danish government gave Bhutan funding to train its judiciary. Instead of expressing outrage we said, 'Hey guys, this is a great initiative. Can you extend it? Can you start talking about democratic reforms in the country? Can you look at the plight of people who were kicked out?' This approach got us a much more sympathetic hearing from Bhutan's donor countries – all except one, the most important one.

India was always our stumbling block. Its relations with Nepal had never been good, while Bhutan, a buffer against China to the north, was a long-time ally. We had some links with India's Congress Party, and the Indian Socialist Party supported us strongly while it was in opposition. But in their periods in government, both parties dropped us. It was a terrible shame. I am confident that if India had pressured Bhutan to repatriate the refugees or stop evicting them in the first place, the Bhutanese government would have backed down. Instead, Indian soldiers and police simply pushed the refugees into Nepal.

Yet it was our best friends who most let us down. Since the fall of the absolute monarchy in 1990, Nepal's political system was new and immature. It had only a few statesmen, like Dr Manmohan Adhikari, leader of the Communist Party of Nepal (Unified Marxist–Leninist), and the third prime minister of the new democracy. He would encourage us to meet leaders of other parties, and not to align with one. He could rise above politics. But he was an exception to the rule.

None of Nepal's three main parties had a consistent policy for dealing with Bhutan regarding the refugees. In October 1993, Bhutan and Nepal established a Ministerial Joint Committee to resolve the problem. Bhim Subba, R.B. Basnet and the rest of us did a huge amount of homework to inform the Nepali delegation going to Bhutan. We wrote briefs on every member of the Bhutanese delegation – his background and character, how to deal with him – only to find that two of the three members of the Nepali delegation were barely on speaking terms and did not share our briefs, or even read them.

At the start of negotiations, the Nepalis made a fatal concession. Bhutan had demanded that the refugees be put into four categories: genuine citizens who had been forcefully evicted; people who had chosen to emigrate; non-Bhutanese; and Bhutanese who had committed criminal acts. The first category required refugees to prove they had been forcefully evicted, which was impossible to do from Nepal. The second enabled Bhutan to produce its so-called voluntary migration forms, which had forced people to state they had left of their own free will. The third and fourth categories were also open to exploitation. When Nepal accepted these categories, they enabled Bhutan to submit the results of its fraudulent 1988 census and say, 'Most of these people are not Bhutanese. Why are you forcing us to take them?' The Nepalis had no answer. It was the biggest win Bhutan ever had.

As negotiations sank into a long stalemate, we had our own problems. By 1994, the divisions between our political parties and activist groups had become so great that a few of us resolved to act. A series of discussions led to the creation of the Bhutanese Coalition for Democratic Movement. The word 'movement' turned out to be too radical for overseas governments – they thought it sounded like we wanted to topple the Bhutanese monarchy – so we changed the name to the Bhutanese Coalition for Democratic Reforms. I was appointed its spokesman, and its first chairman, the new public face of our movement, was a businessman turned politician, Rongthong Kunley Dorji. He was of crucial importance to our cause.

Rongthong Kunley was leader of the coalition's third party, the newly formed Druk National Congress. I had spent my final school years in Kanglung with his daughter Dechen, who remains a friend today. Rongthong Kunley was not a Lhotshampa but a Sharchop from eastern Bhutan ('Rongthong' is an honorific that denotes his home town). He had become wealthy after the Bhutanese government granted him a coal mining concession in the east of the country. Rongthong Kunley could have kept his head down, but he was disgusted by the treatment of the southerners, and fell under suspicion of sending them money. He also spoke about discrimination against the Sharchops by the ruling power, and Bhutan's lack of democracy. Here was an opponent the government could not simply dismiss as a Nepali 'anti-national'. In 1991, Rongthong Kunley was arrested, jailed and tortured for 49 days. He was hung upside down from the ceiling; his head was held under water until he nearly drowned. After the king granted him an amnesty, he fled to Nepal with his wife and two sons.

Rongthong Kunley was a brave, decent man who became a kind of father figure to me. A skilled politician, he threatened Bhutan's rulers, and they decided to stop him.

Late at night on Friday 18 April 1997, I got a phone call: Rongthong Kunley had been arrested in New Delhi. Bhutan, tipped off that he was travelling to the capital, had filed a secret extradition request, alleging that the businessman had committed financial fraud. The king sent his home minister, Dago Tshering, to Delhi on a chartered Drukair flight after cancelling the regular commercial flight. Indian security police would hand over Rongthong Kunley the next day. That meant a death sentence.

Our coalition's leaders said I should go to Delhi at once to assist Rongthong Kunley's political colleague, Narad Adhikari, and others who were working to get an injunction before India's High Court. In Delhi, Narad and I drove to the prison where Rongthong Kunley was being held. He was in a bare cell, without a mosquito net; his face was so covered in bites he was hardly recognisable. I wept. I was also angry. 'This is a disgraceful way to treat an opposition leader of a foreign country,' we shouted at the prison superintendent. Rongthong Kunley's conditions improved after that.

India's legal system – unlike its security forces – respects due process: the High Court granted our injunction, and Dago Tshering flew home empty-handed. But Rongthong Kunley's trials were far from over. In July I returned to Delhi to help campaign for his release from prison. We had meetings at the UNHCR and the embassies of eight countries, including the US. In June of the following year, Delhi's chief magistrate finally granted Rongthong Kunley bail, saying that Bhutan's charges against him looked to be politically motivated. But he was required to remain in Delhi, under supervision, pending the resolution of Bhutan's extradition request. That would take another 12 years, during which he continued to lead the party and our movement from Delhi.

In 2010, Rongthong Kunley was finally allowed his freedom, but time in Bhutanese and Indian jails had broken his health. His family brought him to a Buddhist monastery in Sikkim, where he died, aged 73. He had been in exile for 20 years. He had sacrificed his life for our cause.

*

In 1995, we sent Smriti, aged five, to live in Kalimpong with my mother-in-law and attend St Joseph's Convent School. In Kathmandu she had started happily at the Montessori School but the awful pollution made us worry about her health. Seven or eight of her cousins, children of Saroja's sisters, already lived in Ama's big house, and Smriti could grow up with lots of company. Ama was known for caring for children while inculcating good discipline. Yet when I dropped Smriti at the bus stop to travel to Kalimpong with Saroja's sister Jyotsna, she put her little hands tightly around my neck and said, 'Papa, please don't send me.' I felt a terrible emptiness; my tears flowed. Was there any place where I could bring together my scattered family?

That year, a visit to the camps by Hillary Clinton, representing her husband, President Bill Clinton, briefly drew world attention to our cause. Yet nothing changed in Bhutan. The number of outright expulsions slowed but other restrictive policies remained in force. In 1996, the government passed a resolution terminating the civil service jobs of relatives of dissidents. My sister Punam lost her job as a draughtsperson in the Education Department, and my older brother Rudra Lal was sacked from the army after 23 years' service. He returned to Lamidara to find that the authorities had seized his home. The government was settling northern families on land it had stolen from the southern Bhutanese.

In the camps, life went on. Old people died, babies were born. Conditions improved: water quality, health and education were among the best of any refugee camps in the world. Yet young people continued to move out, seeking a better life. Some teachers, unable to resist the offer of better wages, left to work in Kathmandu and other large towns, and the quality of our schools began to slip. Local villagers often resented aid flowing into the camps, and that money also attracted con men – one group was funded to bring tortured refugees to Kathmandu for convalescence but instead pocketed most of the money. There were some suicides, and a rise in cases of depression and anxiety, especially among women.

On my visits I sensed a growing frustration that nothing

was changing. A suspicion that we would never go back to Bhutan was beginning to take hold. A few of our leaders took opportunities to migrate to western countries. Someone would leave for training or a seminar and not return. The subject of third country settlement began to be discussed more. Some talked of integration into Nepal, but the Nepali government was not keen on that option, fearing it could create a precedent for all Nepalis abroad, especially in India.

In 1996, a violent Maoist insurgency erupted in the Nepali countryside, and triggered a brutal government response. Maoist recruiters were active around the camps. As HUROB spokesman I would speak out on Nepali radio and TV against any use of violence. I said that if we won the fight with a gun, we would have to sleep with a gun, and guns could also be fired at us. My idea of arms was giving young people a book. This angered some people. Word got out, including to my anxious mother, that if I came to the camps I would be killed. I still went, but I was often looking over my shoulder.

India and Pakistan, in perpetual conflict, also had agents in the camps, trying to recruit anyone prepared to detonate a bomb in the other country. Their intelligence agencies saw us as a captive population that would do anything for money. I would get calls from anonymous people who would drop hints about providing arms and suggesting we meet in strange locations. Nothing came of these conspiracies but so-called leaders ran around the camps saying it was time to fight. In 1996, a new body, the Appeal Movement Coordinating Council, resolved to carry an appeal to the king by marching to Bhutan, a 23-day journey. The Indian authorities arrested more than a thousand activists, beat some viciously – the Indians were very free with the baton – and marched them right back to Nepal.

The failure of that march increased our despondency. In late 1996, we closed *The Bhutan Review*. We felt it had outlived its purpose: to educate the international community about our cause. The world was listening to us less – I could feel it. The newspaper needed a new strategy, and therefore more time investment from us. I was already struggling to give it enough time. I couldn't keep doing the same thing and expect a different result. Should I fight on, or should I start exploring alternatives, recognising that life is not always fair but that I had the power to create my own future?

I had some hard conversations with my colleagues. My Kathmandu colleagues were pragmatic and agreed we had to explore new options for the refugees in the camps. But Dr Bhampa Rai, the general secretary of HUROB, was dead against any path that did not involve return to Bhutan. He and I did not confront each other, perhaps because we had been so close in Dacca, but nevertheless our conversations were painful. I still believed in our cause, but there were many days now when I doubted our chances unless we changed course. He, on the other hand, was going to sacrifice his life for the dream of going back to Bhutan.

Saroja and I still had no thought of leaving Nepal, unless it was to return to Bhutan. But we decided to revive a plan we had made years earlier to study for master's degrees. I was fully involved in the movement and would feel very guilty if I left it. I was guardian to Om Daju's wife Pabitra and their three children, and could not leave them. So we decided that Saroja would go first. She applied for admission to the public health degree at Sydney University, where Om Daju had a research and teaching job, and was accepted.

But after much talk, we changed our minds. I did not like

the idea of my wife being on her own in a strange city, having to both study and work to earn money. Saroja did not want to be so far from our daughter.

I was exhausted, and needed time to reflect on where our movement was going. Studying for a master's in business administration would complement my engineering degree and strengthen my capacity to earn and help my family. I could return renewed to the cause, whether that was repatriation of refugees to Bhutan or resettlement somewhere else.

For years I had been working to obtain Australian visas for Om Daju's wife and children, a protracted process involving extensive forms, medical check-ups and trips to Delhi. In 1997, the visas finally came through. After seven years, the family would be reunited. It was then that Om Daju said I should come to Australia.

In all our conversations over those seven years, in calls, letters and visits, my brother had talked little about his life in Australia. He was always more focused on his family: were the children doing well in school? Had his wife got the money he had sent through me? But now, with his family about to leave, he began talking about his wide range of friends in Sydney, the community he was part of. It's a good country, he said.

He had found an MBA program at the University of Technology Sydney that offered a range of subjects I wanted to take. The course was very expensive – A$30 000, when we didn't even have 30 000 Nepali rupees, which was less than A$1000. My Kathmandu colleagues laughed at my plan. But I have always believed in the mathematical concept of simplification: breaking a big problem into smaller parts and tackling one at a time. To get the MBA I needed to study four semesters but we only had money for one. So I would start with one.

Om Daju said he would help me with initial funds, and I could stay with his family. We sold our red van. Saroja offered to sell some jewellery. We took three of her gold necklaces and a ring of mine to a street of jewellers in Kathmandu. The man took a necklace and put it under a fire, the gold went dark and I nearly collapsed in panic. He said, 'Don't worry, the colour will come back.' He paid us 325 000 Nepali rupees (about A$8000). We had to postpone my departure another six months, but after paying expenses I finally had $7500 – just enough for one semester and a plane ticket to Australia.

Saroja and I made a last trip to Kalimpong to see Smriti and Ama, and to Jhapa to see my parents. My father came back with us to Kathmandu, and came to the airport, along with Saroja, my siblings Gopal and Padma, and Om Daju's younger brother Bishnu. As I looked into my father's eyes, I unconsciously removed the gold ring I was wearing, took his hand and put it on his finger. Then I boarded the flight to Delhi.

As the plane rose through a blazing blue sky, my head was full of dark thoughts. Once more, I was leaving behind my wife and daughter and parents. Would I see them again? A memory of Smriti often returned to me. One night in Kathmandu, I had seen her looking longingly at a dress in a shop window. 'What is it, Smriti?' I asked. 'It's nothing, Papa.' But I could see by her face that it was not nothing. I knew that since becoming a refugee, she knew there were some things she could not have. That pained me. I wanted my daughter to feel that if she set her mind to it, she could have or do anything. Was there any place where this could happen?

6

'THERE IS SMRITI!'

On Christmas Day 1999, nearly a year and a half after I arrived in Australia, I opened my emails to read one from Saroja. In the past few months she had called the Australian High Commission in New Delhi 15 or 20 times to see whether she and Smriti could get visas to join me. She had just learnt the government had rejected her application. Sitting in my room in Om Daju's house, I went into a panic. What had I done, coming to Australia, cutting myself off from the people I loved most in the world?

For five nights I did not sleep. I was lonely, exhausted, consumed by anxiety. On my way to work at a Coles supermarket in the city, I was crossing the intersection at George and Liverpool Streets when my vision began to blur and swim. I fell and hit the ground. A stranger grabbed me and dragged me to the pavement. He might have saved my life; he certainly changed it.

Seventeen months earlier, on 25 July 1998, Om Daju and Pabitra and their three children, Sita, Geeta and Ramesh, met me at Sydney Airport. We drove to their university-owned home in Cobbitty, a tiny country town about 20 kilometres west of Campbelltown, on the outskirts of south-west Sydney. The family lived there to be near Om Daju's workplace in the veterinary department at Sydney University's Cobbitty campus.

I had come to Australia's biggest city but Cobbitty felt like a remote village in Bhutan. I would go out of the house and not see a human being all day. My first strong impression of Australia was of kangaroos lifting their heads from grass in the fields to gaze at me. My second was of Om Daju's piled-up trolley of groceries when we visited Macarthur Square Shopping Centre in Campbelltown.

On my third day, he took me to the University of Technology Sydney to enrol in my Master of Business Administration course. Three evenings a week, I would take the train from Campbelltown to Central Station and walk to the city campus. About half the students were locals, and the other half came mainly from Malaysia, Indonesia, China and India. I enjoyed the classes, particularly economics, but I wasn't thinking much about study, and I kept my time on campus to a minimum. I went there only for classes and to use the university computers, as I could not afford to buy one. I rarely got back to Cobbitty before midnight.

In those first weeks, I was all at sea. People would call me Tom, struggle to understand my accent. I could use my Bhutanese driver's licence, and Om Daju lent me his car, but while I managed the roads alright, I could not navigate. Om Daju went to China on a work trip and I used his car to drive to Campbelltown Station to take the train to the city. Coming back at around 11 pm I got lost, could not read the street directory, and had no phone. I finally got home at 2 am. Pabitra and the children were very worried.

More than study, I was obsessed with finding work. I had brought US$1440 from Nepal and handed it to Om Daju on arrival – he is my older brother and I didn't want to keep cash with me. After that I had virtually no money, and

I was desperate to send some to my parents. The train from Campbelltown cost me $35 a week, a small fortune, but I saved a lot on rent and food by living with Om Daju and his family. I never ate out; buying a KitKat was a big thing.

Looking for work was hard. I couldn't knock on the doors of businesses – Cobbitty had none. In my whole life I had never applied for a job, or written a resumé. Driving to Campbelltown one afternoon, I saw a 'Vacancy' sign on the street, and I pulled in excitedly to apply. It was a vacancy in a motel, not a workplace.

Gradually, reality dawned. Om Daju had said I could bring Saroja and Smriti over on my student visa but this turned out to be a dream. Even if I could have gotten visas for them, I had no thought at this time of staying for good. To Australian readers, that might seem like a strange thing to say, especially when I had no secure home in Bhutan or Nepal, but in Bhutanese life the extended family is central, and I was committed to looking after my parents and youngest siblings. Under Australian immigration rules, it was virtually impossible to ever get visas for them. However much I liked Australia and its people, that was a deal-breaker for me. After eight years in this country, Om Daju felt exactly the same. He had a father, two step-mothers and 15 siblings in Nepal and Bhutan. Without at least getting some of them to Australia, even with his wife and children here he would never make this country his permanent home.

So I was stuck, far from home, doing an MBA but unable to look after myself, let alone be a good father, husband or son. I was a burden on my brother and his family. I had always cared for others, never asked them to care for me. I felt selfish every day – selfish to leave my wife alone, to leave my little girl, to leave my parents in a refugee camp with no money to send them, to abandon the cause of getting our people back to Bhutan. I had never been a bad sleeper; now I lay awake for nights at a stretch.

The staff at UTS were wonderful. They allowed me to pay my fees in instalments. One lecturer, Diana Bromley, knowing I could not afford textbooks, borrowed them for me for the whole semester. 'Om, don't worry, it will all work out,' the advisers in the careers counselling office would say. I spent a lot of time there, just to have someone to talk to.

Calling Saroja or Smriti or my parents and siblings, usually from a telephone booth on George Street, became so important. But I could not call often – telephone cards for calls to Nepal cost $1.50 a minute, a little less for India. I craved hearing my daughter say, 'Hello, Papa', but it pained me when she said, 'Papa, why can't you be here? Next week is our school concert and I am in it.' And the connection was often so poor that my $10 phone card would run out before we could say much. Talking to my parents was even more difficult. I had to call the telephone booth in the camp and ask the man who ran it to contact my parents, then wait for an hour before calling again.

So we wrote letters. Saroja and I wrote to each other by hand every week, using email only for visa matters. I have some beautiful letters from her and Smriti from that time. In September 1998, my younger sister Tulasha wrote to me. I was at a particularly low point but as I read her letter I felt loved, and burst into tears.

The following February, I got an email from Saroja. My father-in-law Ganga Prasad Gurung, who had been sick for some time, had died. I was devastated. I had felt very close to him, a man of principle and great simplicity. I had always imagined that after Saroja, Smriti and I were reunited in Australia, one day I would show Guru Babu this country. It would never happen.

But around that time, my luck began to turn. A Nepali friend of Om Daju's, Keshav Kandel, an agricultural scientist, and his wife Rama came over for dinner. Rama worked at a factory in Penrith and she said I should come along the next day and talk to the supervisor, Mrs Habiba. There might be an opening.

A week later, I started at GPC Electronics. I worked 3.30 pm to 11.30 pm, five nights a week, making handsets for Nortel. My job was fitting the telephone foot stand. I held a screw until the machine came down the assembly line and drove it into the device. My eyesight was poor and sometimes I would fail to hold the screw right but Mrs Habiba, a former Afghan refugee, was very sympathetic. My greatest friends were two Assyrian men on the assembly line; they were so warm, always smiling, looking after me. 'Om, not Syrian, Assyrian!' they would insist. They told me I would be manager one day, or they would whisper, 'I think tonight we are getting overtime.' We would get so excited, because then we would make $100 or more a shift – good money.

Thanks to my job, I could now pay the instalments of my second semester fees, buy groceries for my Sydney family from time to time, and send Smriti kids' magazines and lottery tickets. But as a casual I did not always get the 20 hours a week I was allowed to work as an international student. So I applied for a permanent part-time job at Coles, which needed checkout operators for the supermarkets it was opening across the CBD in preparation for the Sydney Olympics. To not appear overqualified, I removed my degree and MBA course from my resumé. Still, when I stood at head office among 200 people, most of them local kids, I thought I had no chance.

We were interviewed in groups of ten. The interviewer asked us to name one of our pets. People named a dog or cat or bird. But we didn't have pets in the family. My turn was coming – what could I say? At home we had cows, so I said: 'Cow.' Everyone laughed. When we walked outside I heard people saying, 'There's the fella whose pet is a cow.' But because I said cow, the interviewer noticed me. I was called in for a second interview, and I got the job.

I worked at the Coles Express in George Street. We were trained to be very courteous and nice, because a lot of foreigners were coming to Sydney for the Olympics. I worked on the checkout for 20 hours a week, occasionally stacked shelves, and made $220. As soon as I had made $2000, I would take it straight to the university to pay my fees.

One day my boss came in and said, 'Om! You want to be supervisor?' 'Of course,' I said. He made me supervisor on the spot. A few months later: 'Om, you want to be duty manager? You're on.' He called me 'Doctor'. When I said I wasn't a doctor, he replied, 'I never finished Year 12. You're an engineer and you're at uni – you're a doctor.'

Being supervisor brought new challenges. I had to answer the phone and I dreaded it. Many customers couldn't understand my accent and I had to repeat myself, often a few times, which made some quite annoyed. Others would ask for things in the store and I wouldn't always know the answer. One lady asked, 'Do you have my dog?' I was quite surprised: no dog could walk around the store without an owner and our regulations allowed only assistance or companion dogs.

Nevertheless, I looked up and down the aisles, and asked the young student from Indonesia on the next checkout; she had seen nothing. I got back on the phone: 'I'm sorry, madam, we don't have your dog, or any dog, in the store.' The measured tones of her reply did not mask her rising agitation: 'I am asking if you have the dog food My Dog in your supermarket.'

But I was starting to understand and enjoy the casualness of Australians, even if some things took time to get used to. One of our managers said to the staff, 'Let's all go for a drink.' In the pub he bought himself a drink. Everyone else bought a drink too. But in Bhutan, if your boss says 'Let's go for a drink' it means they're going to pay for it. Until I worked it out, I sat there without a drink.

It was on the checkout line that I really started to feel at home in Australia. Customers seemed to want to talk to me, and there would often be a queue at my checkout. An elderly couple who lived in The Rocks, near the Harbour Bridge, wanted to know my whole story. They asked so many questions – 'How is Saroja? How is Smriti?' – that I worried other people in the queue were getting angry. This couple in their eighties, who seemed to love each other so much, gave me a lot of perspective. They had children but they no longer saw them much. They lived in public housing, and did not have an easy life, even though they were born in Australia, yet they felt sad for me. They made me think, 'Their situation is not so different from mine. Why am I so full of guilt that I am away from my wife and daughter?'

Yet my anxiety returned. I used to go to a South Indian doctor in Camden, near Cobbitty. I felt he understood me. One day he took out some tablets, gave me five or six, and said 'These will help you sleep.' But I would not take them. What if I became dependent? I would lie awake staring at them on my bedside table, determined not to give in.

One night in September 1999, an extraordinary thing happened – my younger sister Punam called me out of the blue from Thimphu, on Om Daju's home phone. She was very brave to do this because she was in danger if the government monitored her call. For ten minutes I spoke to her, my brother-in-law Bhim Lal and my niece Jyoti, and for days afterwards my loneliness vanished. I wrote in my diary: 'I feel so proud to have such a loving sister.'

Then, on Christmas Day, I got the email from Saroja saying the government had rejected her visa application.

For weeks after my fall in the street, my mind teemed with thoughts: 'What have I done? Would my daughter be proud to tell people her father had collapsed and been killed? Because he was weak? Would my parents, who have such hopes for me, be proud of me for giving up? Why am I magnifying my problems? All this anxiety will not bring Saroja and Smriti here. I need to dwell only on things I can affect: on my studies, on earning an extra $10 at work. I need to start living every moment, to focus on people I love. I love my wife. I want her to be happy, prosperous. I want my daughter to grow up with a sense of abundance about life. Why can I not make these things happen?'

Gradually I calmed down, and my slower thoughts were stronger thoughts: 'I can't control what happens to me but I can control my response. The answers to my problems are inside me. Yet even that mighty idea is only half the truth. I rely for my life on the kindness of others.'

Om Daju and Pabitra took great care of me. At the university, one of my lecturers, Diana Bromley, who already knew a little of my story and had borrowed the books for me, heard about my collapse. 'Om, you should have told me before,' she said to me in her office. She set me up with a counsellor. The university had some spare funds from a scholarship it had created for students from Indonesia and Malaysia and other countries going through the 1997 Asian financial crisis. Diana made me fill out a form and she took it to the vice-chancellor. As a result, I was given a $5000 scholarship. It was such a big thing – almost a semester's fees. And it meant that after more than a year and a half apart, I could see Saroja and Smriti again.

In January 2000, Saroja had called me from New Delhi, where she had flown to visit the Australian High Commission. A year earlier she had left Kathmandu for Kalimpong, to be with Smriti and Ama. It was lovely to hear her voice but she could barely speak. She had managed to get an interview with a visa official, but her application was rejected again. I took a deep breath and said, 'Darling, we will never give up!'

Desperate to see each other, we decided to meet in Bangkok. Three weeks later, Saroja and Smriti were waiting for me at Bangkok Airport. Our little girl, now aged ten, almost reached my shoulders! I hugged her and didn't want to leave her. We took a taxi to the city and talked non-stop, about Smriti's school and Saroja's efforts to get visas. I was amazed to see how much Saroja had grown in confidence from doing this hard work. In our week together, we even went to the Australian Embassy, thinking they might give us a visa if they saw us as a family, with our beautiful girl. When we got knocked back Smriti was devastated. 'Why can't we go to Australia with Papa?' she asked. She didn't want to hear the word 'visa' ever again.

Back in Australia, I decided to go all out to reunite my family. I was worried about being away from Smriti, and my parents were getting old. If I became a permanent resident, after my graduation I could try to find a job in Asia, perhaps in Hong Kong, and fly often to see Saroja and Smriti and my parents. I could work on bringing them all to Australia, without closing the option of returning to Bhutan.

I heard about NSW Legal Aid and made an appointment. A case officer, Bryce Wilson, heard my story and told me I could apply for a humanitarian visa. Bryce was so thorough; together we wrote a 21-page account of my refugee experience. On 17 July 2000, just three months after we had applied, and without having to do an interview, I got a permanent visa. Bryce and I were so excited. 'Right! We apply for Saroja and Smriti straight away,' he said.

Around that time, my life changed in another big way. To be close to my work and study, I had decided to leave Om Daju and Pabitra's home in Cobbitty and look for a flat in Sydney's inner west with a friend, Tulsi Katel, who had just finished a master's in project management in Brisbane after coming from Bhutan on a scholarship. Tulsi was an electrical engineer like me, and I had studied year 12 with his brother.

Our search for a place to live was not easy. Real estate agents treated us badly, they were often rude and disrespectful. They would commit to showing us a property then not turn up. As we didn't have a mobile phone, we wasted a lot of time and money chasing them. But eventually we found a nice three-bedroom flat in a two-storey block next to a church in Dulwich Hill. In time we got a new flatmate: Naresh Parajuli, a doctor and a former classmate of Tulsi's in Bhutan who was studying for a master's degree in international public health.

Occasionally our niece Juliana Dahal, daughter of Saroja's eldest sister Deepa, who had come to Sydney to study a master's in information systems, would visit the flat. Having been fed by others all my life, I finally learnt to cook, and got quite good at traditional Bhutanese dishes such as ema dachi, or chilli cheese curry, although I admit it is quite simple to make. Juliana would be all praise for my cooking: 'Uncle, your chicken was very delicious!' Word of my new skills even reached Kalimpong, and Saroja was apparently impressed, once her initial disbelief had passed.

I kept up with news of Bhutan by reading the website of *Kuensel*, the government-controlled newspaper, and, for a more accurate picture of events, by emailing friends in Nepal. I spoke at some forums about Bhutan organised by Amnesty International, or at Sydney University. In 2000 I got a call from Tenzin, director of Bhutan's animal husbandry department and a friend of Om Daju's. Tenzin was a western Bhutanese whom I had known well in Thimphu. He was keen to meet, and he spent a few nights in our Dulwich Hill flat; we had no spare room or bed so we put him up on the living room floor. One night we stayed up till nearly daylight talking about what happened in Bhutan. But our conversation never went deep. Tenzin was loyal to the regime, and Tulsi and I said nothing that would have forced him to clam up. We wanted to maintain that friendship.

I don't know exactly when I started to feel at home in Australia. I remember wanting to get involved in the life of Marrickville. At a community event I met a local activist, Sam Byrne. We got talking about Amnesty International, and I told Sam about how much it had done to expose the violence of the Bhutanese government. We decided to set up a Dulwich Hill–Marrickville Amnesty International group. The Reverend John Jegasothy, the local Uniting Church minister, gave us the church as a regular meeting place, and we set up a stall at the Marrickville Festival and Saturday market to sell Amnesty merchandise.

Sam, who was a local leader in the Greens party, asked me if I would join, and perhaps run for Council as a Green. I said no. I have never wanted to be a politician or to favour one party. Yet it was at the Amnesty stall that I met Anthony Albanese, member for Grayndler, the federal seat that covers Marrickville, and his then wife Carmel Tebbutt, a minister in the NSW government. I even met the then Opposition Leader Kim Beazley at a community reception. The man who introduced me, a local leader of Indian background keen to rise in the Labor ranks, identified me as 'an Indian brother', which he did with anyone from South Asia. I felt patronised and erupted in anger: 'I'm not Indian, I'm from Bhutan!' I went on a short rant, blaming India for making me a refugee. Everyone was embarrassed – except the Indian leader. 'This is just what we need – people like this young man, who speak with such energy and passion,' he said, not missing a beat. I had to give him credit for that.

In those years, I also learnt about Australia by becoming an investor. Before my arrival I had heard only vaguely about share trading. In 1998 Om Daju got me to join the NRMA, the NSW motorist organisation. In 2000, the NRMA sent me a letter saying its insurance branch was going to list on the stockmarket and was giving all its members shares. I got an astonishing $500 worth – that was big money for me – and I was hooked.

I started reading the share market pages in newspapers.

I went to any share trading seminar that was free and close to home. I bought a few shares in big companies like Telstra. Once I got to $300 profit I would sell them, then I got a little greedy and made my sale point $500. I saw that by investing in blue chip shares you could make reliable but modest profits, whereas if you took a few calculated risks, you could make a little more – and it was more exciting. I also started going to property seminars – free ones at first, but later, when I got a job, to property investment boot camps that cost $5000. I remember learning how negative gearing on investment property worked and thinking, 'This country is fantastic.' The federal government had just legislated to make property investing easier, and lots of people, lots of migrants, were taking advantage of the new rules. I could see that it was trading shares or buying an investment property, not working at Coles or anywhere else, that was going to give me enough money to send home to my parents.

I began 2001 on a much brighter note. The scholarship had solved my financial problems, my studies were nearly finished. Saroja wrote again to the Australian High Commission in Delhi, saying her husband was about to graduate and she hoped to be there for the ceremony. When the High Commission wrote back inviting her to Delhi, we felt optimistic. The immigration official was very friendly and considerate; she seemed to understand the pain Saroja and Smriti were going through. On 11 May, four days before my ceremony, Saroja sent me a long-awaited message: the visas had come through. She and Smriti were flying to Australia the following day. They were coming to my graduation!

Once again, I could not sleep, but this time for the best reasons. I called the graduation organisers and asked for two extra tickets. I got to the airport very early. Om Daju, Bhauju, Sita, Geeta and Ramesh arrived a little after 7 pm and we talked feverishly in the waiting area. Ramesh said to me, 'Kaka (Uncle), you watch on the left and I'll keep an eye on the right.'

Time dragged for 45 minutes. Then Ramesh shouted: 'There is Smriti!'

Above Lamidara, 2022, the beautiful village where I was born. The building with the blue roof is my primary school (although the building has been upgraded).

Left Representing Bhutan at the World Administrative Radio Conference in Spain in 1992.

Below left Welcoming guests at the launch of Bhutan's first satellite earth station and international switching system in Thimphu in 1990.

Contract signing along with Thinley Dorji (not in the picture), with Mitsui & Co. in Tokyo in 1989 for the supply of telecommunication equipment.

My father-in-law with his two wives, relaxing at home in Chengmari, Bhutan, 1990.

My sister and my closest friend, Yoga, at work in her office in Phuntsholing in 1988, a year before she passed away.

One of the classes in Beldangi refugee camp in 1991, which were initially run under trees before the huts were built.

Refugees demonstrate in Beldangi demanding repatriation to Bhutan, 1995.

Smriti (second from left) with her cousins and friends in front of my mother-in-law's house in Kalimpong, India, 1998.

Saroja and I receiving Dashain tika from Om Daju and Pabitra Bhauju at their house in Werrington in 2002.

After 12 years of being stateless, finally, we belong! Receiving citizenship certificates from Sam Byrne, the Mayor of Marrickville, on 28 April 2004.

With family and friends receiving the 2016 Premier's Multicultural Community Medal for Lifetime Community Service from Premier Mike Baird.

The Bhutanese community in Sydney comes together
for a picnic at the showground in Blacktown, 2014.

The SSI Board in 2015, with the visionary
CEO Violet Roumeliotis on the far left.

Smriti joins the Tuladhar family for a photo shoot in Darjeeling after the wedding reception, 2018.

A photo shoot with the students at Bunko University in Japan after my lecture on a strength-based approach to refugee settlement, 2019.

Thank you Australia! Despite what they have gone through in life, they keep smiling – my parents enjoy life in Australia, 2018.

Above The family comes together to celebrate Saroja's birthday at home in Fairwater, 2021.

Right 'Walking in the rain by your side' – Saroja and I take our regular evening walk in Fairwater with our niece, Dristi, 2022.

Below right At home in our garden. I have lately developed an interest in gardening (hopefully providing a little more help to Saroja), 2022.

7

THE THREE OF US

We sat in the university's Great Hall, my wife and daughter shining in their brightly coloured, traditional Bhutanese dresses. Sitting in the student area, I kept looking across the room to make sure they were actually there. Smriti was exhausted from jet lag but determined to stay awake for my big night. As he handed me my certificate on stage, the vice-chancellor, Professor Anthony Blake, said I was the first UTS graduate from Bhutan he had met. I have a treasured photo of Smriti gazing up at him as they chatted afterwards at the reception.

The next month was such a happy time. I showed them the Opera House, the Harbour Bridge, Paddy's Market and the nearby Chinese Garden of Friendship, and level 5 in the UTS building, where I had taken my classes. We took many photos, Smriti chattered excitedly about a school play she had taken part in; there was so much to talk about. A week after their arrival, I left the Dulwich Hill flat and we rented a flat a few streets away in Marrickville. My sorrows had vanished, life seemed so good and kind. We would have taken even more time, but after a month Smriti started complaining that she was getting behind in her studies and insisted we put her in school. In late June she started year 6 at Wilkins Public School in Marrickville.

As soon as she and Saroja arrived, I began thinking about my parents. Someone suggested I approach Anthony Albanese. I had met him earlier but was amazed that in Australia ordinary people could set up a meeting with their MP so easily. He said straightaway, 'Let's try to get your parents here.' He wrote a letter to the High Commissioner in New Delhi, and got shadow foreign minister Kevin Rudd to also write one.

After that, Anthony and I used to meet quite often. I liked him a good deal. Our conversations about skilled migration encouraged me to write a submission to a parliamentary inquiry. Thinking of the Bhutanese experience, I urged the government to consider settling refugees and skilled migrants in rural areas, where those with farming skills could use them, and where they might feel more at home than in the cities. UTS publicised my submission, quite a few journalists contacted me for interviews, and I was invited to speak at forums. With every day I felt more at home in this country, and that I might be able to contribute to it, if I could find a way.

But our bid to get visas for my parents failed. The High Commission replied that it was not taking applications from the camps in Nepal, since the Nepal–Bhutan negotiations to find a resolution to the refugee issue were ongoing. I was very disappointed.

I was now free to focus on finding a job. Next door to Anthony's Marrickville office was the office of an employment provider, MTC Work Solutions (now MTC Australia). Across the road, the May Murray Neighbourhood Centre ran a skilled migrant placement program. I signed up with both, but the job search was a struggle.

I went to MTC every day to look at job notices on their computers. Martin Keil, a friendly and kind man who worked there as a manager, encouraged me to apply for everything, including internal jobs at MTC. After a few months, he got me to apply for a job as a caseworker in the Work for the Dole program. To my excitement I was hired, but just before I began, the federal government withdrew funding for the role.

At the neighbourhood centre, Merryn Jones was the skilled migrant placement officer. A warm, excitable woman, Merryn was like a godmother to me. Like Martin, she encouraged me to apply for everything. I applied for jobs at Telstra, Optus and Vodafone, in telecommunications, engineering, business, government administration, and sales. Over six months I applied for 52 jobs – and got 52 rejections. Sometimes I got to the interview stage but the final answer was almost always the same: 'We are very impressed with your resumé. However, we had more experienced candidates and you were not successful this time.'

Life was still good in many ways. Smriti liked her school, and Saroja was working casual jobs in restaurants while upgrading her credentials by studying for a diploma in laboratory technology at a TAFE college in the city. But I was beginning to despair. I liked working on the Coles checkout – but not for the rest of my life.

People offered me sympathy. It's not your fault, they said. It's Australia's racism, or the fact that you're a refugee. But these views didn't sit right with me. I hadn't experienced any racism, and how would people know I was a former refugee? It wasn't on my resumé. Merryn didn't believe any of that either. Something else is wrong, she said. We have to work out what it is.

After my last rejection, she had an idea. She would do a mock job interview with me, film it, and watch the tape.

I came in the next day to find Merryn in a state of excitement. 'Om, I've got it! You're looking down at my feet! In interviews you have to look at my face!'

In all the interviews, I had behaved like a good Bhutanese. In our culture, to look directly at a person of higher rank, from the king down, is a mark of great disrespect. Merryn had given me a new angle on my job problem: not racism, not being a refugee, but not looking people in the eye.

Around the time Merryn made her video, after many attempts to get feedback from firms that rejected me, I finally arranged to meet with an HR manager, who said she would talk to me in confidence. She said, in words that chilled me: 'How could you lie so smoothly?'

She recalled that the interview panel had asked me whether I had ever managed a large team of staff. I said I had done so in Bhutan, which was the truth. But because I had looked down at the floor as I answered, the panel had assumed I made up the story.

Feeling very uncomfortable at first, I started looking interviewers in the eye. The change was instant. Two companies made good offers, one in marketing, one in sales. I was astonished. I still thank Merryn every day for what she did for me.

At the same time, Martin Keil told me that MTC had a position as a training and placement officer in their Belmore office, just down the road from Marrickville. It was a higher-level role than the one they had previously offered me, and I would need a Certificate 4 in Training and Assessment, but I could study for that on the job. In July 2002, I began work at MTC. Two weeks later, Nadia Lacharite-Morgan from Telstra called. A market analyst job I had applied for six months earlier was now available.

With my background in Bhutan, there was no company I wanted to work for more than Telstra. The job on offer was entry-level, and the MTC job paid about $20 000 more. But it wasn't about the money.

It was an agonising dilemma. MTC had treated me so well. After a long silence, I told Nadia I would feel a sense of betrayal if I left MTC. In despair, I added, 'If only I could come back in six months.' After a long pause, she said, 'You can.' They were happy to hold the position. After talking it over with Saroja, who said I should never take a job just for the money, I was thrilled to accept Nadia's offer.

I threw myself into my new job at the MTC Belmore office. I placed unemployed people in Work for the Dole projects, which they had to do to qualify for their Centrelink payments. For example, Rookwood Cemetery would ring up and we would send down some young people to weed and clean around the graves, making sure we sent the Muslim kids to the cemetery's Muslim section. It made me uneasy. Not many learnt a skill they could take to a job.

The Work for the Dole program had been introduced by the Liberal government of John Howard. The MTC staff, most of whom seemed to vote Labor, disliked it. They were under huge pressure to meet targets, and it was so hard to get people into projects that staff often accepted any employer who rang up wanting free labour. I could see the program's flaws, and its name carried a terrible stigma. Who would hang a certificate on their wall saying, 'I did Work for the Dole'? To most people it would say, 'I am a bludger.'

However, I could also see the program's potential. What

if we asked the young people to choose their own path? One might be interested in tap dance, another in rap dance. Another might like to cook or build a website. Could we not design a program to harness those skills? The camps in Nepal had shown me that everyone has a talent. If we could help a young Bhutanese refugee to fulfil his dream of becoming a doctor, surely we could help young Australians, even those who, like our clients, had never worked and often had parents who had never worked? I wanted to hear their stories, try to understand their goals. Many told us they wanted to develop their computer skills, so some other MTC staff and I developed an in-house IT training program for them.

Yet I was overloaded with administrative work, entering data, taking calls from Centrelink about whether our clients had breached their obligations. We also had to look out for scams: for example, most of the medical certificates exempting people from the program came from one doctor in Lakemba! It was hard to be creative in that system. And Telstra beckoned.

A few months into the job, I told Martin I would leave in the new year. He was disappointed but accepted my decision. Then I got a call from the MTC CEO, Mark Chaffey. He and the board chairman, Peter Longbon, wanted to come to Belmore to talk to me. They offered me the role of acting area co-ordinator, a big pay rise and a work car, a new Ford Falcon. Peter even promised to look at trying to get my parents visas for Australia. After being unable to get an employer to even consider me six months before, it was terribly flattering, and I felt very grateful. But I was set on returning to telecommunications.

In February 2003, I began work at Telstra head office

in the city. I was a market analyst supporting a sales team working on acquiring and supporting government business in mobile phones. After about a year, I won a promotion into Telstra Wholesale. We wrote six-monthly, 100-page reports, situation analyses on aspects of our industry. What are the coming technologies? What are the key global players and our competitors doing? How can we use this knowledge to support a customer?

I found the work thrilling. To me it wasn't a job – Telstra was my family, my new university. I learnt so much from my mentor and friend James Liao, a senior analyst, who would force me to push my thinking to its logical or illogical conclusion by constantly asking me, 'Why?' A later boss, Deena Shiff, showed me how to think through problems calmly, focusing on the facts.

Even after I left the office, I stayed on the job. When I was in a shopping centre I would go around to the Optus shop and find out whether our products matched theirs. On the train into the city I would work on my laptop, using a dongle to access the network. Because dongles were new, people would ask, 'What's that?' It was another way to promote Telstra. I would shoot an email to the CEO – Ziggy Switkowski, Sol Trujillo, then David Thodey. If they liked the idea they would respond, and often they did.

Yet one thing at Telstra troubled me. I was the newest person on the sales team, and I earnt the least. When our team went out for a drink, people would wonder aloud, 'Will I be getting my full bonus this year?' Or 'I haven't met my target and the boss won't be happy – no bonus for me.' It made me uncomfortable. People were working crazy hours, enduring so much stress, to earn their bonus, and in their minds some had already spent it on a new car – a Mercedes or a BMW. But they already had beautiful cars. Their salaries were better than nearly everyone else's in the world, but their whole happiness seemed to depend on getting that bonus. What if they got that car and their neighbour got a better one? I felt they had built that element of dissatisfaction into their lives.

At Monday morning meetings, people would talk about what they did on the weekend: a boat cruise, a great party, dinner at Darling Harbour. I felt awkward – the most exciting thing we ever did was a picnic at Gough Whitlam Park in Earlwood. We didn't even know who Gough Whitlam was!

I had many friends at all levels of the organisation. I was working very hard, aspiring to be like them. And yet, when I thought about their lives, many seemed to have something missing. Even when we were refugees in Nepal, with nothing, we had great parties, great times. Were these people any happier? One senior manager to whom I grew quite close would say, 'Om, I wish I could be like you and volunteer in the community, but I'm not earning enough to have any spare time.' (To her great credit, after she left Telstra and before starting a new job she took a chunk of time and did substantial volunteer work.)

I felt like the problem started at the top. In 2005, Sol Trujillo became Telstra CEO for a salary of $13.2 million, an obnoxious sum. I loved Sol's brashness and courage in forcing the company to adopt 4G through the Next G network. It was a farsighted move, pushed through against internal opposition when the technology was in its early stages. But Sol, whose relations with government were disastrous, got his money by painting a picture of how bad Telstra was, so that any improvement he made, however small, could be justified.

It wasn't just Telstra: across all big companies, money had become everything. At work we read a case study of Al 'Chainsaw' Dunlap, the American executive whose creed was to turn around companies by slashing staff numbers and shutting factories.

Paying our CEO so much led other Telstra people to say, 'If Sol is getting this, I should be getting this.' Senior managers wanted millions. One of my bosses made a speech saying, 'I am not here to make friends, I am here to drive outcomes.' People would shiver when they saw him; he was inhuman. Yet the system rewarded him. I can't blame individuals; that's what the culture was.

I kept quiet in these conversations. In my early days at Telstra, I told one of my bosses, Graham Barr, that I wanted to leave most days at 5 pm so that I could take Smriti to basketball and all the other sports she was crazy about. If that meant no bonus, no upgrade of our old Toyota Corolla, that was OK with me. Graham was very supportive.

I loved driving Smriti to her basketball games, and our conversations in the car. While she played, I talked to other parents or sat in the car and ate the dinner I had brought from home. Most times, of course, I watched the game. But sometimes I could sneak out, go to the pub and have a glass of beer. I liked the pubs, their relaxed feel, especially on a hot day, when I felt I was seeing the real Australia. Every day I tried to speak to a younger and an older person, and someone from a different culture; pubs are a good place to do that. But when Smriti got in the car she would say crossly, 'Papa, you smell of smoke!'

In early 2004, just as I started my new role at Telstra Wholesale, I was at a noisy company event at Darling

Harbour when I took a call from Peter Longbon. Would I join the MTC board?

I felt great affection and gratitude towards MTC, and there was only one answer. Determined to be a valuable contributor, I bought books on governance and how to negotiate, and read them for hours at night. But in board meetings I got a jolt. I was the youngest, the only migrant, a tiny fellow with no board experience, and not a high-flying lawyer or accountant. I lacked confidence. I am quietly spoken, and people would regularly talk over me. They were good people but at times I felt insulted, hurt. I imagined them thinking, 'What would this fellow, a refugee, know?'

Two developments changed my thinking. At first, every time I was interrupted or ignored in a meeting, I made a note in my diary. Then I stopped doing that. Why dwell on these episodes? Most people nearly always did the right thing. I could learn from this situation, but only if I took ownership of it. I had to understand this system. What was troubling these people? Perhaps the financial difficulties MTC was going through, or the fact that its records weren't in good order? That was a much better way of connecting with them.

My saviour, though, was Serge Derkatch, who had just replaced Peter Longbon as chair of the MTC board. Serge, a former senior manager at Lendlease, was a wonderful mentor. He saw what was going on and he would stop the discussion and say, 'Om, can you repeat that?' Over coffee, he showed me that I was trying to be like other board members, when instead I should draw lessons from my lived experience: 'Om, you're the only one on the board who's been unemployed – focus on your strengths.'

On Serge's recommendation, I was made chair of two

board committees: innovation, and CEO evaluation and remuneration. I read the papers thoroughly and spent hours preparing for meetings, a habit I still have. I noticed that some board members did not read the papers or have a clue what was in them. Gradually, I built confidence. People began to say, 'Hey, Om, can we have a coffee?' Thanks to Serge and his faith in me, I spent ten happy years on that board.

Outside work, our lives continued to improve. We were able to regularly send money to my parents. We also saved $2000 to buy a car. At a second-hand auction yard, Smriti got into a silver Toyota Corolla, announced that it was right for us, and wouldn't get out. The only problem was the cost: $4200. The auction yard offered us finance; we paid it off in six months.

After Saroja graduated in 2003, Merryn Jones helped her to find a work placement at St Vincent's Hospital in the city. The placement led to a job at a pathology laboratory in Macquarie Park. Saroja worked the afternoon shift, and sometimes would not finish until 1 or 1.30 am, so I would make the 40-minute drive from Marrickville because there was no late bus. I wouldn't leave Smriti in the flat on her own, so often I would carry her out of bed and put her in the car, still asleep. I sat in the dark outside the lab, remembering days I used to wait for Saroja outside Thimphu General Hospital when we were first dating. Then we drove home along empty roads, talking quietly while Smriti slept. Sometimes we wouldn't get home till 3 am, but they were beautiful times.

After finishing primary school, Smriti went to Casimir Catholic College in Marrickville. It had a similar feel to her Kalimpong school, St Joseph's Convent, and she loved it. She was both academically gifted and very sporty; she took up netball, basketball, soccer, cricket, even touch footy. At the end-of-year function for year 7 she was called onto the stage five times. I couldn't control my tears, which Saroja, far less sentimental than I am, teased me about.

On 28 April 2004, nearly 12 years to the day after we lost our Bhutanese citizenship, Saroja, Smriti and I became Australian citizens. Sam Byrne, who had become mayor of Marrickville, handed us our citizenship certificates at Petersham Town Hall. Trembling a little, almost as if someone might snatch it from me, I grabbed the paper so hard I almost tore it. I had been stateless for so long, and so much wanted to belong somewhere. Becoming Australian gave me that sense of belonging.

That year was a big one. We had saved some money. On Saturdays, while Saroja worked, Smriti and I went house-hunting. Liverpool and Blacktown were two areas where prices were in our range. Both had such diverse populations that they felt like the United Nations, which I liked. Some of my Telstra friends were worried about Blacktown, though. Dangerous place, lots of crime, they said. But none of them had been there, or lived anywhere near. So I did my own research. I spent time at Blacktown Station at different times of the day and night. I could see that in the evening it could be a little scary, and Smriti would have to be careful coming home late from school, but the fact that it was always crowded made it safer.

We trudged around that suburb for months. Late one Saturday afternoon we were in a street called St Pauls Way when we saw a real estate board lying on the ground. We picked it up, matched it to a nearby townhouse, and called the number. 'Stay right there, I'll come now,' the young woman said. We walked in and bought it on the spot for $300 000, subject to Saroja's approval. She came the next day, and told the agent the backyard was full of rubbish and we would pay no more than $295 000. The agent said, 'Yes, ma'am.' Naresh and Dukka offered to lend us some extra money for the deposit – and we were homeowners.

The very week we moved in, Saroja heard that she had got a job doing laboratory testing at Nepean Hospital in Penrith, just 25 minutes' drive from Blacktown. A keen gardener, in St Pauls Way she could finally plant herbs, tomatoes, chillies and Bhutanese vegetables such as chokos and rayo saag, a form of spinach. We started frantically looking for a school for Smriti before choosing Trinity Catholic College in Auburn.

Living in Blacktown would change my life, and once again, Om Daju had a big role. In 2001, he and Pabitra had bought their first house and moved to Werrington, a suburb of Penrith. A lot of Nepali people lived there; for a time, Werrington's second-most spoken language after English was Nepali. These people were not refugees but skilled migrants. Many had bachelor's degrees in engineering or agricultural science from universities in Nepal or India, or from the Asian Institute of Technology in Thailand. They were part of the big wave of skilled migrants that came after the mining boom got going in the early 2000s and the government ramped up immigration in response.

As I began to mix with these friends of Om Daju, I saw a problem. Some of their children were growing up speaking only English. Even parents who were not very fluent in English would use it to talk to their kids. As a result, they and their children were losing their common language. At one gathering I said hello in Nepali to a beautiful kid aged three or four, but his father said, 'He doesn't speak Nepali.' He was proud to say that, but I felt sad. Some parents had invested so much in their children, had come to Australia for them, but all they did was work. They had moved into nice houses, with lovely cars and a good holiday once a year, and they gave their children whatever they wanted, hoped they would become true-blue Aussies. But many weren't spending enough time with their kids, and it was causing everyone sorrow.

The worst disconnection was between children and grandparents. The parents were working so hard they would bring out their own parents from Nepal or India to look after their children. But the grandparents, here on temporary visas that could last six months, couldn't talk to the children. They were all living in the one house, but the children watched TV or played video games. I looked at those old people, tried to imagine myself in their place, and felt their hurt.

Saroja and I talked about it a lot. We wanted the material things these new migrants had, but not to this extent. Smriti had been to an English-language school in Kalimpong; her English was perfect but her Nepali was beginning to fade. We decided that outside the house she would speak English, of course, but inside the house she would speak Nepali. Om Daju and Pabitra had made the same decision with their kids. Smriti resisted at first, but she accepted it, and today her Nepali is excellent.

Om Daju was also thinking about these problems. He and some other Nepali friends decided to set up a community organisation. The Nepalese Community of Western Sydney, or nCOWS, began with modest aims: organising some social events, helping people to hold funerals. It advertised an event to celebrate Dashain, the Hindu festival that all children in Lamidara used to love. So many people showed up that the organisation had to book a bigger hall. Five hundred people came, and nCOWS really took off. A committee was established, elections called. With my experience managing organisations in Nepal, I was asked to help, and in 2006 I was elected the first general secretary.

That same year, I was made a Telstra hometown ambassador to promote the Next G (4G) network. I went to business breakfasts in Penrith and similar events, all in the early morning or evening, all voluntary work. At night I worked on getting nCOWS registered with the NSW Fair Trading department, publishing its magazine, and creating an award for the Nepali young person who got the highest mark in the HSC. I did my Amnesty work and I mentored some skilled migrants, helping them write resumés and apply for jobs. In 2007, the year Smriti was sitting for her year 12 exams, I was invited to apply for a senior competitive intelligence analyst role at Telstra Business and I got the job. Life had become very busy.

Through these years, I kept close tabs on what was happening in Nepal and Bhutan. Over there, things were starting to stir.

After seven years of fruitless negotiations between Bhutan and Nepal, international pressure had finally forced Bhutan, in 2000, to agree to establish a joint verification team to begin screening refugees to establish their bona fides. The team assessed more than 12000 refugees in one camp, Khudunabari. Despite Bhutan's claims that they were not genuine citizens, more than 90 per cent of those assessed were able to produce a citizenship card or land tax receipt proving their Bhutanese origin.

It took three more years and many tense exchanges between the two countries' teams before the result of the verification was announced, in June 2003. As soon as it was, the Bhutanese team abruptly halted its work. The protests from Nepal and other governments were depressingly muted. Sixteen rounds of negotiations over ten years had given Bhutan what it had always wanted: to stall the process at every step. In 2003, foreign minister Dawa Tsering even admitted in Bhutan's National Assembly that some 'people in the camps' were 'bonafide Bhutanese who had been evicted forcibly'. Yet the government never allowed one refugee to return.

In 2005 we sent money to my parents to enable them to rent an apartment large enough for them and my three youngest siblings, Gopal, Tulasha and Padma, in Birtamod, a town near the Beldangi II camp, in which my parents had lived since 1992. That year, Saroja, Smriti and I were also able to travel to Nepal and see them, after a long separation. My youngest sister, Padma, had married earlier that year and we met her husband, Ishwari Subedi, a dashing young man who worked as a lecturer in a college in Darjeeling. We had been fortunate in Australia, and on that trip we gave varying amounts of money to 55 different family members and friends in Nepal, India and Bhutan.

In Nepal, much had changed. My sisters-in-law Jyotsna and Usha had migrated to Canada with their husbands, Bhim Subba and Mandhoj Tamang, and their children. For the 107 000 refugees in the camps, countries and organisations that had supported them were beginning to feel 'donor fatigue' and to cut funds. Officials in the US Embassy in Kathmandu had stayed focused on the plight of the refugees, and as a result State Department officials kept coming to the camps to assess their suitability for US citizenship. The officials' impressions were favourable, but the US and other potential host countries, as well as the United Nations, wanted to be sure the refugees were open to resettlement. In other words, that they had set aside their dream of returning to Bhutan.

Ten years earlier that would have been unthinkable. But by 2005, the mood had shifted. There was a small but steady flow of people out of the camps to Kathmandu and other cities, where they could find jobs, or to other countries. The once excellent schools were struggling. By 2002, a fifth of all people in the camps had been born there, and still there was no sign they would ever see Bhutan, a place many could not remember, or had never known.

In 2007, I got an electrifying phone call from D.P. Basnet, my former colleague and friend from HUROB, now living in Washington, DC. The US had just announced it would take 50 000 Bhutanese refugees.

Other western countries were bound to follow suit, as has been the pattern in formal refugee settlement over the past 50 years. In time, Canada, New Zealand, the Netherlands, the UK, Denmark and Norway also made commitments. In August, the Australian Embassy in Nepal announced that Australia would take a share of the refugees. More than that, it would take whole families, including grandparents, which almost never happened in migration intakes. The goal was to clear the camps.

That announcement provoked huge excitement among the Sydney Bhutanese – all 17 of us.

At that time, we were four couples and nine children, after Naresh had managed to bring out his wife Dukka and their child Namika, and my first flatmate, Tulsi, had gone to Nepal

159

and married Poonam Khatiwada, from the Pathri refugee camp, and brought her to Australia. We were essentially an extended family: we took holidays together, marked cultural events, celebrated our successes, even ones as small as getting a driver's licence, and we helped each other combat the isolation and loneliness we sometimes felt, living away from our larger groups of family and friends. We sought to maintain our Bhutanese identity while also joining the larger Australian community, which had welcomed us so warmly.

After Australia's announcement, we talked constantly about how we could give our countryfolk as good an experience of Australia as ours. On 26 August 2007, at a function at our home for Smriti's 18th birthday, the four couples formed the Association of Bhutanese in Australia, the ABA. Our friends Parsuram Sharma-Luital and his wife Tanka, former Bhutanese refugees based in Melbourne, also dialled in. The group asked me to be the first ABA president. I was ready to do it. I think I was hungry to do it.

I contacted the NSW office of the federal Immigration Department, and began an ongoing conversation with Sam Zjakic, manager of the Multicultural Affairs and Settlement Branch, who would oversee arrival of the Bhutanese into Sydney. Sam told me that a migrant organisation had never initiated contact with him before to offer help with settlement, and he was delighted to work with us. We talked about settling them in Blacktown, where housing was relatively cheap, and where I could dedicate time to helping them get a start. In a city as expensive, busy and challenging as Sydney, the department also showed foresight in choosing most refugees from among family members, close or distant, or people who knew each other, and could support each other.

In December, on a driving holiday with Om Daju and his family in Tasmania, I pointed out that many places, in their weather, size and environment, felt very much like our homes in Bhutan. 'Our people would love Launceston,' we agreed. The day after we got back to Sydney, Sam called to say the first arrivals would be here the following year. 'That's fantastic,' I said. 'Will they be coming to Blacktown?' No, Launceston and Adelaide.

I had urgent conversations with my family and friends in Nepal. We got a message to people in the camps: if you want to come to Australia, get in touch with us. There was a lot of tension between those wanting to resettle and those determined to stay put until they could return to Bhutan. Hard-headed people in the second group were laying down the law. In May 2007, the secretary of Beldangi II camp, Hari Adhikari Bangale, who supported resettlement, was physically attacked, and in an ensuing clash involving Nepal's Armed Police Force, a refugee was killed. A group that claimed its mission was to 'foil' resettlement shot another refugee in Damak, a town near the camps. The UNHCR had to clandestinely contact potential candidates for resettlement: the first people who jumped into International Organization for Migration (IOM) vans to attend interviews had to make up stories about what they were doing.

Yet when the vast majority of refugees heard about resettlement, they breathed a sigh of relief. They had endured their years of exile 'with extraordinary dignity and patience', wrote historian Michael Hutt. Finally, it seemed they might not stay forever in their tiny huts, sandwiched between banana plants in a corner of Nepal.

In May 2008, I decided to travel there, to learn about the

situation first-hand. Mum told me not to come: 'There is no way you can go to the camps. They are too volatile.' Around the time of my visit, nine masked men attacked an IOM bus that was carrying refugees being processed for resettlement. I stayed out of the camps, but refugees came to see me at my parents' place in Birtamod and in two other nearby towns. We kept it confidential as we didn't feel safe, but I think people appreciated hearing directly from someone they trusted. I advised them to apply for Australia, where they would have great opportunities. When Australian immigration officials asked people if they had a close relative in Sydney, many would say 'Om Dhungel', prompting an amused outburst from one official: 'Om, are you related to everybody?'

Most people were accepted, except for those with serious criminal records, or men with two wives, who got a visa only after producing papers showing they had divorced one wife, who was then settled in another country.

Back in Sydney, I met Sam Zjakic, and Jill Gillespie from the service provider ACL, which was responsible for settling the NSW group of Bhutanese. I was briefed on what support the new arrivals could expect. I spelled out an early version of the ABA's plan to ensure the immigrants would not become dependent on service providers but would stand on their own feet.

That month, the first Bhutanese families to get visas under the resettlement program began to arrive. Australia would grant 205 visas to Bhutanese refugees that year, and about half of them would come to Sydney. The ABA was ready for them.

On the morning of 3 September 2008, my mind was racing as my car raced down the M4 towards Sydney Airport.

I had been in Australia for ten years. The nCOWS role had given me practical skills in running an organisation but many experiences here had also shaped me. I could have found a job so much sooner if I had only had work experience and a reference and known how to conduct myself with an Australian interview panel. I had seen how Work for the Dole missed the chance to prepare people for jobs by using their skills and firing their passions. I thought we could learn from the emptiness I had seen at Telstra and among some of the Nepali families of Western Sydney.

I was determined to ensure the Bhutanese got a good foundation that was not just material but cultural, moral, even spiritual. In a way I felt in debt to the newcomers. I had not languished in the camps for 20 years, losing confidence and hope. When I left Nepal I had left not only my wife and child, parents and siblings, but our great cause: returning to Bhutan. Here was my chance to repay. And the great cause was lost. There was no going home. We had to find another home.

I cannot say that all these thoughts were in my head, but nor were they far away, as I pulled into the car park and hurried towards the customs gate, where our small party – Tulsi and Poonam from our community, Sam from the Immigration Department, and Anita Adhikari Ale and Naima Wisse from the service provider ACL – were gathered, ready to welcome the flight from Kathmandu, via Singapore.

8

THANK YOU, AUSTRALIA

'Hamro Kamal ra Reeta!' Poonam let out a shout as her brother Kamal and his wife Reeta walked out of the customs hall. Then came a group from my village: Om and Narapati Kafley – brothers, and cousins of mine – and their wives Pabitra and Sita, each couple with two tired children traipsing after them. Next were Deepak Sharma Dhimal and Bhim Kumari Adhikari, a brother and sister, also related to Poonam. Last through the doors were Lachi Maya Dhaurali, a single mother, and her four children. The 17 arrivals doubled Sydney's Bhutanese population at a stroke. I would have spotted them even without the IOM tags around their necks. Every adult, apart from Lachi, was known to either Poonam or me.

The minivan belonging to the settlement services provider ACL drove the group to furnished apartments in Blacktown and nearby Rosehill, where they would spend four weeks as part of their entitlement under Australia's refugee program. At about nine that night Saroja and I knocked on Lachi's apartment door. Mum and the children were all sitting in the living room, the younger daughter and son drifting in and out of sleep. 'Have you eaten?' I asked. It turned out Lachi had been too scared to light the stove, after the IOM orientation session in the camps had warned new arrivals to avoid triggering the smoke alarm. Saroja and Lachi got to work and, with the spinach and beans we had brought and rice provided by ACL, cooked dinner, our second of the night.

What would life in Australia be like for Lachi, I wondered, escaping a violent marriage in Nepal and raising four children? They were in our care now. That Saturday, we invited all five families for dinner. I brought each family to our house, Lachi's requiring two trips since I could not fit six in the car.

Chatting with Kamal and Reeta, we realised that I knew some of Kamal's relatives from Chirang, our district in Bhutan, and that Reeta's grandfather and my father were meeth, meaning they had made a formal pact of friendship and were like brothers. I knew Reeta's father Talman Kharka, a national soccer player, and that her grandmother cooked delicious chamre, fried rice, that I ate on visits to their house during the Dashain festival when I was a boy. 'So now you can call me Kaka (Uncle),' I told Reeta.

When I visited their apartment few days later, Reeta said to me: 'Kaka – this girl comes into our room every second day and changes the bed sheets. This is something I could do very easily. Can I find this job?' I was impressed. Reeta had spent 15 years in a refugee camp, and was already keen to work.

In coming months, people arrived in groups of ten or 15, usually spaced a few weeks or a month apart. I spent a lot of time at the airport. One morning in early December Ama and Baa – Mum and Dad – walked through the arrival doors alongside my brother Gopal and his wife Pabitra, whom he had married only in 2005 and whom I had never met.

Unable to contain my emotions, I bowed down to the ground, first to Dad, then to Mum, and touched their feet with my head. Both of them placed their hand on my head and said, 'May god bless you.' I hugged Gopal but only bowed slightly to Pabitra, both of us saying 'Namaste', since I am not allowed to touch a buhari, a younger brother's wife. Pabitra was carrying their year-old daughter Mona, and I reached out to hold her but she was cranky after the long flight and clung to her mother. She looked as enchanting as Smriti did at her age.

Our Blacktown house had only three bedrooms, so my parents took one, and Gopal, Pabitra and Mona slept in the living room. When we bought it in 2004, we had decided to postpone our housewarming until my parents could be there – an act of blind faith, since we had no idea at that time that my parents would ever be able to come. Four years later, Harihar Acharya, a pandit, newly arrived from Nepal, performed a puja, a ceremonial rite, and 150 people crammed into the house for a very happy party. My parents and Gopal's family lived with us for three months, until we found a house for the five of them a few minutes' drive from us.

In this way, Sydney's Bhutanese community was born. The Association of Bhutanese in Australia had reached an unusual understanding with ACL and its settlement services manager, Jill Gillespie. Australia's humanitarian program funds a case worker to take newly arrived refugees to a local school, bank, doctor and Medicare office, register them at Centrelink, help them to enrol in English classes and find a permanent place to live. It's a generous program, but Jill and I thought it could be even better if the newcomers were introduced to Australian life in the presence of Bhutanese people already living here.

'Everything was new,' an early arrival, Ran Maya, later told me about her first days in Sydney. 'Bathrooms, bedrooms, kitchen, backyard, train stations, bus stops, pedestrian crossings …' People did not know how to board a bus, let alone open a bank account and handle a bank card. The four families who created the ABA spent a lot of time showing people how to work the lights and flush toilets of their new dwellings, how to not get burned by the hot tap or trigger the smoke alarm. At a workshop we organised with Blacktown City Council, we explained how rubbish disposal worked, and what recycling was. Since some families struggled with using their stove and all cooked rice twice a day, Saroja and I bought more than 50 rice cookers as gifts. We also left food, especially Bhutanese vegetables such as chokos and rayo saag, in the fridge.

We drove people to visit friends, pointed out South Asian stores. Neither the camps nor Bhutan had supermarkets or the profusion of soft drinks or lollies you get in Australia, so we tried to show parents what their children should be eating and drinking, and why they should not fill the fridge with Coke or other fizzy drinks. We described local etiquette: the need to queue, to not drop litter, smoke indoors or get your children to buy you cigarettes; ideally not to smoke at all. We showed people how to stand on the left on an escalator – and what an escalator was.

My days were long – I almost never got to bed before midnight. But my bosses at Telstra could not have done more to help me. They virtually let me set my own hours of work. At times, I would leave my job, drive to the airport, then drive to a family's furnished apartment. Once they were settled for the night, Saroja and I, sometimes with my father, would visit another family or two before I went home to work on issues affecting the new arrivals.

Many early challenges were about housing. An ACL staff member would get in touch to say she had found a house for a family, and would I come along to have a look? I often helped people fill out application forms, telling real estate agents that ACL could authorise Centrelink to pay them directly, since agents are often wary of new migrants without a credit record or a job. I wrote many letters guaranteeing to pay the rent in case of default. At one point Saroja and I were guarantors for about 15 families, which the agents might not have allowed, had they known.

For every family that came, Saroja and I, or another of the four families, would host a meal. We would start conversations by finding out what district in Bhutan people came from; perhaps we had friends in common or were even related. Sharing stories of what we had suffered in Bhutan built a bond. Before long, the meals would stretch to 60, 70, even 100 people. Our kitchens were full of women and men cooking as children careened around our small backyard. No one sat there doing nothing: by the time the last person left the dishes were done.

No one had a car and poor English speakers were nervous about taking public transport, so the four families did a lot of driving. One day I made 11 trips. Most years I drive about 10000 kilometres a year but in 2009 it was 39000. Luckily, I like driving, and it helped that Telstra gave me a new car every other year.

That early period of settlement was a happy time. Old friends were reunited; people had not fully turned their minds to what might lie ahead. We urged people to relax, enjoy life after the camps. I knew many of the elderly were anxious about Australia. Refugee camps are nests of rumours: they won't let us be Hindus there; they'll force us to eat beef; they'll put us in the desert and we'll be bitten by snakes and spiders (Australia's detention of people seeking asylum in remote centres at that time no doubt provoked this rumour).

To allay these fears, one morning in early 2009 we organised nearly the whole community – 108 people – to take a train to Wollongong. Commuters would have seen two noisy, colourful compartments full of people carrying picnic baskets, older women in saris, men in traditional Nepali dress known as daura suruwal, and topis, Nepali caps. As the train raced through the beautiful green bush south of Sydney, people looked out the window and shouted, 'This is like Bhutan!' We visited the Nan Tien Temple, one of the biggest Buddhist temples in the southern hemisphere, then we had a picnic. I ate far too much dhakaney, a delicious, heavy rice pudding, but it would have been rude to refuse.

That day, I could see the influence of the camps on our people. No one ever wants to be a refugee, to grow up or grow old unable to set their life path, knowing no other home than a tiny hut. But life in the camps in Nepal wasn't all bad. People lived as families, often three generations under one roof. Most migrants to Australia are people of working age or students, who cannot bring their parents or grandparents as permanent settlers. But under the refugee program, the Bhutanese mostly came to Australia as intact families. This difference would profoundly shape our community. On the train to Wollongong, I watched young people help elders find seats, carry food. The confined spaces of camp life had taught them to care not only for their grandparents but for neighbours too.

As our population grew, our impromptu meals and gatherings, while great fun, got harder to manage. We saw a growing need to bind our community, to convey consistent messages about the settlement challenge, to prevent loneliness, and to encourage people to integrate into Australian life.

In early 2009, Blacktown Council approved our request to stage a gathering at Alpha Park Hall in the Blacktown CBD on the last Saturday evening of every month. The venue was close to Blacktown railway station, with parking. Nearly the whole community would show up. We had guest speakers from the Department of Immigration, ACL, other service providers and the police. I or another member of the ABA leadership team would give updates about our activities, or maybe announce an upcoming wedding. Young volunteers ran painting and dance classes for children in a room beside the hall.

A highlight for me was watching new families walk shyly onstage to be introduced, some children hiding behind their parents' legs. People who had arrived earlier were invited to share an achievement in the new country, and would hold up their L plates or a school award, to great applause. In time it would be year 12 certificates or letters offering a job. In those days people were very connected – excited, fearful, alive to the adventure of Australia. All stories were shared; we had not yet retreated into private life. When my brother Gopal got his driver's licence, having never driven in Bhutan or Nepal, the news went around the community like electricity.

From the start, four groups of Bhutanese faced particular challenges: elders, youth, women, and anyone looking for a job. We realised that the ABA had to shift from being a loose grouping to a formal community organisation. In early

2010, we sought nominations for an eight-member executive committee, including four coordinators to look after women, youth, culture and general welfare respectively. Two years later we moved to formal elections every two years. We held them first at Alpha Park Hall, with booths to ensure a secret ballot, and later by a combination of online voting and printed ballots delivered to people's homes. We worked hard on our democratic process, even appointing a three-person electoral commission. It was vital the ABA had the authority to speak within and for the community.

Every year we held a community AGM and a Bhutanese Annual Day celebration to mark our arrival in Australia. We started an annual Bhutanese Sports Day, which included a walking race for elders, a chocolate race for children, a tug-of-war, guessing the weight of a watermelon, and Cockfight, a popular Bhutanese game in which people with one arm and one leg tied behind their backs bang into each other until only one is left standing.

The first Annual Day celebration was held at Blacktown's Masonic Centre in October 2009. Our guest of honour, Laurie Ferguson, then a Western Sydney MP and parliamentary secretary for immigration, spoke of the progress the 800 Bhutanese had made in Australia, and revealed, to cheers, that another 2000 would be settled in 2010. In my welcome address, I said we would never forget our roots in Bhutan, but it was time to move on. 'We were thrown out of our own country but have landed in the warm and welcoming lap of a beautiful country called Australia.'

From all these events, an ABA strategy gradually emerged. The key to it was participation, based on volunteering. In my speeches, I said that everyone has at least one skill that he or she can share to help others, and I encouraged people to come forward and make their skills and passions known. Someone could fix computers, another interpret in English, or cook, cut hair, drive a car, or look after children. One immigrant, Nakul Chhetri, who had been involved in food distribution in the camps, had great skill at resolving arguments within families, and we called upon him several times in that role.

Our job as ABA leaders was to bring these people together. Could anyone do our books, keep records, set up a website? If so, could they teach others? Did anyone know how to register an organisation with the Department of Fair Trading? Only when we reached a point where we lacked the resources to get something done ourselves would we turn to outside help from a service provider, institution or the government.

Volunteering taught people about local norms, like maintaining eye contact in job interviews. Volunteering was a guard against loneliness, as it got people out of the house. It brought so many benefits. Through volunteering, people would not just settle but become part of Australia.

To further speed the integration process, we decided that half of all ABA activities had to involve people outside our community. Bhutanese people joined tree planting and bush regeneration events organised by Blacktown Council. In early 2009, Hari Khatiwada, who had taught in the camps, brought together a group to take part in Clean Up Australia Day in Blacktown, a tradition that continues today. Hari said he wanted 'to showcase our sincerity and commitment to the nation.'

The most powerful way to integrate was through work. When I had first looked for a job in Australia, the chain I could not break was having no local experience or referees.

But volunteering might break it. We said to the new arrivals: 'You cannot get what you want straight away, but volunteering can give you vital experience. If you want to work in aged care or childcare, offer to visit seniors regularly, or take care of children at our events. If you want to drive a bus, learn to drive a car and transport people. An ABA leader will mentor you and write you a reference.'

We did not think that people should take any work they found. Far better to gain or upgrade a qualification than to start hunting for a job that might be out of reach, or end quickly. We urged people to first improve their English, and to accept the difficulty of transferring skills from overseas. We said: 'Look at jobs in demand and tailor your aspirations accordingly. Whatever you were at home, you might have to park it for now.' Some struggled to accept that in the beginning, but it was true.

Finally, we urged people to aspire to own a home, as they had done in Bhutan. Home ownership meant belonging. When some people asked us to support their applications for public housing, we agreed for only a disadvantaged few, fearing that once people got into it they might never own their own home.

Would our strategy succeed? The question haunted me. I had struggled so hard to get a job, and I had been privileged, with degrees, management experience and good English. Many newcomers had never been to school and were illiterate in Nepali, let alone English. All had waited for years in camps. Would they have the confidence, and the persistence that goes with it, to find work?

Yet I emphatically did not believe our people were simply vulnerable refugees in need of help. In the camps they had taken jobs as health workers, teachers, carers, for little or no pay. They had learnt leadership skills in the camp management committees, the Women's Association or the Children's Forum. The success of the camp schools meant that at least one person in every family, usually a youth, spoke English. Our people were strong people. They had helped each other to survive a great ordeal. These strengths would surely help them to build a life in Australia.

Nevertheless, many of our elders had suffered violence and torture when they were expelled from Bhutan. None spoke English and their chances of integration seemed low. To make our seniors feel at home, we showed them their corner of Australia. They went to a Hindu temple, to the zoo – a concept many had never heard of – and to a dairy farm, where my mother, who had milked cows by hand all her life, was astonished to see rows of machines milking, all up, a hundred cows a minute.

Soon after my parents arrived, I introduced my father to Mark Wright, then commander of Blacktown police, at a function. Mark is a warm and energetic man, but also very tall, and when he came forward to shake hands, my father looked nervous, even afraid. I encouraged him to extend his hand, but instead he simply put his hands together and said, 'Namaste.' On the way home in the car, I asked, 'Dad, why did you not shake his hand?' He said he was scared of Mark's uniform; it reminded him of the soldiers who had tortured him.

I did not want to let this stand. Soon after, we organised a group of seniors to visit the police station. Before going we told Mark a little of what some of them had suffered in Bhutan. Mark got my father and others to wear his hat and sit in his chair; some went for a ride in his car. He got the seniors laughing. Mark's welcome eased people's minds, and I think they began to see that the police were there for their safety.

Many elderly people adapted far quicker to their new life than I could have imagined. Most did not want to languish at home. In 2010, the ABA and SydWest Multicultural Services, a migrant resource centre, started a regular Friday morning program for seniors at SydWest's Blacktown office. They chatted, went on many excursions, did a yoga class. The program expanded to include an English-speaking session after Damber Bahadur Budathoki, aged 94, said to a SydWest interpreter, 'Why don't you teach us English so you don't always have to interpret for us?' Later the program also took in fortnightly visits to Riverstone Community Garden, where many elders who had been farmers in Bhutan started plots and grew vegetables to take home.

Perhaps our liveliest elder was Tika Ram Acharya, a man in his eighties, and alert to everything. If people around him spoke English, Tika Ram would ask, 'What are they saying?' On walks with his wife Menuka, he would excitedly point out 'For Sale' signs and pass on the news to house-hunting families. He could not read a word of English but he had worked out that 'For Sale' was one letter less than 'For Lease'.

Tika Ram's openness influenced others. When my brother-in-law Puspa Acharya, who co-ordinates the seniors program at SydWest, decided to take the seniors group to Manly Beach, some people were uneasy, saying it was wrong to expose the elders to all those nearly naked people lying around. But the day was a great success. People took their lead from Tika Ram, who said the beach scenes were fine: 'Yes, people behave differently in Australia. So what?'

Young people presented a different challenge. On

Saturday mornings I would pick up teenagers and drive them to soccer training. Hemanta Acharya, the pandit Harihar's daughter and Tika Ram's granddaughter, had come to Australia at the age of 15. In the camps, boys had played with a ball made of socks and plastic, but girls were not welcome. In Australia, Hemanta followed her brother Parshu, a good player, and found that she also had a gift for the game. In June 2010, 19 months after arriving in the country, she represented Australia in the FIFA Football for Hope festival for youth from refugee backgrounds, held during the World Cup in South Africa. The ABA held a special event to celebrate her success.

From the time they arrived in Australia, girls and young women quickly found their balance, and started looking for opportunities to earn or learn. With boys it was much harder. Some felt isolated and missed their friends from the camps. Australia offers so many opportunities to study and work and succeed, but also so many opportunities to get into bad habits and trouble. I had sleepless nights thinking about that. 'Come on, guys, let's get into the car, go and play soccer,' I would say cheerfully on Saturday mornings. I was a little pushy sometimes, but I also tried to be accepting: 'Oh, this kid's sleeping in every Saturday, but that's what kids do.' Both boys and girls, trying to make sense of a strange place, seemed to have given the older generation their trust. Could we hold it?

That question arose very quickly, when we invited pandits and seniors to open our monthly gatherings at Alpha Hall with Hindu chants of praise known as bhajan. This was popular among the target group, but not among young people, who began to call the gatherings 'bhajan sessions', and to drift away. So we had to change, ask young people what they wanted to do.

They wanted to sing and dance, hold quizzes; a few wanted to recite poetry. So the nights became a glorious mishmash of old and new: ancient Hindu chants mixed with hiphop, speeches advertising job opportunities, resumé writing or domestic harmony workshops, followed by a dance or a poem, or Tulsi Sharma, a founding ABA member, jumping up to croon one of his beloved country-and-western numbers as little children carried half-finished paintings into the hall.

At these gatherings, young people naturally chatted about their talents and passions. Five youngsters got talking about their love for soccer. One thing led to another, and one Saturday morning a group of us stood in a park in Blacktown and announced the formation of Druk FC (football club), Druk being the dragon of Bhutanese mythology. A young man who had been active in the camps, Damber Dhungyel, was appointed captain. A men's team began to play regularly against Nepali, Tibetan and South Sudanese sides, while two women's indoor soccer teams were formed and came second and third in a tournament organised by SydWest.

In 2010, the ABA started a regular, open planning process for the year ahead. We held Saturday workshops for women, youth, and people transitioning to work. The youth workshop was especially exciting. The 50 young people in the room named their three priorities as sport, art and information technology.

A lot of kids love to draw, and some older ones had been artists in the camps. Nawal Khatiwada, a 26-year-old fine arts student who had won art awards in the camps, volunteered to run classes with my daughter Smriti, who had studied art in year 12. A service provider I approached said it could do a class for a few months if it could find around $5000 in funding. Not having that kind of money, not wanting to apply and wait for it, we decided to do the classes ourselves.

We asked people to hunt in their houses and garages for paints, pencils, paper. Smriti used to work in an art and crafts supplies shop in Blacktown's Westpoint mall and knew that it often threw out reject paper, brushes and pencils. The shop owners were pleased to give her these materials for free. The first classes were held under trees beside the Blacktown Council building. I suggested to Smriti: 'Don't do it by yourself. Get kids in the class to help you organise and manage it.' We were delegating as much as we could, to bring on new leaders. The workshop, which in time moved to a classroom owned by my old employer, MTC, ran for about six months. It cost us a grand total of $37.50.

Many young people were also keen to develop their IT skills, and they had the ABA website to work on. Tulsi Sharma built the first version, with some help from Naresh and me over a few nights and a few beers at Tulsi's house. We created an IT team to advertise events and share achievements and stories. Young people and children were encouraged to contribute articles, poems and pieces of writing. The website was vital in holding the community together in those early years.

But not all adult–child relations were strong, and not all families stayed close. In Bhutan, the family was a collective. Parents ran the show and set standards of discipline; children contributed to the upkeep of the house and consulted parents before making big decisions. In Australia, children could make their own decisions as soon as they turned 18, or even earlier, with little or no regard for what their parents thought. In some families discipline totally collapsed, with children coming and going as they chose. Mothers would cook meals and wait for children to come home, only to be told they had already eaten.

Some of these parents were devastated. They had sacrificed everything to live among strangers so that they could give their children the very best. Now these children felt like strangers too. Some would inadvertently hurt their parents when they saw material goods on television or at their friends' houses and ask for the same. Saroja and I visited one family soon after the mother had come home from taking her boy, aged about eight, to a shopping centre. He had demanded a jacket; she said no, it was too expensive. Knowing she spoke no English, the boy said, 'If you don't buy it, I'll leave you here alone.' He didn't carry out his threat, but he left his mother very worried.

A few parents, struggling in Australia, asked me to be an alternate guardian who could speak for them at their children's school. One 15-year-old, a lovely boy from a troubled background, could not speak English well. In a remedial class, another boy taunted him mercilessly, eventually saying, 'F... your mother.' The Bhutanese boy had lost his mother. He lashed out with his fists and the incident was caught on a school security camera. He was suspended for several days.

When I sat down with the boy, he was no longer angry but felt a keen sense of injustice. I said I understood his feelings, but he had to manage his anger. I said, 'You may have bad days but look at all the care you are getting. In the camp you were one student among 30 or more, with one teacher who was not even qualified. Here you are getting one teacher to yourself all day (through a remedial English program).'

The boy looked despairing: 'Uncle, I am trying!' Over the next few months, both the school counsellor and I spent time with him. The boy began to share his feelings. He told me he could cope with any taunt, unless it was about his mother. Gradually, his life improved; he changed schools, the family moved interstate. Today he is a different person, and works happily on a fruit and vegetable farm.

Another young man, the eldest of six children, arrived in Australia at 18. It's a dangerous age for a migrant – too old for school, with Centrelink money rolling into your bank account. This young man took English classes at TAFE and enrolled in a course, but he struggled. He started drinking, taking drugs, getting into bad company. His family was ashamed: he had brought them disharmony and dishonour, yet he was such a quiet, nice fellow, doing the normal things young people do. I said to other community members, 'He is not our son, but we are responsible for him.'

I started taking him for coffee or a drive. Our early talks were short and one-sided: I asked questions, he gave mumbled responses. After about three months, I dropped him home one night and accompanied him to his room. I said good night and was leaving when he took my hand and said 'Thank you, Uncle'. Then he began to sob. I hugged him and kept him in my arms for a while, my faced turned away so that he could not see my own tears.

I'm not sure why, but after that night our conversations changed. Perhaps he put his trust in me, or perhaps he felt that if someone was looking after him he needed to take more responsibility for himself. He started asking me questions:

can I do this, can I do that? What should I study? Soon he enrolled in a university course, and graduated three years later. Today he has a well-paid and valued job and a wonderful family.

But I did not always do well with young people. SydWest had agreed to support one of our youth programs. I passed the news on to our youth committee and asked for a response. I got none. At a meeting I pointed this out, frustration creeping into my voice. A young man who knew me well enough to call me Uncle stood up and said defiantly, 'Who are you?'

I fretted about this exchange all day. I had acted like a Telstra executive, expecting a quick response to my query, but these young people were volunteering their time. And they faced challenges in their lives that I could not begin to grasp. I apologised to the young man and got a gracious response. That was a big lesson. I had to sit back and listen, then to suggest, not insist. I had to discard my assumption that with my education, experience and longer time in Australia I knew what was best for the Bhutanese.

I also learnt that I could hinder others through my very desire to help. In the early days, I regularly picked up my cousins, the two Kafley brothers and their families, and drove them to various appointments or to buy groceries. One day Saroja and I visited their newly arrived younger brother Dambaru and his wife Damanta in Werrington, half an hour's drive from Blacktown. We didn't bother to call beforehand – they spoke no English and couldn't drive, so where could they go? But we arrived to find no one home. I called Dambaru, who said, 'We're in Westfield, in Liverpool!' That was a long way – two trains – from Werrington. There was pride in Dambaru's voice. Maybe driving the other Kafley families everywhere had been a mistake. Once or twice is OK, but if you keep doing it you make them dependent. Sometimes people need to work out things by themselves.

Every day I felt I was learning a little more about the best way to motivate and empower other people, when to step in and when to step back. These lessons were valuable even inside my own family. I would often pick up my father and take him for a drive. Because his torture in Bhutan had left him with scars and a rigid back, he found it hard to get into the car and to turn around and fasten his seatbelt, so I would reach over and do it for him. But one day I thought, 'What if a stranger gives him a lift? That person would expect him to fasten his seatbelt – how would he do it?'

The next time we went for a drive I suggested he clasp the seatbelt himself. He shifted his body gingerly and fumbled for a while with the clip. It was painful to watch. While he held the belt with one hand, I held his other hand and made him feel the hole and put the belt in the clip. I made him try again on his own. 'I can't,' he said.

The same thing happened on our next few drives. 'Keep trying,' I said. One day he reached over, took the belt, and put it into the clip. Click. His face lit up. And it would still light up years later, when he was in his nineties and got into a car, fastened his seatbelt and grinned, as if he had just landed on the moon.

I vowed never to make that mistake again. By doing the task for him, I realised, I was taking away his chance and his right to take charge of his own life. I was taking away his smile.

9

FROM CORPORATION TO COMMUNITY

In 2010, I was promoted to competitive intelligence manager in Telstra's Innovation, Products and Marketing division. My pay increased but so did my hours. I also joined the board of SydWest Multicultural Services in Blacktown, while still on the MTC board.

I would leave Telstra's head office in George Street at 5 pm, my phone pinging with questions about work in progress, and start responding as soon as I sat down for the 50-minute train trip to Blacktown. My car would be parked at the station or Saroja would pick me up for the drive to an ABA or board meeting, a dinner with a newly arrived and anxious family, or to Smriti's basketball game, the one family commitment I never missed in those hectic years.

That year, Smriti decided she wanted to raise funds for Haiti, which had just suffered a terrible earthquake. The three of us would get up at four on Sunday mornings, collect a pile of second-hand goods that Smriti's friends had dropped off at our garage, and take them to a local market, where Smriti would sell them.

In Monday morning team meetings at Telstra, everyone shared what they did on the weekend. Someone had been on a harbour cruise, or eaten a delicious dinner at a Thai restaurant on the North Shore. I spoke about meeting people at the airport or driving them to English classes. As the train raced to Blacktown from the city I felt I was moving between two worlds, each largely blind to the other, and two ways of thinking about the world.

At Telstra, we would analyse a situation, identify all the factors that contributed to it, focus on important causes and discard others, recommend a response, then stick to that path until new information suggested a better way. It was a rigorous, powerful method, but it was black-and-white thinking.

Telstra had many command-and-control leaders who moved fast and did not have to spell out the reason for every decision. In Bhutan I had also given and taken orders without question. This approach will never work in a community setting. People giving their own time must be engaged and encouraged; they must be asked, not told. Consensus decisions are best, but if that is not possible, the way a decision is reached and enacted has to be clear to all. Leaders do have to push sometimes – for every person who steps forward, more sit back – but they must do so gently. Community building is confidence building – bringing on many leaders and teaching them to work together in a spirit of trust, equality and mutual respect. It requires patience, humility, a democratic mindset, and a lot of hours.

In our ABA work, women played a vital role. An early inspiration was Pabitra Kafley, wife of my cousin Om Kafley. When she arrived in Australia Pabitra had spent 16 years in a refugee camp and was in her early thirties, with only a basic education and almost no English. She could not take a paid job because she had to care for ageing in-laws and a son with poor health. But she helped to organise regular picnics for seniors, and the songs and hymns known as bhajans at our monthly gathering. She studied English and was the first Bhutanese woman to get a driver's licence. In 2009, she was elected the ABA's first women's co-ordinator. In Bhutan or Nepal such achievements and roles would have been closed to a woman like Pabitra. Our culture is very male-dominated. A new wife – or wives, since a man can take two or more – disappears into the husband's family home, to cook, clean and raise children. But migration can help to level those traditional patterns and power relationships.

Of people who grasped their opportunities in Australia, many were women. Reeta Khatiwada never chased that job folding bedsheets that she asked me about days after her arrival in Sydney. Instead, she did an aged care course and quickly found a job, before going back to study to take a Bachelor of Nursing; she works as a registered nurse today.

Other women opened businesses. Four set up childcare centres catering to children from our community. My sister Tulasha, who had arrived in Australia with a Bachelor of Arts and long experience teaching in the camps, enrolled in a Diploma of Child Care, then became the first former Bhutanese refugee to open a day care centre. Krishna Acharya and Goma Dhungel opened centres in Blacktown, and Uma Chamlagai in Kingswood.

In my generation in southern Bhutan, it was rare for women to drive, let alone start a business. In Australia, women saw that getting a driver's licence was the key to getting ahead. But many still faced opposition – and that is where our monthly gatherings were important. In our messages, we were able to show that people would have a better life in this country if both husband and wife worked and drove. Without such encouragement, a woman would have had to convince her in-laws or her husband that it was OK to drive. They, in turn, would have started talking to other seniors, who would have tut-tutted that a woman was having driving lessons with a man. Before long, she would have given up. But when Pabitra got her L plates, then her licence, we called her to the front of our Alpha Hall gathering and everybody clapped. Men anxious about their wives taking new roles saw her being praised, and stopped objecting, at least openly. Other women were inspired to have a go too.

It helped a great deal that four of the ABA's eight founding members were female: Saroja, Poonam, Dukka and Pabitra. All had jobs, all were active in the ABA, all mentored new arrivals. Dukka was the ABA's first treasurer while her husband Dr Naresh was involved, but initially had no formal role. Women influenced the ABA's work in large and small ways. For example, we preferred to call events 'gatherings' or 'get-togethers' and to combine them with a meal. If we called them 'meetings', women were much less likely to show up.

Migration to Australia also undermined class or status hierarchies. Jagat, a senior community member, considered himself much more competent than Hasta, who was virtually illiterate when he came here and whose family was considered 'backward' (I have changed names to protect their identities). But Hasta persevered more than most at learning English. Jagat confided to me that he had never imagined learning how to use a computer to sit for a driving test, let alone driving a car, until he heard that Hasta had acquired a licence. He said, 'If it wasn't for Hasta, I wouldn't be driving today.'

But for people to participate, they had to have an adequate level of English. That understanding led to the most ambitious project the ABA has ever undertaken.

By 2011, most Bhutanese had been in Sydney for two years. Most were doing well but two groups in particular – wives at home and former farmers – were struggling to learn English. They blamed their parents for never sending them to school, they blamed the long years in the camps, or they blamed themselves. I spoke at length to seven or eight women in this group. 'I'm too old, too dull, too dumb,' they would sigh. Some husbands sapped their confidence. One told me, when his wife was in the next room, that she was stupid. I replied, 'She's just cooked this incredible meal we've eaten. You and I couldn't cook it. And you say she's dumb?'

Tara Nidhi Bhandari, a young pandit, was keen to improve his English. I suggested he take the lead and organise a conversation with people who might benefit from a special class. One night he invited to his home 12 students who were studying in the government-funded Language, Literacy and Numeracy Program at the Blacktown campus of MTC, where I sat on the board. The students made it clear they were not learning much. People with wildly varying levels of English, such as a man with a bachelor's degree and his illiterate wife, were put in the same class. A few teachers were excellent, but some didn't even show up. Students wanted to practise spoken English more. They wanted individual mentors, tailored learning plans and homework. To build their confidence, they wanted to be able to ask questions and talk with each other in class.

From these and other discussions emerged the ABA Spoken English School. The school was designed to comple-ment, not replace, official language programs. For our students, even the basic English levels of the Adult Migrant English Program, in which they were entitled to 510 hours of free tuition, were too high. We needed to start them at level zero. We also felt that only a school created by our community, not by service providers, could understand the students' situation. While our classes would be in English, teachers who could speak Nepali and translate key words were essential.

We also thought the school could help teachers in our community. Lots of smart, committed people had taught in the camps, and enjoyed respect. But in Australia their qualifications were not recognised, and many were struggling as a result. The school could rekindle their motivation, and give them work experience that would help in their search for a job.

The MTC managers were keen to work with us. They accepted our request to use their empty Blacktown classrooms on weekends. Three classes began on Saturday mornings with 45 students. Most were uneducated and illiterate women, ranging in age from mid-thirties to Bishnu Maya Khadka, who was 78 and an inspiration to all. We focused on everyday language that would help people to shop, use computers and get their driver's licence. After a while, we started offering citizenship classes since a core ABA principle was to encourage people to take the test and become Australian citizens.

The school ran on volunteers. Puspa Acharya, my brother-in-law, who had run a motorcycle spare parts store in Nepal, worked tirelessly to run the school and teach in it too. Leela Bhandari and Hari Khatiwada, former teachers in the camps, developed the curriculum. Over time, about 15 volunteers taught. For a year I spent my Saturdays on school administration and when not enough teachers were available, I would take classes myself.

I would launch into simple conversations in English:

'What is your name? What did you do today?' A lot of women would not come forward. If I invited a few to the front of the class they would get nervous, go quiet. But I persevered: 'OK, let's stand at the front together and talk.' Sometimes we would walk together around the room, and then I would sit, leaving the woman out the front alone, and for a moment she would forget she was already talking. Students said they came home with a sore throat from laughing and talking so much. Slowly, their confidence grew.

We had a lot of early obstacles. Teachers would leave when they found jobs or started courses, and some classes had to be merged. But the biggest challenge to the school came from within our community. Some people tried to discourage family members from going by saying the organisers must be doing it to make money, when we were volunteering all our time and spending our own money on petrol. Some husbands and even some children didn't want their wife or mother to come to the Saturday morning class. They had no faith she could learn, and anyway, who would cook their breakfast? They would refuse to drop her at the station; quite a few times I had to collect female students and drive them to Blacktown myself.

Similarly, in three or four families where women did not get citizenship, it was their men who stopped them. One man, whose wife started taking English classes, said, 'Why are you bothering? In this country even the dogs understand English.' He's a very funny fellow, and we all laughed, but he was putting his wife down; he could not bear her getting ahead of him. Today, she speaks English well, and he doesn't.

The school lasted three years, until most people found jobs, and the need for it faded. But its influence has lasted.

An academic study in 2014 found that the school had helped Bhutanese migrants, especially older people and women, to fill gaps in their education that were stopping them learning English. Tika Ram Adhikari, who had been a farmer in Bhutan, told me he 'didn't know ABC and had never touched a computer' when he came to Australia in 2011. Thanks to the school, he says, he got his driving licence two and a half years after his arrival.

Even as their English improved, people did not find jobs overnight. Often their paths to work were long and tortuous. But we kept repeating the same messages: study; get work experience; volunteer; persist. Most did exactly that.

Many Bhutanese found work as cleaners. Kamal Nepal had finished high school in the camp, but knew he had to improve his English, so he took a vocational education and training (VET) course in English language while working as a cleaner. He then took a VET course in laboratory technology, but could not find work in that field. Disappointed but not defeated, he took two certificates in cleaning. He now runs his own thriving business, and has employed several other Bhutanese.

Another person who took a long time to find good work, who overcame many setbacks, was Champa Rai Adhikari. While raising two young children, she completed a VET course in English, then another in hospitality. She got a job, but the workplace was far away and she didn't have a car. So she left and returned to VET to study retail and customer service, while learning to drive. She got a casual job in a grocery, but it wasn't stable, so once more she went back to study, completing a certificate in aged care. She now has a full-time job in a nursing home, and she and her husband

Chabi, another aged care worker, have bought a house in Blacktown.

Another couple, Ram Krishna Gautam and Ran Maya, were farmers in Bhutan and hoped to work on the land in Australia. After studying in the Adult Migrant English Program, the ABA Spoken English School and at TAFE, they found work as hands on a cabbage and lettuce farm near Penrith. Ten years later they are still there. The owner treats them as part of his family, and often leaves the farm in their care when he is away. He has employed other Bhutanese based on his trust in Ram and Ran Maya.

At ABA, our work writing references often led to jobs. One aged care provider would even contact me asking for more workers.

Yet not all newcomers did as well. Some could not come to terms with the changes in their life. 'I was the boss at home. I want to be again' – that mindset was a big barrier. There were episodes of domestic violence, anger and frustration, and of sheer loneliness. A few lost fortunes on the pokies. One man, out of pride, bought a house he could not afford without telling his wife, then lost his job, and his deposit. Late one night, I had to go to the police station to prevent a child being taken from a parent – a good person but given to sorrow – whom the police had found drunk in Blacktown CBD.

Some did not easily make the journey from a life of scarcity to one of overwhelming abundance. Some could not manage their budget, and would have no money for an electricity bill while being on the hook for monthly instalments to buy the latest model phone. Or they would visit friends and relatives with a new sofa and big screen TV, and not realise these things come only with effort. We encouraged them to work to improve their position, rather than compare themselves with others or listen to those who blamed Australian society for 'injustice'. We urged people to value what they had, and to teach that gratitude to their children.

A few people got stuck on Centrelink benefits. These payments had a mixed impact on our community. On the one hand, they were vital in helping some families buy a home, especially when parents, grandparents and adult children could pool their payments for a deposit. The money also helped people to adopt ABA's advice to study or gain work experience rather than jump into the first job they could find. On the other hand, Centrelink payments allowed some husbands to insist their wives stay home, and sometimes to stay home themselves. They enabled some religious practitioners to go out in public and preach the worst Hindu traditions, such as segregating and shaming people based on caste, while relying on easy money from the government. Welfare payments are important in the short term, and to support the very disadvantaged, but over time they can entrench bad habits and oppressive traditions by keeping people out of society.

Yet despite a few setbacks, by 2015, six years after arriving, most adults were in work or study. Many jobseekers had focused on fields with skills shortages, especially in health, the care sectors, and hospitality. As a result, of a total Sydney Bhutanese population of about 500 people, more than 50 were health care workers and related professionals, including eight registered nurses; another 25 were in aged and disability care. These skilled people could mentor others. When Damber Dhungyel, the ABA's first youth co-ordinator and a captain of Druk FC, became one of our first nurses, I would refer would-be nurses to him.

By 2015, Australia had settled more than 5000 Bhutanese former refugees. The then Home Affairs minister Peter Dutton praised the community for 'supporting each other to quickly gain employment and independent living'. A survey taken a few years later showed that more than 60 per cent of people owned their homes.

In April 2013, I got a call from my nephew Teku Kafley. His parents, uncle and aunt would become citizens at a Blacktown City Council ceremony that evening – would I be there? I was excited to see one of the first groups of Bhutanese take out citizenship. The ABA had always stressed the importance of making this commitment, and when Teku called I felt proud. A survey we did showed that nearly everyone in our community had volunteered at some point since arriving in the country. Nearly everyone had done a huge amount of hard work.

But I was starting to realise that success had come at a personal cost. I was on the board of MTC Australia, and in 2010 had joined the SydWest board. In 2013, I had also joined the board of Settlement Services International, New South Wales's biggest provider of services to refugees. I was spending weekends on ABA business, all while working full-time at Telstra. I often got rundown and sick. One day, Smriti, who was studying for a Bachelor of Interior Architecture at the University of New South Wales, asked me whether she could organise some time with me the following week to discuss an assignment. I was shocked: my own daughter felt she had to make an appointment to see me. I had never fully gotten over my guilt at leaving her and Saroja on their own when I came to Australia. When Smriti told me that I pretty much decided on the spot that something had to change.

I am blessed to be married to Saroja. She never once made me feel that my work was taking me away from her. And she was deeply involved in the ABA work too. Still, I got a shock when Serge Dekatch, my former MTC board chair and a friend and mentor, took me through an exercise in which I divided up all my activities across a week. We worked out that I left 5 per cent of my time for leisure. Serge asked: 'What about your time with Saroja?' I said that she came with me on visits to families. 'That's ABA business, not time together,' he replied.

I had got to know Kalyan Ram, the founder and president of Social Entrepreneur Ventures Australia, or SEVA International, an organisation that provides a platform for South Asian communities in Australia. Kalyan had invited me to join SEVA's board as a representative of the Bhutanese. He was in his eighties, and when he decided to step down, he and his board asked me to become CEO.

That role promised a new direction. I had thought a great deal about the way that migrant and refugee communities could thrive in Australia. I could stay at Telstra and increase my own wealth, or I could try to help migrants with few resources to prosper, and in that way increase Australia's wealth. It was a no-brainer for me.

Over the past 30 years or so, various psychologists, social workers and community organisers have developed a theory they call 'asset-based community development' or a 'strengths-based approach'. The core idea – compelling to me – is that individuals and communities thrive by focusing not on their limitations and needs but on their skills and strengths. There is a vast academic literature on this idea, but at that time I knew none of it. I only knew that we had tried to take our own strengths-based approach with the Bhutanese refugees.

I loved my work; I was proud to be a Telstra hometown ambassador, giving talks and helping to organise events to promote the company, and I was well paid. Leaving would mean a huge salary cut, but Saroja fully supported my decision to follow my heart.

There was one other reason for my decision. My time at Telstra had got me thinking: 'We live in this paradise, one of the richest countries on Earth, yet people are so stressed. On our way home in a nice car, we can remotely switch on the air conditioner and get into a house that is already cool, then make a video call to a friend on the other side of the world. Yet for many of us, happiness seems so far away. What is missing?'

That question troubled me. I was an engineer, trained to be logical, but I had learnt that logic helps us to understand only the material aspects of life. While I never believed in a particular god, even as a boy I thought that religion – its teachings, not the rituals applied selectively to suit its priests and gurus – provided the ground for a good life. Yet I saw that religion often divided people and societies, creating disharmony. I longed for something beyond religion. Leaving Telstra might give me time to search for it.

In a long email to about 300 Telstra colleagues in March 2013, I thanked many by name for all they had taught me, for their support and friendship over the past ten years. I said that long before I called Australia home, I had been connected to Telstra: as a bureaucrat in Bhutan I had recruited experts from Telecom Australia to work on the national telecommunications master plan, and had sent engineers and technicians to train at Telecom in Melbourne. I expressed my sadness at leaving, told them of my plans, and hoped we could stay in touch. Several people told me they cried as they read it. The CEO, David Thodey, responded while on a trip to Bangalore in India and set up a meeting to say goodbye.

It was an emotional farewell, but it felt right. Although I was never an engineer at Telstra, working for a national telecommunications company had felt like the culmination of one part of my life's journey: from my headmaster Mr Nair's advice to become an engineer, to studying in Bangladesh to working on Bhutan's telecommunications plan. On this path I had learnt one way to think about the world. Now it was time to think about another way. I wanted to move from corporate life fully into community life, to try to shape the public debate on refugee settlement, and to share what I had learnt with other people.

10

BEYOND CHARITY: RETHINKING REFUGEE SETTLEMENT

Around the time I left Telstra, I began keeping a piece of paper and a pen by my bed. I would wake in the middle of the night, mind racing, and scrawl another thought in the dark. Soon the papers were crowded with words in circles, and arrows shooting between them. Some I understood in the morning, some looked like drawings I had done when I was four years old.

One day I put my ideas onto a sheet of paper and took it to Smriti, who was studying interior architecture and knew a thing or two about design. She took one look and said, 'Papa, I can't make any sense of this. What are you trying to do?' Smriti is a tough taskmaster.

What I was trying to do – my obsession in those years – was to document what the ABA had done with the Bhutanese, what the Bhutanese had done for themselves. A UNHCR plan had enabled more than 100 000 refugees to find homes in eight western countries. It was one of the most successful resettlements undertaken since the end of World War Two. At a time of much despondency about the fate of refugees around the world, I thought more people needed to know about this story, and Australia's part in it.

By refugees, I meant people admitted through the humanitarian program, not the people seeking asylum who came to Australia by boat in the 20 or so years before 2013. People often confuse the two categories, in part because most of the latter group were also found to be refugees, having a well-founded fear of persecution.

Those who came to Australia through the formal refugee program – the so-called front door – received services that were as good as any in the world. Those who came through the back door, who were put into indefinite mandatory detention, were treated in a manner that was needlessly cruel. While this second group was not part of my argument, it was nevertheless relevant. I hoped to show what refugees in general could do for Australia, and in that way try to persuade the country to take more.

The Bhutanese, who had spent years in refugee camps, in many cases without jobs, clear roles or a sense of a future, had put themselves on the road to fully integrating into their new society within three to five years of arrival. I believed they had taken such strides not in spite of, but because of the fact that they had been refugees. Many lacked skills and confidence but no one could say they lacked perseverance or drive.

Yet they had not taken their new path alone. Through a community organisation, the ABA, they had been guided and supported by people who spoke their language and understood – in many cases shared – their history. A government-funded settlement service provider, ACL, was there to offer accommodation and essential advice in their first months in the country, when they were most in need. Other government services – Centrelink, Medicare and free schooling – ensured they could start to build a secure, long-term base for new lives. Could Smriti put all that on a diagram?

She got to work, and after many drafts devised a hub-and-spokes wheel that showed how each ABA initiative – the monthly gatherings, sports days, art and Spoken English classes and so on – linked to the others and reflected the organisation's larger goals. I was delighted with her colourful, catchy design. I knew from my time in the civil service and at Telstra that diagrams, elaborated with short, sharp sentences, were a great way to clarify a complex issue for busy people, and it was busy people I hoped to persuade. Smriti's one-pager proved very useful when I briefed Liberal Senator Concetta Fierravanti-Wells, who was responsible for settlement services in her role as Assistant Minister for Social Services in the Abbott government.

In those days I was always rushing to see where I could influence public debate. I gave speeches, ran workshops, helped to create a toolkit for establishing community organis-ations. I met many public servants, and attended roundtable consultations with immigration ministers such as Scott Morrison and Peter Dutton. I wrote a report for the Westpac Foundation after being awarded a Social Change Fellowship to study refugee settlement overseas. I even wrote a book manuscript that was part memoir, part manual of refugee settlement the ABA way.

At the top of my diagram I had written, 'The local community is the basic productive force. Help the community understand what skills it has within so that it can identify what support is required from outside. What service providers can do comes next – it is secondary.'

These three sentences captured the essence of the ABA's model of refugee settlement based on volunteering. Sadly, they rarely reflected the reality. Jill Gillespie, manager of ACL, provider of settlement services to the Bhutanese refugees, had fully supported the ABA's model. Yet other service providers criticised our approach, asking, 'Why are you making people volunteer at such a hard time? They have their hands full just getting their lives together.' That question made some of our people doubt themselves. What worried me was that anyone would ask it.

The question seemed part of a bigger problem, one that still troubles me today. Over time, I have seen responsibility for settlement being shifted from migrant communities and their organisations to private and not-for-profit service providers. Service providers spend too much money on tasks – some as basic as arranging barbecues or picnics – that communities could do themselves, learning valuable skills along the way. The settlement sector's stated objectives are all about empowering former refugees, yet increasingly it has come to see them through a social welfare frame: as vulnerable, often traumatised by their past, needing ongoing support.

I come to this problem not as an outside critic but as someone with deep roots in the settlement system, and a deep desire to work with colleagues to improve it. As I wrote my first critiques of the system, in 2013 and 2014, I was on the boards of SydWest Multicultural Services, Settlement Services International (SSI) and MTC Australia, all of which still provide services to refugees. Violet Roumeliotis, Elfa Moraitakis, Melissa Monteiro and Cath Scarth, the CEOs of SSI, SydWest, the Community Migrant Resource Centre and AMES respectively, are all respected colleagues and friends who want only the best for their clients, as do the case workers who deal with refugees every day. No one wants to paint refugees as passive recipients of services, as victims. But such attitudes have become baked into the funding model.

While doing research for my book manuscript, I was excited to read that the ideas behind the ABA model had been advanced in the founding document of Australian multiculturalism, the 1978 *Report of the Review of Post-Arrival Programs and Services to Migrants*. This report, known to all as the Galbally Report after its chair, Frank Galbally, announced Australia's move away from a postwar migration program built on assimilation, on requiring migrants to merge into the dominant culture. The government of Malcolm Fraser adopted the report's principles and recommendations nearly in full.

One of these principles was what Galbally called 'self-help'. In the months just after their arrival, he wrote, migrants could not be expected to fend for themselves, or to immediately find work. That's when the settlement services proposed in the report were essential. But after that early period, policy should be geared to helping migrants and refugees take charge of their own lives.

Galbally believed that migrant organisations, not govern-ment agencies, were best placed to understand and meet communities' needs. The report recommended the establish-ment of Migrant Resource Centres to enable migrants to develop their own programs in areas such as language learning, advocacy, help for the elderly, media and oral history. 'Ethnic groups themselves must take on the task of advising governments of the needs and priorities of migrants, and ensuring that ethnic cultures are fostered and preserved.' Such an approach would both speed migrants' integration and reduce government spending on welfare services.

Galbally's proposals were communal, participatory, democratic in spirit. But in the years since his report came out, for reasons I do not fully understand, that spirit has been lost.

From the late 1990s, the federal government began to contract out many services to private and not-for-profit providers, rather than delivering them itself. It was a revolution of sorts and it transformed refugee settlement services, along with many other program areas.

Over time, the government found it cheaper and more convenient to deal with fewer service providers. In my ten years on the board of MTC Australia the number of organisations that won tenders to provide services to job-seekers fell dramatically. In refugee settlement, by 2022 just five organisations would be responsible for all services across Australia.

As the number of organisations has fallen, their size has grown. They often expand into other fields: NGOs that began in employment or settlement services now bid for contracts in family, community or disability services.

In some ways the change has been good. Large service providers are run with greater efficiency and rigour. They are strong enough to represent the sector and lobby for more resources in Canberra.

However, the more organisations grow, the more they are locked into winning government grants to support that growth. The larger ones have taken on marketing departments and multi-million-dollar budgets. They hire people whose sole job is to bid for more business. When I met with Senator Fierravanti-Wells, then the Assistant Minister for Social Services, I sensed her displeasure that service providers were using taxpayer money to employ professional fundraisers, who would lobby government for more money. Some of these organisations have come to resemble corporations. I heard a senior figure in one say that it aspired to be a 'one-stop shop' for services to refugees. But its role is to provide human connection and build human capacity, not to sell mobile phones.

The growth imperative also shapes the nature of the case the sector makes to Canberra. In bidding for a contract to run a settlement program, NGOs typically start with a 'needs analysis' of the community the program will serve. Once you start looking for needs, you find them everywhere. The remedy? Another program. Inevitably, that attitude infects migrant community organisations as well. The leaders of one asked me, 'What can we get from the government? How can you help us to apply for grants?' The promise of Galbally's grassroots democracy has been supplanted by the risk of dependency.

Many of these changes have been justified by the need to bring specialist professional expertise to the settlement of migrants and refugees. Counselling, for example, increasingly cannot be provided unless it is 'trauma-informed', which requires a qualification to practise. One effect of the increasing focus on professional expertise is to shut out migrants and their organisations that lack such qualifications.

I identify two kinds of expertise. Governments and service providers are full of *content* experts, usually well-educated professionals with a lot of knowledge and formal power. They know how the system works and how to work within it.

A *context* expert, by contrast, has lived experience of a situation or a local environment. They may not know how the system works but they know first-hand how their local community works.

Both kinds of expertise are important. But our society champions content expertise over context expertise. People with high qualifications are consulted on every report, called to speak at every function. They start wearing their learning as a badge of honour, and their ego builds. By contrast, if you turn to the end of virtually any review of refugee policy or outcomes, you will find a list of former refugees who are thanked for sharing their experiences. They are given the honour of telling their stories! They are almost never asked for their views on policy; that is for the 'experts'. Yet someone with little or no schooling can often know more than someone with a PhD.

I think of Pabitra Kafley, the ABA's first women's co-ordinator. Sixteen years in a refugee camp deprived her of a formal education. But Pabitra played a crucial role in helping to run ABA gatherings and other major events. She knows what food is needed, what relationships and traditions must be observed, how to look after elderly people, who can mind children or bring the chairs.

For the same reason the ABA asked two teachers, Hari and Tulasha Khatiwada, to run cultural transition or family harmony workshops, with the support of the NSW Service for the Treatment and Rehabilitation of Torture and Trauma Survivors (STARTTS). Hari and Tulasha were not experts or trained in the issue, but the couple had lived in the camps, and understood how much family violence had occurred there, and why. They were best placed to gently but firmly explain to our people why attitudes and behaviour had to change in Australia.

In the early days of Bhutanese settlement, I occasionally acted as a guardian to speak on parents' behalf to their children's school. Two brothers, not long in the country, had gotten into an argument. Both were struggling at school, and with English. Their single mother was struggling to cope. The older boy, who was 16, was overwhelmed: he had to handle Centrelink money, manage the house, do the shopping, and his ten-year-old brother would not help.

One day he snapped at his younger brother, who then arrived late at school. Asked to explain why, his English failed him, so a Nepali interpreter was brought in on the phone. The interpreter explained that the older boy had told his younger brother: 'Mardinchu hai!' A direct translation is 'I will kill you', but in Bhutan the phrase usually means 'I will hit you' – a difference the Nepal-born interpreter did not understand. When the school heard the word 'kill', it panicked and called local youth service providers. After getting a phone call, I arrived at the school to find two or three youth workers and a school official sitting around a table. There was talk of removing the younger boy from home and putting him in institutional care for his own safety.

When I asked to speak to the older brother, who was under guard in a corridor, I was refused: the boy was an 'aggressor', and even I was potentially at risk. I persisted; I knew the boys well and saw this as just a fight between two brothers under pressure. Finally, after assuring the officials that I was practically part of the family, they let me approach the older boy. At once he said, 'Uncle, namaste!' We hugged. The idea that he might have planned to kill his brother astonished and appalled him: 'I just told him I would hit him if he didn't listen, and he kept ignoring me.'

The whole thing had been blown out of all proportion. Fortunately, we were able to defuse the situation, but if the younger boy had been removed it would have devastated that family, to no earthly good. Despite being trusted by the family, I was not able to talk on its behalf once the department took over, because I'm not a relative, and don't have a counselling certificate. This is the risk of institutionalising problems, of ignoring context expertise.

Of course, when a family is dangerously dysfunctional, a woman is beaten, a child horribly neglected, the state must step in. Some people have physical and psychological injuries that require professional help. The ABA has worked closely with STARTTS, which does an excellent job. And yet I often think of the case of Hem Lal Paudel.

Hem Lal is a lovely man, a few years older than me, quiet, but with a smile never far from his face. A farmer, he was arrested and tortured when the army took control of southern Bhutan. He fled to Nepal with his wife, Bhim Maya, and they spent 18 years in a refugee camp, raising three children, before coming to Australia.

Despite the passage of time, Hem Lal could not overcome his memories of torture. He was referred to counselling. Yet he found that counselling, by forcing him to focus on his traumatic memories, made them worse.

Hem Lal had a gift for cooking, especially samosas and other snacks. In Sydney he would cook for family and friends, until an ABA executive member heard about his talent, and asked him to help at community events. He would cook samosas and make tea at home, then turn up to serve them at Alpha Park Hall. 'How was it?' he would shyly ask.

Two years after arriving in Australia, Hem Lal enrolled

in a cleaning course at TAFE. He and Bhim Maya found jobs as cleaners in the same school in Blacktown. In 2017, they bought their own home, from where they sent their daughter and son to university. Hem Lal's Facebook page shows him and Bhim Maya standing arm in arm in their Blacktown backyard, he in a suit, she in a sari, in front of their Hills Hoist.

Hem Lal will tell you his life began to change for the better the moment he began cooking for so many grateful people. He is just one of many former refugees who simply needed a chance to get started – not charity but inspiration.

I think also of Hemanta Acharya, who represented Australia in a global soccer tournament 19 months after coming to the country with her family. Until the age of 15, she had lived her whole life in a bamboo hut with eight other people, under a leaky roof that meant rainwater pooled on the floor.

Hemanta was so hungry to learn that, after a long day in the camp school, she would go back to her books under a dim lamp. Her parents would tell her, 'Go to sleep! You don't have to study so hard.' But even then, Hemanta knew she wanted to be a doctor or a nurse. Why? She had seen people get sick from cholera and malaria; her good friend had died of typhoid.

She would watch aeroplanes crossing the sky and think, 'One day, if I'm lucky, I'll be on that plane.' When she finally learnt she was going to Australia, she counted every day till departure. As she boarded the flight, she said to herself, 'Let this be the last day I am a refugee. As I land on Australian soil, let my refugee tale stay inside this plane.'

Whether it did or not, Hemanta's refugee tale has shaped

her Australian life. Her short stories are published on a Bhutanese literature website. She runs a dance academy, is a presenter at My Nepal Television Australia and a coach at Football United, a soccer development program. Having completed a master's degree, she works full-time as a clinical nurse specialist.

When I began to document the ABA model, some people told me it could not be applied to other refugee and migrant communities. The Bhutanese were only a small group. Our families were not divided and broken by the refugee experience, and had not faced hostility in Australia. These were valid points, yet I was adamant that while individual histories of settlement differed, the core principles remained the same. But I needed some proof beyond the Bhutanese community. The search for it took me down a surprising path.

*

It was raining hard in Blacktown, the roads were clogged, and I knew I would not get to the event in Fairfield by 6.30 pm. I called the organiser, who was very relaxed: 'Don't worry, Om. Take your time.'

I walked in at 6.45 to find just one person in the hall. Slowly, it filled up. I sat at a table next to Julie Owens, at that time the federal MP for Parramatta, who had walked in well after 7.30. 'How long have you been here?' she asked. More than an hour, I said. She laughed: 'You don't know African time.'

Not long after, I went to a hall in Granville to celebrate the birthdays of the year-old twins and 10-year-old daughter of Emmanuel Kondok, chairperson of the NSW Community of South Sudanese and Other Marginalised Areas, and my friend. By then I knew the start time might be loose, but it was a birthday, so I arrived punctually at 6.30 pm. One other person was there, an official from the federal Department of Social Services. At about 7.45 pm, one more person showed up – the MC. Finally, a stylish black Toyota cruised to a halt, and out stepped Emmanuel, dressed in a long white robe, which he called 'royals attire'. Emmanuel says he is from royalty in South Sudan. He was followed by his wife and daughter, each carrying one of the couple's twin boys. They were quickly surrounded by an entourage of about 15 people; we entered the hall, and the party began. And what a party it was.

In 2014, I started going to African community events. I went to as many as I could. No event ever lacked dancing, and after 9 pm the night would go full swing. I would venture onto the packed floor but not for long – I love dancing, but I can never get my body to cooperate.

These fabulous events taught me about the lighter side of life. I realised that at the ABA we were far too rigid in the way we ran our functions. When we invited Laurie Ferguson, the federal MP from Western Sydney, I asked him to come to our event at 6.30 pm, ready to speak at 6.47 pm. He said to me twice: 'Om, what time do you *really* need me there?' I repeated the times. Laurie came on time, and we got him to the podium at 6.47. That was too uptight. If an event is late or goes a little wrong, who cares?

But the big lesson I learnt from the African Australians I met in those years was not about event management.

South Sudanese refugees began arriving in Blacktown only a few years before the Bhutanese. They were a larger group than we were and, unlike us, they got a harsh reception. When young South Sudanese men gathered in groups around the centre of Blacktown, as all young people do, there were complaints to the local council, even occasional demonstrations in the street. I saw Africans being targeted in the media. I didn't like it. Yes, a small number of young men were violent, but why single out a whole community? If the Bhutanese came under hostile scrutiny in the media, could we defend ourselves? Who would stand with us? We had to solve our problems together. And in Blacktown we had a model for that.

In the late 2000s, there was trouble around the streets of Blacktown CBD, especially between young men of Islander and South Sudanese backgrounds. The railway station was scary in some ways; you had to navigate through the crowds and try not to get pushed. On Thursday nights young people would come by train from all over Sydney to watch 'fight night' – open punch-ups on the fourth floor of Westpoint shopping centre. Something had to be done.

The task fell to the Blacktown police commander Mark Wright, whom I knew quite well.

Soon after taking the Blacktown job, Mark got leaders of community organisations, service providers and churches around a table to talk about youth violence. He asked the question that the ABA always asked: 'What can *we* do?' These Blacktown leaders formed a group called Com4Unity, the name meaning 'connecting our minds for unity,' with the '4' referring to Westpoint's fourth floor, where the fights were happening. Community leaders began walks through the mall, talking to young people. Regular soccer matches were organised between teams from local schools and the police.

Following a suggestion from JoJo Tau, a youth worker who was part of Com4Unity, young people were surveyed about what events they would like to see at the mall. They said they wanted to perform and watch music, dance, rap. The result was Switch, a regular Thursday night concert involving 300 or 400 young people. Switch lasted for three or four years, and its impact has lasted much longer than that. Police statistics show that crime rates fell in this period. Blacktown CBD and station are safer places even today. It was a marvellous example of what communities determined to make change can achieve.

In 2012, SEVA International staged a concert with a similar theme to Switch. There had been clashes between young Lebanese men and South Asian students in Harris Park, a suburb near Parramatta known for its Indian restaurants and shops. SEVA had won a grant from the federal Department of Social Services to promote social cohesion in the area. Working with local organisations, SEVA brought together young people of Middle Eastern, South Asian and other backgrounds to stage a concert, Rhythms of Peace, in a packed Parramatta theatre. The night also featured a short play that used humour to act out and resolve – at least on stage – the conflicts in Harris Park.

The department was impressed, and encouraged SEVA to apply for more grants. It asked us to partner with some African organisations with which it hoped to build relationships. If the partnership did not work, we would not be penalised in future grant rounds. The department's far-sighted offer encouraged us to take a risk.

I met Olivier Kameya, president of the Rwandan Community of NSW, and Noël Zihabamwe, its cultural, social and engagement coordinator. I liked both men from the start but Noël was the one I got to know well. He was in his thirties, a softly spoken ambitious gentleman, extremely proud of his wife, Marie Delphine, and their children. He would hug me while exclaiming to others, 'Oh, he is my mentor!' Unable to speak English when he arrived in Australia in 2007, Noël was now studying for a master's degree in policy and social research. I was not prepared to ask him or Olivier direct questions about the Rwandan genocide, but I knew that many of their close family members had been murdered. Noël would later co-write a book, *One Thousand Hills*, loosely based on his life and the genocide, which won the NSW Premier's Young People's History Prize in 2016. If these Rwandans felt any hatred over the fate of their families, I never saw it.

Another person I met was Nadine Shema, who had grown up in the Democratic Republic of the Congo with her Rwandan family. A doctor by training, she had come to Australia to study public health, became a permanent resident, and co-founded the Great Lakes Agency for Peace and Development (GLAPD). This community organisation worked to help migrants and refugees from the Great Lakes area of Africa find a home in Australia, including in regional areas, where many of them felt more at ease. Nadine belonged to an African dance troupe and when she danced, any struggles she faced seemed to vanish in her joyous movements and contagious laughter.

Then there was Sarjoh Bah, a former refugee from Sierra Leone who was a leader of Bantal Pulaar, an organisation representing the Fula people of West Africa who lived in Western Sydney. Sarjoh, a warm, quietly spoken man, had contacted me to learn about the Bhutanese experience in

Australia as part of his research for a master's degree in social work. To help his countryfolk, Sarjoh was determined to learn how things worked in this country. At Centrelink, where he worked, he had designed a computer program in 60 languages to help people navigate the Centrelink, Medicare and child support systems. I started contacting him for advice when any of our people had problems with Centrelink.

They amazed me, these leaders. After they reached Australia, it would have been so easy to focus on their own careers, or simply go on to Centrelink payments and relax, but none of them did. They were all studying or working and raising children, while using whatever spare time they had left to run their organisations and build on the strengths of their people. Like the ABA, they hoped to work across ethnic lines, and form new, blended communities in the quiet suburbs of Sydney. But I feared such leaders were being left to burn out, their organisations living from grant to grant, with little formal support from government or NGOs.

I was not starry-eyed about migrant organisations in general. Most were far from perfect. Very few were demo-cratically elected. They could be hierarchical, unrepresent-ative, male-dominated, and wracked by internal conflict. Their leaders could be self-selecting and self-serving, prone to perpetuating the political divides of the home country.

Yet for all that, they were genuine grassroots. When governments wanted to explain a policy, political parties wanted votes, or NGOs needed a partner for delivering a program, these were the organisations they turned to. They had a raw, albeit undirected, energy, born of the immigrant's fierce need to put down roots in the new country. Sarjoh had formed Bantal Pulaar at his house in Auburn, Western

Sydney, after a chance meeting with some other Fula people at a railway station sparked an urgent conversation about how to get ahead in Australia.

It was to help such organisations that SEVA founder Kalyan Ram and I created the Empowering Communities project. With the support of a federal government grant, I engaged Dee Brooks, a former youth worker based at Newcastle University and a global leader in the asset-based community development movement. Dee ran five or six workshops in which leaders from the Afghan, Bhutanese, Fula, Nepali, Punjabi, Rwandan and Sindhi communities debated how to build strong, representative organisations. We loosely followed the ABA model: what can *we* do? What skills do we have? How can we bring people together to teach and learn from each other? How do we create the right mix of activities within our own community and within the larger society? Only when we had tried to answer those questions would we seek outside support.

As the workshops progressed during 2014, the ABA was putting these principles into action. The Sydney community was scheduled to host the third Bhutanese interstate soccer tournament. We decided to expand the event into the first Australian Bhutanese Youth Festival. It gave us an opportunity to show politicians and public servants what one community organisation with skills and energy but no money could do. Our young people, who took the lead, wanted to put on a blockbuster event, with other sports, music and dance thrown in.

But in our early planning, we hit a snag. About 250 interstate visitors were due to come to Sydney for the event. We planned to accommodate them in hotels or hostels, but I made a few calls and realised the cost was sky high. Perhaps the whole festival idea was a dream.

Then an older man piped up at a meeting. At least ten people had lived in his house in Bhutan, he said. In the refugee camp, five or ten visitors often slept on the floor of his hut. 'Here in Blacktown, I've got a huge, three-bedroom townhouse. I can take ten, even twenty.' That was our eureka moment: we all looked at each other and began counting how many visitors we could take.

Our volunteers – about 80 in all – designed T-shirts and banners. They cooked momos, set up a first aid team, made sure the PA system was plugged in. They picked up interstate guests at the airport and Blacktown Station, often late at night. They were integral to the planning and execution of an event that ran over four days in a Penrith park in July 2014.

About 500 people – Bhutanese and other migrants, Aussie-born locals and lots of VIPs – came to the festival each day. Alongside the soccer tournament were athletics and volleyball competitions, Chinese and Iraqi musical performances, and a multicultural parade featuring Western Sydney communities – all kicked off on the first morning by a welcome from event manager Suman Chettri, a lamp-lighting ceremony organised by Hindu pandits and a soccer game staged by Sydney schoolgirls.

The whole festival cost us less than $20 000. If we had hired service providers to run it, the bill would have been about $90 000. We got great support: SSI, STARTTS, SydWest and the Community Migrant Resource Centre in Parramatta all donated funds. STARTTS did our printing and seconded a youth co-ordinator for the whole festival. SydWest lent us its mini van, and six other organisations also provided help. Yet while their role was crucial, we solved our biggest problems ourselves.

Seven years later, that festival remains a model of the community organisation–service provider relationship that I would like to see. I believe service providers should continually be asking themselves, 'How can we be guides for communities, not top-down program deliverers? How can we genuinely consult community leaders and activists, rather than pulling them together only to meet consultation requirements for a grant or to respond to some emergency? What should we *stop* doing, to give communities the space to do things by themselves?'

But while the power balance has to change, that does not mean service providers have a minor role. On the contrary, I want to see them forge even stronger partnerships with community organisations than they have today. I want to see them funded to co-design the kind of leadership and management training that so many community organisations desperately need. I want service providers to push community organisations to be more representative: to ensure their structures and activities include women, young people, seniors, and people from different backgrounds in their home country.

Finally, I would like to see service providers help community organisations to manage public funds. I have seen organisations virtually destroyed by amounts as paltry as $2000. One organisation gets the grant, others complain about discrimination, or ask, 'Where has the money gone?' The leader is blamed, often cut down, and a cycle of failure goes on. In nearly all cases it is better if service providers deploy their usually strong accounting and reporting systems to handle taxpayer money, allowing community organisations to access it as needed.

Governments must also play a stronger role than they do today. They need to monitor much more carefully how their settlement and multicultural dollars are spent. As with many service providers, government consultation of communities tends to be shallow and ad hoc, focused on finding problems, and outsourced. The consultant brought in to do the job typically speaks to a few people, tries to avoid those who are vocal or ask difficult questions, and misses many people who have valuable things to say.

Governments need to develop a way to capture advice from communities and ensure it is fed back into policy development and implementation. They need to ask whether their programs, usually delivered by NGOs, actually benefit communities. Are they empowering people or making them dependent?

The changes I am proposing might mean some extra money at first. But already the amount of money government throws around is crazy. During the COVID-19 pandemic the NSW government is reported to have distributed $19 million in the locked-down local government areas of Western Sydney. What impact did that money have? Just 10 per cent of it could have been used to upskill organisations, service providers and community champions in a new approach. Instead, a lot of it went on events that communities could easily organise on their own. The ABA held two picnics: one government-funded and managed by a service provider; the other we ran ourselves. The first involved much less work, but the second strengthened our community, and was much more fun.

These views are not mine alone. In 2020, Hazara, Khmer and South Sudanese organisations all testified to an inquiry on diaspora communities, held by the Senate's Foreign Affairs, Defence and Trade References Committee, that the move over time from a community-based funding model to one dominated by large service providers had been damaging. STARTTS, which works with many communities, told the inquiry that some activities 'are much better run by refugee organisations themselves'.

All these ideas, and others like them, were discussed by the community leaders involved in SEVA's Empowering Communities project. In December 2014 we launched our toolkit at an event in Auburn for about 60 people. Nadine's troupe danced, and in a speech Sarjoh said, 'Many people work within their own communities and that's a good thing, but Om has had the vision to go beyond his own community … that's what Australia needs today. Om, from our perspective, you've touched the sky.' That touched me.

*

In 2016 I got a further chance to develop my thinking after being awarded a Westpac Social Change Fellowship to research refugee settlement by looking at the experiences of Bhutanese communities in four other countries: Norway, Canada, the US and New Zealand. In Stavanger, Norway, I was excited to meet Ramesh Gautam, an energy engineering student who also taught in a high school, mentored teenagers, wrote stories and blogged on websites in the Bhutanese diaspora. In Nova Scotia, Canada, Rupesh Dhungana and Kharga Bahadur Bhandari, two students in their early twenties, were leaders in their community of around 500 people. I was astonished to hear Rupesh and Kharga talk about creating events to reduce loneliness among elderly Bhutanese. Why would they, or Ramesh in Norway, do what they did when they could be out nightclubbing or otherwise having fun with people of their own age? I could only put it down to the refugee spirit, and the culture of supporting each other, across the generations, that people had built in the camps.

On the other side of Canada, I was reunited with Saroja's sister Usha Tamang, and her husband Mandhoj, who were among the leaders of the 1000 Bhutanese who lived in Lethbridge, a town of 100000 people. In every country I visited, organisations were vital to building strong Bhutanese communities. But those that had been set up in a traditional, male-dominated manner often provoked splits. Atlanta, Georgia, had 17 Bhutanese organisations. That made it hard to get things done.

In Harrisburg, Pennsylvania, I visited my sister Kaushila and her husband Mukti Nath. He had been so entrepreneurial in Bhutan and Nepal but now had to depend on welfare in the US. Mukti Nath was feeling a lot of angst. He wanted to import betel nuts from Nepal, but how? 'I can see money everywhere. But I don't have the language,' he told me sadly. On the other hand, his son Khagendra was working in IT and making good money; he proudly showed me his convertible and his huge motorcycle.

All communities worried about the same things: the isolation of the elderly, a future for the young, domestic violence, the cost of buying a home. Parents feared losing touch with children whose values and behaviour were western, not Bhutanese. Shared religion and culture helped people to cope, but more than anything, I saw that close-knit families were critical to successful settlement.

Everywhere, the almost irresistible pull of individualism was eroding communities and quality of life. Yet strong families operated as a unit, making well-thought-out decisions that balanced individual and collective aspirations. Migration had upended old power structures; many women, in particular, had left their old roles behind. Families that accepted and absorbed such change, while keeping a communal spirit, were harnessing the best of the East and the West.

More than anything, mindset mattered. From Norway to Western Sydney, life in a new country is difficult – that's the hard truth. Not everyone can get the job or life they want, at least not at first. Some migrants are afflicted with traumatic memories; more common is a deep, sometimes disabling, sense of loss. For some, the job, status and power they held in the old country are gone, and they feel bitter. They do not accept their new country and life. They are stuck. The people best placed to help them overcome their loss are fellow migrants. For example, only a person with a shared refugee experience can say, 'This country has given us asylum. Our safety is no longer at risk. Let's be grateful for what we have and build on it.'

The capacity to have such hard conversations is another reason why community organisations are so important. Service providers cannot do it; they would be seen as putting pressure on their clients. Instead, they tend to empathise and say, 'You are an engineer, highly skilled. We will be your champion, and find you the job you deserve.' Their intentions are always good, but it puts the onus for a good result only on the host society, not also on the refugee.

Even worse, if the job does not materialise, there will be staff and volunteers at some organisations who tell their clients that the problem is not them but Australia, which refuses to properly recognise overseas qualifications, puts a low value on refugees, or is racist. Such remarks, which were made to me when I was job hunting, never do justice to the complexity of the problem. To tell people the situation is so simple is to set them up for failure, and to provide them with an excuse when, through no fault of their own, they fail.

At many speaking engagements, I would thank Australia for giving us a home. This did not go down well with Paul Power, CEO of the Refugee Council of Australia, and he had legitimate reasons. He would say, 'Why do you always thank Australia? It's Australia's obligation to take refugees. It should take more.' I would reply, 'But Paul, I *feel* gratitude to Australia. I'm grateful to you, too, because you work hard to support refugees.' Later, Paul and I developed a friendship. I think he came to respect my position, even if he didn't agree with it.

Australia took me in, gave me opportunities to make new friends and develop parts of myself that even I, a privileged person, could never have dreamt of in Bhutan. Such gratitude does not mean subservience. But ultimately my feeling of gratitude is about much more than Australia.

Gratitude creates happiness; it creates hope. If we want Australia to take more refugees, merely pointing to our international obligations will not do it. We need to tell well-founded stories of success and hope. With such stories, and the goodwill towards people fleeing persecution that I encounter in Australia and overseas, I believe we can start to reduce the global refugee crisis, as overwhelming as it appears to be.

By the time I published the Westpac report, in 2017, I had left SEVA to establish my own consultancy. I had decided to work on a 50-50 model: half my time in paid work, half volunteering. In 2018 I pulled together a consortium that included service providers, a university, and people with lived experience of unemployment, to seek government funds to find jobs for former refugees living on income support in Blacktown and Penrith. We wanted to involve nearly 400 former refugees, more than half of whom were female and in the prime working years of 26 to 49, in co-designing services that directly affected them. We did not get the grant, but we'll keep trying.

I also began to work closely with the Syrian and Iraqi communities that have established themselves in large numbers around Fairfield in Western Sydney. They also have inspiring leaders, such as Dr Bushra Al-Obaidi, president of the Iraqi Australia University Graduates Forum. She works as tirelessly for her communities as do the African and South Asian leaders I know, and faces similar struggles, risks and uncertain rewards.

A few years ago, SydWest hired me to host a camping trip near Wollongong for a group of 26 recently arrived refugees from Syria, Iraq, Afghanistan and Bhutan. On the first night, I asked each person to stand up and speak about themselves. When some began in Arabic, I would say, 'No, let's try in English. If you speak in Arabic, you have two minutes. If you speak in English, you have ten.' That got a laugh.

One older man, who had been a professor of design in Iraq, was visibly nervous. He asked to speak in Arabic; I gently said no. Speaking very slowly, in broken English, the man told his story, and told it well.

As the group got ready for bed, he approached me. 'I have been a professor for 30 years, and I have never before stood up and spoken in English in front of such an audience,' he said. 'Thank you.' On the drive home I called Smriti, now an interior architect with lots of contacts, and asked her whether she could investigate getting the man registered as a designer. 'What can *we* do?'

*

Perhaps I spread myself too thinly in these years. Or perhaps one former refugee's voice will never be enough to shift policy. The senior bureaucrats I spoke with in the Departments of Immigration and Social Services were always polite, but either did not seem too keen on my ideas, or expressed interest but did not follow up.

Apart from our local MPs, most of whom warmly supported our projects, I got furthest with two senior politicians. After Senator Concetta Fierravanti-Wells, at that time responsible for settlement services, attended our youth festival, she or one of her advisers was quite often in touch. She invited me to write a briefing paper on our strength-based approach, but she moved into a new role soon after and our conversation lapsed.

Another who expressed interest in my work was Senator Kristina Keneally, Labor's Shadow Minister for Home Affairs from 2019 to 2022. She contacted me after we met at a small dinner organised by SSI, and we had a long conversation, after which I wrote her a brief. When we met at another event, we spoke again and she gave me her private number. But before we could meet again she lost her seat in the 2022 election.

Most politicians I met were distracted, even elusive. They would listen carefully, then I would not hear from them again. I was not always sure I expressed my message clearly or strongly enough. Yet over time, I have also shifted my focus.

I had hoped to shape the national debate not only on refugee settlement but on how to build a strong multicultural society. I still have that hope. But I have come to believe that the best place for me to do that is in the place I know best, my local area and home.

I saw Bhutan try to construct a multi-ethnic society with full rights for all citizens, then reverse course, with devastating results. Australia faces a different challenge, yet the principles and the ultimate prize are the same. If we are going to come together as a complex yet harmonious society, it must happen in places like Blacktown.

11

A BLACKTOWN BOY

I remember the moment when I decided Blacktown was the place for us. Smriti and I were looking at houses on St Pauls Way, before we found the house we bought. While Smriti waited in the car, I got out and talked to an older woman of Eastern European background who was working in her garden. 'Oh, it's lovely, very quiet, the neighbours are nice,' she said. 'It's only five minutes' drive to the station and the 274 bus is good, too.'

She said nothing about rowdyism, or the crime-ridden Blacktown I had heard about from other people. That was real for me: a woman who felt safe. I got back into the car ready to buy.

Our new house had south Indians on one side, north Indians on the other. The northerners, Ajay and Ketki, were from Gujarat and had a young child. We had frequent cups of tea, and occasional meals or walks with them, or with other neighbours. Across the road lived a Filipina woman alongside a Chinese family. On our evening walks, Saroja and I would chat to an older Anglo couple a few streets away. They were surprised, and I think impressed, by how many people came and went from our place, especially after the Bhutanese migrants came to Blacktown and two families moved into our street. 'Our son and daughter-in-law are coming to visit us at Christmas,' the older couple said. I was startled: Christmas was five months away. Their other children would visit, but only now and then. I felt the couple were longing for these visits.

Over time, the residents of our street got talking, and we realised that the strata management company that ran our estate was overcharging us. We formed a management committee and said to the company, 'From now on, if you spend more than $50, our committee has to approve it.' Residents started meeting, mostly in an open area in front of our house. Someone would say, 'I've had this problem with my roof', and another would say, 'Oh, I can fix that. I'll do it tomorrow.' Some of us started having meals together, becoming friends.

A couple from Sierra Leone with a young child moved in across the road. At first they kept to themselves, but they were friendly and would always wave. The man kept piles of scrap metal in his backyard and would make a lot of noise when he came home late at night from his nursing job. He never tinkered for too long but still, some neighbours were annoyed. One day the man and I got talking in the street. He told me he was repairing old bikes and shipping them to Sierra Leone. Many young people lived in villages and could use the bikes to ride to jobs which otherwise they could not get to. When the other neighbours heard this story, they stopped complaining.

In St Pauls Way, I saw people from all over the world navigating the pleasures and annoyances of suburban life. No stereotypes – such as uptight Anglos versus fun-loving migrants from looser cultures – fitted the reality of our street. When a car that was parked outside a big gathering slightly abutted an adjacent drive, the indignant neighbours were South Asian. The family most upset by the bike-maker's noise came from that most communal of cultures, the Bhutanese.

My experience gave me a deep loyalty to the ordinary Australian street. No one in ours knew or cared that we were once refugees. By contrast, in those early years we got to know about ten Nepali families living around Blacktown, and had big gatherings with them. I liked these people, but some Nepalis from neighbouring suburbs didn't treat us so well. They looked down on us. They were skilled migrants, and we were refugees.

Being Bhutanese of Nepali heritage is central to who I am. I want to preserve my culture and pass it on to my daughter, and I hope that she passes our culture on to her children. But this is a culture I already know. In Australia, in my street, I have an incredible opportunity to learn about other cultures and lives.

I am worried by the current trend towards identity politics, especially based on race or ethnicity. It encourages us to focus on our differences and to nurture grievances around them, when we should be thinking of how we can strengthen all that we have in common, as Australians, as human beings, and, in my case, as fellow citizens of Blacktown.

Moreover, my identity is made up not only of my ethnicity, history and family, but also my activities, passions and values. It's a fluid state of many moving parts that cannot be narrowly defined as 'Bhutanese of Nepali heritage'. At one point in my life I was socialising with the tiny number of Bhutanese in Sydney, while at the same time building relationships in the Nepali community, working at Telstra, writing letters for an Amnesty campaign on behalf of a political prisoner in Saudi Arabia, and driving Smriti to her weekend basketball matches with her two friends Anna Pengai and Anna Lee, whose parents were working and unable to take them. Why should only the first two of these activities define who I am?

I always looked forward to those weekend drives, sometimes all over Sydney, as Smriti and the two Annas sat in the back and laughed and chatted about school, fun, gossip, or the game they'd just played and my enthusiastic cheering. I threw in the odd question or comment, sometimes pulled their leg, or said, 'Hey, you've got to be on time.' These girls' cultures were Pacific Islander, Chinese and Bhutanese but they were one culture, teenage girl culture. I saw the two Annas as an extension of my daughter, and I was glad to play a father role with them.

Within the Bhutanese diaspora we talk from time to time about our identity. Some people are looking for a simple answer to who we are. About two years ago, some of our youth organised an online radio program that brought together various people from around Australia. I put forward my view that we should focus less, not more, on our ethnic identities. While lots of people nodded and agreed, others were not satisfied – they did not get the answer they were looking for.

A few years ago, some South Asians, smart fellows with a lot of business acumen, got in touch with me. They had bought a big plot of land near Riverstone, in the north of the Blacktown LGA. They wanted to build an aged-care facility for the 'South Asian community'. I wasn't sure what they meant. The term 'South Asian' represents so many cultures – how could they build a common facility for them? Still, from a business perspective, it was a no-brainer, and if I had joined them, I could have made millions.

But the idea didn't gel with me. Of course, an elderly Hindu woman might be uncomfortable in a mainstream aged-care home that serves beef and doesn't allow statues of deities in a common area. Yet even with $10 million in the bank I would never be happy away from my parents, knowing I hadn't done my duty of looking after them. And tomorrow, when I'm walking with a stick, I'll want to be with my children, grandchildren and neighbours. We can't build separate aged-care facilities for every community; we're struggling to build enough as it is. If many families from migrant and refugee backgrounds already care for their parents at home, why not support that?

Sadly, though, separatism is a growing trend. One community wants to build its own temple, another its own church or mosque. There just isn't enough land to accommodate all these demands, as federal communications minister Michelle Rowland, MP for the Blacktown seat of Greenway, has pointed out: 'Every ethnic group wants their own hall – "my hall!" That is not going to happen.' I have heard Bhutanese people also make that demand. But we rent a perfectly good hall in Blacktown; let's share it with other groups.

If I am a Hindu from Bhutan, there is already a temple at Westmead, near Parramatta. I don't need a separate one in Blacktown. Australia has Hindus from north and south India, Sri Lanka, Nepal and Bhutan – do we all want separate temples, burial sites, cremation places? Even if there was enough land, we are moving away from each other. That's not how multiculturism will flourish in this country.

If communities want to fund their own infrastructure, I guess that's their business. But federal and state governments should not fund projects that keep communities apart, no matter how hard they are lobbied. The following story has exact parallels in many communities and on both sides of politics. In the 2019 election campaign the then immigration minister David Coleman promised $1 million for a Nepali community centre in his south Sydney seat of Banks. The community has many factions, so after Coleman made his pledge, Labor supporters went to the shadow immigration minister, who promised to match the funding. It's like an arms race. During the 2022 campaign, a Nepali friend in Penrith told me he had locked up the Nepali vote for the Liberal Party by obtaining a $15 000 grant for a sports club. Will politicians try to build communities or to buy them?

The problem is bigger than politics. Many heads of community organisations increasingly identify themselves first as a Hindu or Muslim or Buddhist leader. Once I start with that narrow identity, I will work hard, often subconsciously, to protect it. In doing that, I am creating division. If we don't start with what we have in common, rather than on our differences, we could be heading for disaster if we have more pandemics, or when other hard times hit.

Similarly, the Blacktown City Council Multicultural Advisory Committee, on which I sit, has some great people, but I also think we should aspire to put such committees out of business. At some point the concepts of multiculturalism, diversity and inclusion have become rigid, but everybody wants to keep them because that's how people wield their power. I am not worried about whether I am a Hindu or a Christian or Muslim. I am concerned about the people around me. I am a Blacktown resident first.

In 2016, we left St Pauls Way and bought a property off the plan in the Fairwater Estate, a new housing development just 15 minutes' walk from the Blacktown CBD. Saroja and

I loved the place from the start and were determined to put down roots there. Houses are built around a lake and a park full of ornamental pears, with a community centre and café overlooking the water. The estate is the first in Australia to extensively use geothermal technology, via copper pipes that descend to 90 metres, enabling the ground to serve as a heat dump during summer and a source of warmth in winter. Two days after moving in, on our evening walk, we saw roses outside the house of a neighbour, Baskaran Gunasundaram, and Saroja told him how beautiful they were. Next day, Baskaran came over with a perfect red rose in a vase. We planted it, and we still have it.

Fairwater's developer, Frasers Property Australia, had a plan for community-building on the estate. It appointed a community development manager and established a residents' committee. Over time it has sought to involve active residents such as Erin Stokes, who has organised Easter egg hunts and Halloween trick or treats, Sanjeeta Aggarwal and Vijay Chennupati, who run the residents' meetings, and Camille Abbott and Prakash Panthee, who get involved in almost everything (Camille leads the Green Fairwater committee). I was also active from the time I moved in, and in 2020 Frasers asked me to become a part-time community engagement consultant. The CEO, Anthony Boyd, said his company wanted to create a sense of belonging, and to work with residents to achieve it. I liked Anthony's ideas. I had not realised how challenging it would be, at first, to make people understand what I could deliver. Residents started contacting me for everything: building issues, neighbours' noisy children, dog poo left in front of their house. That wasn't quite my role.

Nor was my role like the one I had at the ABA. While the Bhutanese faced much greater material difficulties than Fairwater residents, they also shared a common culture and history and, in starting new lives in Australia, a sense of a common fate. At Fairwater we were a group of people who just happened to live side by side.

About 2000 people live on the estate in detached homes and townhouses. The population is highly diverse. People of Indian background are the largest group, followed by those of Chinese, Anglo-Celtic, Nepali, Korean and Filipino backgrounds, and many other groups as well. It is a middle-class community, with average property prices of about $1 million, which sounds a lot until you remember that Sydney's median house price in 2022 was a crazy $1.245 million. Many residents work long hours, often in distant places such as the Sydney CBD. About half of the estate's 700 families have school-aged children.

Many residents told me they simply had no time for volunteering. The same faces tended to show up at residents' committee meetings. Those who did volunteer often felt despondent when they got little response from others.

Yet I was excited by the challenge. Talking to people is my favourite pastime. With Sarah Melody, the estate's community development manager, I ran two workshops applying the ABA approach: what are our strengths and passions and how can we build on them? What do people like about Fairwater? Residents said it was clean, green and safe. How, then, could we embed those qualities even more deeply? How could we encourage people to say hello to each other, turn strangers into neighbours?

These questions inspired many initiatives, on top of those

already underway. The Green Fairwater committee ran an annual gardening competition, tree-planting days, and a Sunflower Festival – it sent sunflower seeds and planting instructions to 120 houses that showed interest. Another committee successfully lobbied for the creation of a dog park, and residents opened a book club. Two resident Facebook pages highlighted events. Another, run by Frasers, encouraged residents to support small businesses run by people on the estate, including a candle-maker, a printing company, a seller of beef jerky, and a woman who sold very popular seafood.

Based on my ABA experience, I tried to involve people early, and encourage them to share their knowledge. When a resident, Prasenjit Sarker, won a gardening competition, we invited him to run a workshop in his own garden. A Hindu resident offered to run an event to celebrate Diwali, the Hindu festival, while a Christian offered to run a Christmas party. That didn't seem very communal, so we decided that members of the events committee, irrespective of their religion, would organise all activities together.

Initially, the advent of COVID made the work even harder. An evening doorknock to welcome new residents and give them a picnic rug had to be suspended, and a communal barbecue cancelled. Yet I told the organisers that even if the events didn't happen, 90 per cent of the most important work, the relationship-building, had been done. In fact, the pandemic did a lot to bring Fairwater closer together.

There is loneliness and vulnerability in this community, as there is everywhere. For a while I had noticed that routine conversations with individual residents, usually over some matter affecting the estate, would often turn into deeper ones. Someone was going for an important job or promotion, or was struggling to keep a business afloat, and needed not just advice but counselling. These conversations became more common with the advent of the pandemic. People posted on our Facebook page that they were struggling with isolation. Others would quickly reply, offering to have a chat over the phone, and a coffee when restrictions were lifted. Photographers shared beautiful photos on Facebook to cheer up residents, while Frasers funded a well-being webinar with three expert panellists, including Dawn O'Neil, a former CEO of Lifeline and Beyond Blue. When I desperately needed a COVID test kit for my mum and put out a call on Facebook, three people knocked on my door with a kit within an hour.

I saw that same spirit in the larger Blacktown community. For about two years before the pandemic hit, SydWest Multicultural Services had run a leadership forum for community organisers. Some of these people were on the Zoom call described at the start of this book, when eight activists got together to talk about how to spread reliable information about the pandemic in our communities, and created the hashtag #WhatCanWeDo?

In July 2021, after Sydney embarked on its longest and most severe lockdown, we renamed the SydWest leadership forum the Blacktown COVID Emergency Taskforce. Clement Meru, SydWest's community engagement and disability services manager, led the taskforce while two other SydWest staff members, Saurav Shrestha and my brother-in-law Puspa Acharya, co-ordinated it. Eighteen people attended the first Zoom meeting; over time the number would swell to close to 30.

That first meeting was dominated by complaints: Blacktown and the west were discriminated against; the politicians were communicating badly; the vaccination centres were too far away; the food being delivered was culturally inappropriate, and so on. I understood that people needed to vent their fears and frustrations, but when the second meeting began in the same way, when someone said the food being brought right to people's doors was not warm enough, I began to lose my patience. We faced an emergency – the issue was life, not lifestyle. Saurav, Puspa, Clement and I spoke, and decided to try to shift the conversation onto what we could do. When asked to speak, I described what the Association of Bhutanese in Australia was doing – especially what we called our virtual doorknocks.

A month earlier, we had begun calling community members asking about their health and well-being, and asking them to call others. We created a telephone tree, along with Facebook sessions, to spread reliable information. As soon as I explained that idea, members of the Blacktown taskforce picked it up at once.

Each taskforce member was asked to call or Zoom ten people in their network, and ask each person to call another ten. When we contacted someone, we would ask after their health, then spell out three messages: follow the lockdown rules, get vaccinated, and get tested at the first sign of symptoms. Callers tried to clear up any misunderstandings – for example, the word 'household' does not mean 'family'. A lot of people confused the two, and thought it was OK to be with parents, grandparents, aunts and cousins. In our communities that could mean gatherings of 50 people.

If someone resisted these messages, saying the jab was useless, dangerous, or a plot by Bill Gates to plant a chip in people's bodies, the caller would not argue, but offer to set up a call with a doctor or nurse. Doctors were only too willing to help. One doctor the taskforce often called on was Dr Jan Fizzell, a senior medical adviser from NSW Health, who was endlessly available to speak to communities. Dr Fizzell also spoke to the Fairwater Residents' Committee, patiently and articulately responding to many queries.

Our virtual doorknocks, a pyramid scheme to save lives, lasted for more than a month. A few hundred people made calls, comparing notes and refining messages as they went. I was on Zoom or the phone almost every night, and most weekends. One morning, Rishi Acharya, general secretary of the Nepalese Australian Association (NAA), called me: 'Om Dai (older brother), can you come to the Clubhouse tonight to talk about virtual doorknocks?' I replied, 'Rishi-ji, we can't do that in a lockdown, even if no one sees.' He said, 'Om Dai, it's a video conference. I will send you a link.' We both laughed at my ignorance: Clubhouse was an app! Rishi and NAA president Dr Madhu Pudasaini were in the Clubhouse almost every evening.

When I came on at 7.30 pm, I was overwhelmed to see that more than 100 people from about 20 organisations linked to the Nepali community had dialled in from across Australia.

Just as inspiring was the work of the South Sudanese Task Force, which emerged from our Blacktown Emergency Taskforce. A lot of South Sudanese Australians were getting sick with COVID, and the community had a very low vaccination rate. It also wasn't a community that watched a lot of mainstream TV. Clement Meru, who led the Blacktown taskforce, began meeting with about 20 other South Sudanese leaders on Zoom every Saturday afternoon.

The South Sudanese Task Force also created a telephone tree. People called their wider families; religious leaders spoke to their congregations. Messages went out in Dinka, Bari and Juba Arabic languages. People as far away as Maitland and Newcastle were told not only to test, mask and vaccinate, but also how to get emergency food through Foodbank. Clement also involved Mayor Chagai, who has a big reach in the community through Savannah Pride, his basketball club in the highly disadvantaged area of Mount Druitt. With help from a small grant from Multicultural NSW, Mayor got young basketballers to take food hampers and vouchers that had been donated to Savannah Pride to people's homes. No one was paid for this work – it was all done to strengthen communities, to keep people alive.

Mayor is another example of what someone can achieve through the brutal experience of being a refugee. Before reaching Australia he trekked through three countries, lost nearly all his friends to famine and war, nearly died himself many times. In a Kenyan refugee camp he discovered that he was a great basketballer. He turned all these lessons into a fierce desire to do something for troubled young men and women from all cultures on the streets of Blacktown. 'I see myself in them,' Mayor has said. Savannah Pride has sent 23 young men to play college or high school basketball in the United States.

In July, the NSW government decided that hundreds of Australian Defence Force soldiers would work with police to provide food and medicines to Western and South-Western Sydney residents who needed them, and to ensure that all complied with the lockdown. The announcement worried some migrants, whose past experiences made them think that the presence of soldiers, helicopters and police spelt political trouble. Once again, some community leaders alleged that Western Sydney was being discriminated against, because it is more disadvantaged than the rest of Sydney. Helicopters weren't hovering over the Northern Beaches, they complained. The media would carry the story and the leaders would share the coverage they had got on social media. I felt they were making an issue out of nothing. The helicopters and soldiers were there for our safety. After my brother Gopal got COVID a soldier knocked on his door and asked, very politely, if he was isolating, and did he have enough food?

But not all police messaging was good. I sit on the NSW Police Multicultural Advisory Council (PMAC), along with Clement Meru and Melissa Monteiro, CEO of the Community Migrant Resource Centre in Parramatta. At a hastily organised Zoom meeting of PMAC to discuss the escalating impact of the pandemic, we were shown a draft media release, scheduled to go to all Western Sydney communities, announcing an 'operation'. Alarmed, we asked senior police officers what they planned to do. 'Knock on doors,' they said. 'To catch criminals?' we asked. They said, 'No, to make sure people are eating and isolating. If they need food, we can drop it off.' 'But this is welfare and well-being work,' we said. 'If you call it an operation and bring out soldiers, people will be upset. So let's use community language.' The senior officers got it at once, and ordered a change of wording on the release.

In October, just as the lockdown was lifted, we learnt that Blacktown was one of the most highly vaccinated local government areas in New South Wales. Government figures showed that nearly 95 per cent of our residents aged 16 and over had been vaccinated twice. Our rate was by far the highest of 12 local government areas that the government had designated 'LGAs of concern'. At one stage, only five other NSW LGAs, none of them in Western Sydney, recorded higher rates of double-dosed residents.

Our virtual doorknocking wasn't the only reason for Blacktown's success but it was a big one. We had reached deep into our communities, using language they understood, spoken by people they knew and trusted. Service providers, working alone, could never have done that. Yet SydWest had provided vital support. Staff members Puspa Acharya and Saurav Shrestha had set up Zoom meetings and contacted community leaders to ensure their attendance. Clement Meru helped to invite guest speakers, including federal and state MPs. It was a model of the kind of community organisation–service provider partnerships that we need.

Now that the worst stage of the pandemic seems to have passed, the Blacktown Community Leadership Forum is talking about how it can stay active. Involving young people is a big challenge. A recent Saturday meeting was attended by leaders from Ethiopian, Bhutanese, South Sudanese, Lebanese and Sikh backgrounds, to name just a few. But apart from 18-year-old Mahatma, from the Ethiopian community, most of us were past 40. How can we engage Mahatma and others of his age? When the ABA appointed its first youth co-ordinator, Damber Dhungyel, we realised that being the only young member of a ten-person executive committee might feel pretty lonely, so we created a subcommittee of three young people to support him. In the same spirit, the leadership forum is exploring ways to train and mentor ten or 20 young people and challenge them to each bring another three people into leadership training. Sixty young people thinking about the change they want to see in Blacktown – it could be magic.

Blacktown is so young. Nearly 44 percent of the LGA's population is under the age of 30, which makes it much younger than Sydney as a whole. Our biggest problems, I believe, are not racism or crime but inequality and lack of opportunities for our young people. But education can lift people's lives, as it lifted mine. The number of Blacktown residents with tertiary degrees has soared over the past 50 years, and a few years ago we got our first university, the Australian Catholic University, in the heart of the Blacktown CBD. Stand at the entrance of Westpoint mall after school hours and watch the youth of all colours and cultures stream in, wearing school uniforms, slinging heavy bags and heading for the fast food counters. Watching all that rowdy, jostling life it's hard not to be optimistic about our future.

Blacktown is coming together as a community, I feel it. In 2022, about 30 non-Muslim leaders attended the iftar meal, organised by SydWest and the Afghan Community Support Association, to celebrate Eid, the end of Ramadan. A year earlier I attended a Harmony Day discussion over lunch organised by the Mount Druitt Ethnic Communities Agency, where I renewed my acquaintance with renowned Blacktown Indigenous elders Uncle Wes, who turned 100 in 2022, and Uncle Greg. Blacktown's population includes 10 000 Indigenous Australians, more than any other urban local government area in Australia.

I told Uncle Wes that the momos I had brought were pretty spicy. 'Fine, fine, no explanation required,' he said as he tucked in. When he talked about welcoming us to the circle, as a migrant I felt gratitude. I also loved Uncle Greg's observation: 'We don't own the land, the land owns us.' Uncle Wes spoke of his people being forced to wear dog tags in his lifetime, and how he was so hungry sometimes he learnt to steal sheep to survive. 'We won't chase that one up, Wes,' said Bob Fitzgerald, then Blacktown's chief inspector, whose own grandmother was Indigenous and part of the Stolen Generation.

At the lunch, I said that as one of the newest migrants, my story in this country was just 23 years old, not 60000. I said I was fortunate that so many people had made such sacrifices to make Australia what it is today. The lunch made me think about an idea that Aboriginal leader Noel Pearson has proposed: that we can build a deep sense of belonging in this nation on three great Australian stories – our Indigenous foundation, our British history and institutions, and our multicultural present and future.

For me, these stories resonate most powerfully in Blacktown. I have lived here for all but six of my 25 years in Australia, among the Australian-born and migrants, including my parents, two sisters and two brothers and their families, my wife, daughter and son-in-law Sudeep. I am a Bhutanese Australian of Nepali heritage, a son, husband, brother and father, a community advocate in Western Sydney and a resident of Blacktown. That's my identity, my story, my blended life in Blacktown.

In Fairwater, just as in our last house in St Pauls Way, our neighbours on both sides are of Indian background, with Chinese and Anglo families across the road. When a neighbour had COVID, Saroja cooked food for the family, and the neighbours did the same for me when Saroja was overseas.

One night in December 2021, a resident called me. He was due to play the lead in our 'Santa comes to Fairwater' event the following day, but a close contact had COVID and he had to isolate. Now we had a Christmas crisis: the prospect of many disappointed children. I called Smriti for advice. 'You do it, Papa,' she said. 'But what does a Santa do?' I asked. She said: 'Go on YouTube and find out.'

The next morning, wearing a white beard and heavy red robe, and trailed by ten adults and children who had come to offer support, I headed out into a blazing 33-degree day. 'Wake up, Fairwater! Santa's here. Kids, come out for lollies!' I called into a hand-held microphone, as Saroja drove ahead with 'Jingle Bells' pumping out our car windows.

Children came out in droves, thrilled that in many cases Santa knew their name; one four-year-old was astonished when Santa spoke to her in Nepali. Their parents came out with them. They were Indians, Chinese, Nepalis, Koreans, Filipinos, Pacific Islanders, Thais and the Aussie-born; Hindus, Buddhists, Muslims, Christian and Sikhs, all following this tiny and far from roly-poly fellow from the North Pole, via Bhutan, booming 'Ho, ho, ho!'

But the going was slow, there were many streets left to cover, and after two hours I was drenched in sweat. My support team, worried that Santa might get heat stroke, called a halt.

When we got home, we found a rush of Facebook posts from parents on behalf of children who had missed out. So at 6 pm I hit the streets again. I looked ridiculous, but who cares? We have to get to know each other.

A year later, Saroja and I still take our walks together in the evening, as we have always done, enjoying the shifting colours on the lake around sunset, and meeting other people. The other night we heard a kid in a pram tell his dad, 'Oh, there is Santa Uncle.' And just the other day, my niece Dristi and I met a schoolgirl at the bus stop whose family is from Africa. We introduced ourselves; her name was Beyoncé. I invited her to sing at our next residents' committee meeting. She laughed, but did not commit. I'll keep trying.

12

HOME

When I was a boy in Lamidara, at the time of the Tihar festival, Yoga and I would grab a lamp from the house and race into our front yard. There we would sit under the night sky, with other brothers and sisters, and wait anxiously for the deusi singers.

They came singing folk songs in groups of about eight, men and boys. When I was little, they sang without accompaniment, but as I got older singers would bring a madal or a tabla, two kinds of drum, and even – a wonderful rarity – a harmonium. When the music finished, Mum would go inside and bring out a nanglo, a flat, woven bamboo tray on which she had spread sel roti, some pickle, fruit, rice and money, with a diyo, a lamp, in the middle. The singers would take her offerings and bless our house, return the tray with the lamp, then move on to the next house.

Forty years later, in Blacktown, there was a knock on our door. On the porch stood a group of singers led by a young man, Bhakti Khatiwada, carrying his harmonium. About 20 people were there to hear them. A few had walked from nearby houses but most came by car – we were in Australia now. Bhakti and his group came into our living room. He sat cross-legged on the carpet facing his harmonium; his tabla player and guitarist began to drum and strum. Deusi can be slow and plaintive, but soon the drums and harmonium got into gear, and young women in bright saris got up to dance, fingers twirling, bangles jingling, as the beat kept building, haunting, almost delirious, unstoppable. Bhakti has a beautiful voice, and as I sat on the carpet, with my wife and daughter beside me, Baa and Ama on a couch, amid so many family members and friends, some from my own village, I began to weep.

It is now nearly 15 years since the Bhutanese migration. In Sydney we're about 100 families and 450 people, part of a national population of 7000, the third-largest Bhutanese diaspora in the West, after the US and Canada. We are still clustered around Blacktown and Penrith, with just a few families in Campbelltown in south-west Sydney. Numbers have shrunk a little over the years, as some families moved to places like Adelaide and Albury-Wodonga to buy homes more easily, a high priority among our people.

About a year ago, a group of ten Bhutanese of different ages got together to discuss how our community was going. A few lamented that the common bond they felt when they arrived in Australia had gone. People were working, studying and staying in their own friendship groups; fewer came to community events. That first rapture had been lost. One person asked, 'How do we get back to 2009?'

But other people replied: the reason our Bhutanese gatherings are smaller is that people are socialising in the wider community. They play sport with other Australians. Many young Bhutanese are nurses, and they are going to drinks, joining Facebook groups with workmates, and buying homes. One person said, 'This is such a good problem to have.'

There is a paradox to Bhutanese families – we live both scattered around the world and as close to each other as we can get. I have two siblings in each of Bhutan, Nepal and the US, and four here, all of whom live in Blacktown. Parbata, my brother Devi's first wife, lives in our Fairwater estate with her son Bedanidhi, his wife Geeta and two children. Parbata's other son, Rohit, lives nearby with his wife Rupa and young child. In 2020 my daughter Smriti and her husband Sudeep also bought a house in Fairwater.

Each Bhutanese family used to be much larger, but that is getting rare. I know one household that used to comprise grandparents, parents and five sons. Now every son has married and moved out, all living as nuclear families, all Australian now. I think some of these couples are struggling – working, racing to take kids to day care, all payments coming out of one couple's pocket. By contrast, when Dil Bahadur Budathoki, one of our great old men, died at home at the age of 95, his house contained his son, his grandson and their families – four generations under one roof.

Coming to Australia as three and even four generations, from Amas and Babas to babies, makes the Bhutanese unusual. Because Australia's migration program is built around the economic value that migrants of working age bring, it has tended to exclude older people, who are seen as a likely drain on health and welfare systems. I understand the government's reasoning, but I think the program is based too narrowly on economics.

The migration of our parents and grandparents has made our community strong. Living in extended families has helped to keep our young people tethered to a sense of care and compassion, which in the long run will do more to make them good citizens than any economic benefit they bring. In my own family, my brother Gopal's children, 14-year-old

Mona and Manish, who is nine, grew up with my parents living in their house. From the age of six or seven, Mona has always offered any visitor a cup of tea or juice. Similarly, Manish would get up early and cook pancakes for my father, and they would eat them together. My nephews and nieces who live in nuclear families do not do this.

But the older generation that has shaped my life is passing. In July 2022, Saroja, Smriti and I flew to Kalimpong, in India, to be with Ama, Saroja's mum, in her last days. Her other five children and five grandchildren came from Canada and other parts of India and Bhutan. There were 18 of us in her house, taking turns to sit with her and hold her hand. When it was my turn, I whispered that we had come back to her, as we had promised we would. Through her severe pain, she nodded and smiled. I owe Ama so much – not only my life with Saroja, but a model of what it means to be an honest, courageous human being.

In Australia, a few years ago, we lost Hema Khadka – Meeth (friend) Ama, as we fondly called her. Even in her eighties, she was an elegant, beautiful woman. She loved to sing and always joined the young ones on the dance floor. She came from my district in Bhutan, and I loved her stories of her younger days. She was married at the age of eight. She often talked of the day King Jigme Singye Wangchuck, the same king that I met, visited her district and complimented her on the golden bangle she wore.

After a few years in Australia, Meeth Ama began to suffer from dementia. She became bedridden and needed 24-hour care. When she started losing her memory, I sensed her frustration. She said, 'Don't stop visiting me just because I may not recognise you sometimes.'

The doctors suggested she go into a nursing home, but her family said no. Meeth Ama's daughter-in-law Chandra Maya took the lead, with support from her husband Talman, and their children and their children's spouses. Chandra Maya's daughter Reeta and daughter-in-law Sumitra both worked in aged care and provided professional expertise. Reeta said, 'In our culture we don't take grandmother to a nursing home. If I cannot look after her, another member of the family will.'

Caring for our elders has had another significant impact. Of the many Bhutanese Australians who are nurses, slightly more are male than female. One reason why these young men have been able to break the Bhutanese stereotype that nursing is a woman's job is because, in many cases, they have looked after their grandparents. Suman Chhetri, who managed our Australian Bhutanese Youth Festival in 2014, is a case in point. Suman had completed a diploma in civil engineering from Ultimo TAFE. To be an engineer had been his passion, but when he started looking for work, he found that employers always wanted local work experience or an engineering degree. So he enrolled in a degree, but he started to worry: what if he struggled to find a job even after finishing it?

Suman is an eldest son, with parents and a grandfather to care for, and by that time he and his wife Goma had two children. His friends in the Bhutanese community were starting to buy houses; he had to act to fulfil the family dream of all four generations living in a home they owned. Looking at the job market he could see huge demand for nursing and health care roles. Six months into his engineering course, Suman gave up his life plan, as migrants must often do, and switched to a nursing degree. He now works as a clinical nurse consultant in a mental health facility, is studying for a master's of nursing, and has bought a home close to us, where he lives with his large family.

Our old people have taught us so much. They overcame their struggles and took to Australia happily and graciously. What I lost in Bhutan was nothing compared to them. I only bought my house in Blacktown, whereas my parents had built theirs in Lamidara: they carried the stones, planted the orchard. Bhutan is in their hands and bodies as well as their minds. To lose all that and still to be able to smile – it astonishes me.

Perhaps we children have helped them too. My mother has children in the US, Nepal and Bhutan, and the scattering of the family can at times fill her with sorrow. After coming to Australia, she struggled for a year until my sister Tulasha arrived. During that time, we worked hard to keep her optimistic. When Smriti got her degree or when I won an award, I would head straight to my parents' house, even late at night, and say, 'This is what you created. This is what you have done for us.'

In 2018, the ABA leadership moved to the next generation, when Damber Dhungyel, the young nurse who set up Druk FC, was elected president. He was succeeded by two young men in turn, Padam Kafley and Nanda Lal Bhandari. Together with Padam, Indira Sharma was elected general secretary, the first woman elected to the position.

In 2022, Hemanta Acharya, who had earlier been youth co-ordinator, became women's co-ordinator. Hemanta, now 29, has been one of our most active ABA members. She is a clinical nurse specialist, fulfilling the dream of working in health she first had in the refugee camp, after she lost a friend to typhoid. None of this would have been possible if she had stayed in Nepal – she says herself she would have been a housewife. Even if she had been allowed to study, she would have had to rely on her husband for money. Here she can pursue whatever path she wants.

But Hemanta also expresses a sense of loss that many of our people have felt after leaving the camps for Australia. 'I don't miss the leaking roof in our hut, but I miss the human connection,' she says. 'In Sydney we had a flood recently that didn't even get into our houses and we complained. We are on our phones even when we are eating. I will be watching a dance show, my brother a football match, Dad something in Nepali. In the camp we were together. My mum would leave us with neighbours or relatives, they would feed us, there was trust. That human connection is hard to see when you have everything.'

Hemanta's words remind me of a woman I met in New Zealand, who had shared a hut wall with my parents in the refugee camp. She cried and hugged me, and would not let go, as she told me how they would share food through a hole in the wall. Once, seven or eight people shared a mango. 'Look at these fruits here. Nobody eats them,' she said, pointing to a bowl on her table. 'I have to throw them away.'

Hemanta says she feels gratitude for her old life – 'It keeps me humble.' But some in her generation struggle to express their identity. They are Australians of Nepali heritage, brought up in a refugee camp in Nepal, with no memories of Bhutan, whose parents call themselves Bhutanese. Many have friends and sometimes partners among Nepali Australians. No wonder they often leave out the Bhutanese bit when telling others about their background. I met a young woman of Palestinian heritage who had grown up as a refugee in

Lebanon and was now an Australian. 'It's very complicated,' she said. I said she sounded just like us.

How do we nurture the best, and cast off the worst, of the old world and of the new? I know people from Nepal in Sydney who feel such disappointment at how their lives have turned out. One highly qualified and well-established couple has two beautiful kids who came to Australia before they turned five. The parents wanted them to have freedom, iPhones, everything. But they worked so hard that they didn't spend enough time with their kids. They say to me, 'Om-ji, we cry almost every night because we don't have that close connection with the children. One of them is marrying someone we don't even know, who doesn't speak our language. We spent all our lives focused on the children, and we've lost them.'

When children grow up in an environment where they think it's good to distance themselves from their culture and language, they find it difficult to come back. Both they and their parents are suffering in isolation. I see that same pain in the Syrian and Iraqi communities: 'Om, what to do? Our children have become Australians.' They get so angry about it. It's not that it's bad to be Australian. What's bad is losing your culture and tradition, your parents. If we don't address this loss, the next phase of our journey is going to be much harder. We can't preserve our culture in a jar, but equally we can't just buy kids iPhones and forget them.

Yet some old ways must go. The caste system still produces so much misery. Even in Australia a Dalit – once known as an untouchable before the offensive term was discarded – is not allowed to enter the house of other castes that are considered 'higher'. If it happens, the family is supposed to call a priest to clean the home and clear it of demons. In Adelaide, an elderly mother wanted to do a puja to mark the passing of a relative, but the priest wouldn't come because some low-caste families had visited the house.

A few years ago, a man from Adelaide came to an Australian–Bhutanese Conference in Sydney. He and Saroja were from the same village, so he called me brother-in-law. He remembered how, although he was a Dalit, Saroja's father had welcomed him into his home. He hugged me and said, 'I will never forget what Guru Babu did for me.' He was so hurt by the discrimination he faced from some Adelaide families. With tears in his eyes, he said, 'Guru Babu did this for me thirty years ago in a small village in Bhutan. And in this country, Australia, with all its freedom, this is how I am treated.'

So much pain over such silly things. Those Brahmins who follow the caste system do not eat rice and certain other foods cooked by other 'lower' castes, and never anything touched by a Dalit. Yet it could well have been Dalits or lower-caste people who donated the food that our people ate gratefully in the camps. No one asked who provided the food – until some of them came to Australia and once again this caste system became a sacred law. If our very survival as refugees depended on the goodwill of others, how could we treat those same people with disrespect and contempt in our new country?

Even today, some people will come to our house and expect to do the cooking themselves. Or they will say, 'We are fine with roti' – one of the few foods made by Saroja they can eat. A Brahmin from Adelaide called me and asked if he could drop by. He insisted there was no need to prepare food since he would not be eating. It was obvious what he meant.

I was very upset, told him why, and ended the conversation. He tried to visit a year later. I said I was not available.

It is time people of the 'upper caste' recognise the social torture of these practices. As religious people, do they believe they will go to heaven by inflicting pain on others?

In some ways, Centrelink payments have made these problems worse. Welfare benefits are not in themselves the problem: at key moments they have helped people to get started, study, put a deposit on a home. The problem is that a lot of people who practise untouchability and discriminate against others are on Centrelink payments. They don't have to take jobs with people who think differently, and so integration doesn't happen.

I used to be quite aggressive about these issues, but now I walk a line. If I am too vocal, my Mum will feel so distressed I might have to take her to hospital. And my parents' generation will never change. So some of us have a saying: accept but don't promote. In other words, we invite everyone to all gatherings; we let our parents sit at a distance from some other people and don't force them to mix, especially while they are eating. But we don't point out other people and say, 'I've moved them to one side so you don't have to sit near them.' That's promoting.

On the other hand, I have come to see that if we concede to these demands, the religious hardliners will put pressure on everyone to follow them. In our kitchen one day, in front of ten or 12 people, I heard someone say, 'Oh, guru-ji (priest) must not be served with this plate or that cup.' I flared up: 'Do not utter those words here. If there is anyone who doesn't want to eat off our plates, they don't have to eat.'

It was Saroja who calmed that situation, which was

remarkable, because such discrimination is to a large degree directed at her. Of course, she gets upset – who would not? – but she responds so much better than I do. Sometimes people will invite only me to an event. I will say, 'If Saroja can't go, I won't be there either.' She has married someone for love. If I do not support her, if I take a family member's side against her, where would she go? I need to be with her every step of the way.

We haven't talked about it much, but from the time we got married I think we developed an understanding that we would face this problem together until we died. If she gets angry, I have to be the cooler person; if I get angry, she has to calm me. Our marriage is the vital thing.

For all that, our caste problem is minuscule compared to other people's. I don't have to depend on anybody for anything. If you are Dalit or another lower caste, and you are poor, your situation is a thousand times worse.

The caste system is dying with the generations growing up in Australia. They cannot understand it, let alone accept it. They don't accept a lot of things we once saw as normal. Not long ago my nieces Dristi, Mona and Divyanka, all in their teens, stormed out of a big family gathering and took up positions on a couch. They said, 'All the women are working and the men are just sitting there. If the men don't serve the women, we refuse to eat.' They put up a big fight; their parents couldn't do anything. So I went to talk to them.

I let them speak for about half an hour. When they started to repeat themselves, I jumped in. 'You made a very good point, and it took courage. But if you get angry and walk away, no one will listen. And how much did you do? Who made the lunch? Who cooked your breakfast? Your mums. If you put your principles into practice, rather than just making this protest, a lot of people will respect you.'

In raising our children, we need to balance rights and responsibilities. If we ignore their opinions, we are failing them. But if we just praise them for standing up, without asking them to also contribute, we are turning them into desktop activists, setting them up for failure.

*

In 2022, my old friend Dr Bhampa Rai died in a Nepali hospital at the age of 72. I spoke about him both at an ABA event and one organised online by the Bhutanese community of Harrisburg, Pennsylvania. A stubborn, wonderful man, Bhampa Daju did heroic work caring for people in the camps. To his dying day he insisted on his right to go home to Bhutan. Yet those who followed his principle remain in Nepal, in just two camps containing about 6300 people, largely forgotten by the world.

In 2005, King Jigme Singye Wangchuck announced that he would abdicate in favour of his son, Jigme Khesar Namgyel Wangchuck, then 25 years old, and educated in the United States and at Oxford University. The international media again faithfully sang the older king's praises. He had promised to give up the throne as a prelude to Bhutan becoming a democracy, but progress has been mixed.

The first elections for the National Assembly, in 2008, were carefully controlled, with just two parties allowed to run. The number of parties has grown over time, and I am optimistic that democracy cannot be stopped once people have had a taste of it. The media is more open than it has ever been, and is even willing to carefully criticise the government. Yet free speech is always fragile in a monarchy. MPs, especially southerners, are very careful in parliamentary debate, lest any criticism is seen as directed against the king or royal family. Bhutanese democracy still rests on the proclaimed benevolence of the king. I believe the abdication was a strategic move: even today, the old man remains the power behind the throne. Like his father, the new king has travelled the country, consulting citizens, but he has also returned none of the properties stolen from the southerners to their rightful owners, including my family.

Lhotshampas still make up about a fifth of Bhutan's population of 800 000, down from about a third in my time. Yet many people remain stripped of their citizenship: a 2005 census classified 13 per cent of Bhutan's population as 'non-nationals'. Repression is less harsh and overt than it was. But a 2021 US State Department report on Bhutan found that some Nepali-speaking citizens still face discrimination in employment and cannot obtain police security clearances that would allow them to enrol in higher education and obtain passports, government jobs and business licences – even to move freely around their own country.

Australia could play an important role in Bhutan's future. In 2022 Bhutanese newspapers published a rush of stories about a 'mass exodus' of both students and professionals to Australia. Even the subservient government newspaper, *Kuensel*, printed an editorial entitled 'What alternatives to Australia?', in which it estimated that '50 000 Bhutanese [were] vying to leave for the southern hemisphere'. *Kuensel* said that most gave the same reason for wanting to go: 'Gokap ra mindu!' – there are no opportunities in Bhutan.

Australia provides Bhutan with more higher education scholarships than almost any other country; it is a major donor to Bhutan's development projects. Four of 11 members of Bhutan's current cabinet, including Prime Minister Lotay Tshering, studied in Australia. With such leverage, Australia could lobby Bhutan to enable resettled Bhutanese to visit relatives and friends, among other initiatives. The older generation long to see what happened to their homes and villages. The young ones want to see where they or their parents came from. None can get a visa.

The Bhutanese diaspora remains active on all these issues. The Global Bhutanese Organization, created by resettled communities in eight countries, supports education and other services in the camps. The Global Bhutanese Literature Organization works to keep our Bhutanese culture and Nepali language alive. American youth leader Suraj Budathoki and others have formed Peace Initiative Bhutan in a bid to find common ground with the Bhutanese government and people. But the continuing internment of political prisoners in Bhutan remains a huge concern: all communities in the diaspora are discussing how they can support a campaign led by Ram Karki, a Bhutanese human rights activist living in the Netherlands, for the prisoners' immediate release.

In April 2022 Suraj led a group of 17 Bhutanese-American professionals who met with US State Department officials. With these and other initiatives, I hope that a dialogue will eventually begin with Bhutan; that Saroja and I can even look forward to one day visiting the country, to sit together again in Punakha, where the two rivers meet under the mountains by the old Buddhist fortress, where we sealed our love. Yet I know that many things would not be the same. As part of its ethnic cleansing policy, the government changed the names of major places in the south from Nepali to Drukpa names. Saroja's Samchi district is now spelt Samtse, to sound more like a Drukpa word. The name of my beloved Lamidara has been entirely changed, to Mendrelgang.

I have lost touch with Thinley and other dear Bhutanese friends. Some tentative connections have been formed on social media, but for their safety we cannot be seen to be in contact. When people travel between Australia and Bhutan, I pass on my best wishes. I hope one day to start a scholarship for a young student from Lamidara. I may never get back there. But the place is always with me.

A few years ago, I had lunch with a Bhutanese official of Nepali background, with whom I had studied in Bhutan. When our conversation turned to the conflict, he parroted the government's line: nobody was evicted, the Lhotshampas left of their own accord. Not long after, the man left Bhutan and went to teach in India. I was not surprised. I thought he was miserable, unable to speak his mind. You get one life, and if you are constrained all the time, always saying what the king or any powerful person wants you to say, that's not a life worth living.

Becoming a refugee, I lost much more than this man in a material sense, but I gained in every other way. Being a senior Bhutanese official makes you snobbish. In such a small place, you are always comparing yourself to others, trying to protect your position and ego. It was a big deal to call myself head of Planning and Development in the Telecommunications Department. I flew to Japan, Spain and many other countries on government business. I had met the king. I wore the white scarf over my shoulders but I badly wanted the red scarf that was given to the highest in the kingdom. In effect, I would be knighted, and people would call me Dasho. I remember thinking: 'If someone junior to me got a red scarf and I didn't, how would I feel?'

Then, overnight, I had nothing. No title, no status, no money, no nationality. I lived in a small apartment in Kathmandu, and spent my days entreating foreign governments to pay attention to the plight of my people, usually to no avail. Yet I feel only gratitude for all that I lost and found.

The Bhutanese elders who meet every Friday in Blacktown always talk about how this country has comforts even our king did not have 20 years ago. You want your house to be warm, it is warm; you want it cool, it is cool. The elders are right. So many of us seem dissatisfied, always wanting more. Yet great wealth is only meaningful if others have less of it. If I envy my next-door neighbour for buying a Porsche, I am outsourcing my happiness to him. If I buy a Porsche and he is envious, my happiness requires his misery. And then he buys a better car, and my misery resumes!

*

Visits from Bhutanese living overseas would sometimes cause my father to brood on what he had lost in Bhutan; on his torture, and on the fact that some stranger now lived in his home. I would work hard to lift his mood. I would tell him that he had donated his property to the king; how many people could do that? I think these conversations helped my father to cope with his loss.

Overall, my parents accepted their fate and were happy in Australia. All his life my father took sugar in his tea. Not everyone in Lamidara could afford it but he stocked it in his shop. Even in the refugee camp, my siblings made sure he always had it. At my nephew's wedding in Sydney, someone serving guests asked if he wanted tea with or without sugar. My father sat back: 'In all my 85 years I have never taken tea without sugar, and you are asking me, at my grandson's wedding, if I am going to do it now?' We roared with laughter.

In Bhutan and Nepal, Dad always carried a couple of chocolates or coconut pieces in his pocket to give to kids. In Australia we said, 'Dad, you can't give sweets to children in this country. People will get upset.' A little baffled, he stopped, but he never stopped saying hello to everyone. One day he turned up with spinach seeds in his pocket. How did you get them, we asked. 'A very nice couple gave them to me. They were planting spinach, and I asked them to keep some seeds for me when the plant flowered.' That had been four months earlier. How he had managed to conduct this exchange in English I'll never know.

'Morning! Morning!' he would say to the reception staff, with a big smile and his right hand raised, as he walked into the Westmead Hospital eye clinic. 'Good morning, Mr Dhungel. How are you today?' the staff responded, smiling at him and at each other. 'Thank you,' he said, with another salute, pleased to be using two of the dozen or so English words he had picked up. After an hour or so in the packed waiting room he was called in to see the specialist, Dr Paul Mitchell, one of the finest men I have ever met, never too busy or important to give his time and warmth to an old man with no English. He would inject a fluid directly into my father's eye to slow the macular degeneration he had begun to suffer in the camp but that was diagnosed only in

Australia. It was a grim procedure – when Smriti watched it one time, she fainted – but my father bore it with good humour.

In his late eighties, he began to experience chronic pain inside his body. Unlike Mum, who had given birth to 14 children, he was not good with pain. He had trouble sleeping; he would twist and turn, get anxious, and often sit at the prayer room we created in his house. I am not one for observing many rituals, but when Saroja and I visited Char Dham, a famous temple in Sikkim in India, I called my father to say we were there, praying for him: 'Dad, we have handed over your pain and sleeping problems to God. Now you will be able to sleep.' I don't know what effect the message had on him, but for the next two years his physical problems disappeared. At the Bhutanese Sports Day, in December 2019, Dad, by then 92 years of age and the day's second-oldest competitor, just lost the seniors' 50-metre walking race to a woman 11 years his junior.

When my brother Gopal and his wife, Pabitra, rebuilt their house in Blacktown, Baa and Ama lived at our place for about three months. Every day, as we crossed the boardwalk, Ama would stand on the bridge and pose for a photo, while Baa took a seat next to the Fairwater Café to enjoy the ducks swimming in the pond. When the pandemic came, Saroja worked long hours at the hospital, analysing COVID tests, and I worked from home. In the morning, I would make my parents' bed, prepare their prayer rituals, bring flowers from the garden for their altar and get warm water for them to drink. Baa would say: 'Add a pinch of turmeric.' Before bed, he would often say, 'There is not a single day that the bed is not made well.'

In April 2021, my father was diagnosed with bowel cancer and spent eight days in hospital. After we brought him home, we decided he would never go back there. He didn't need more medical procedures; he needed love and care from his children and grandchildren. But New South Wales had gone into lockdown and under the rules, he could see only Gopal, who he lived with. So I wrote to the Ministry of Health and the police and obtained permission for Bholanath, Chandra, Tulasha and me to be able to visit him in turn.

My father was in severe pain, and very anxious if no one was around him. We didn't want him to go through chemo, but we consulted a reputable ayurvedic doctor in Delhi, who prescribed medicine to boost my father's immune system. It was delivered by courier every fortnight, since it had to be fresh. The job of mixing drops from ten or 15 bottles four times a day fell to Pabitra and her daughter Mona, aged 13. Mona did it perfectly. At times when Dad wouldn't listen to others, it was Mona who would make him drink, eat and take his medicine. I called her the chemist.

Those last months were good times. We bought my father a wheelchair. When he wasn't using it, Manish, Mona's eight-year-old brother, would ride around in it. One day, working on my laptop in the living room, I could hear Mum and Manish talking in the corner. Mum was saying, 'Manish, can you teach me how to use this?' She was almost begging him to teach her how to ride the wheelchair. Often, Mum would call Manish bekamey, a friendly word that means 'no good', when she felt he wasn't listening to her. Now he replied, 'No, you call me bekamey. I'm not teaching you.' He would not budge. The next day, after I brought Dad back home from a walk,

I said, 'Mum, it's your turn now.' She was elated as I pushed her along the creek next to the house.

My mother had changed. The first of 11 children, she had always behaved like the serious, eldest child. Now she became childlike, playful. She did yoga. At family gatherings she would get up and dance. Feeling awkward to be the first on the floor, she would whisper to a young one, 'You go and dance', so she could get up too. My sisters and brother took my mother and her sister, Nar Maya Adhikari, to a park and the two of them, aged 89 and 87, took turns on the swing, colourfully dressed, as high as kites. Dad sat there, maybe wondering, 'What's happened to this woman?'

By July, it was clear my father didn't have much time left. Again, I obtained permission from the Ministry of Health for all his children to be present when his time came. On the evening of 27 September, he ate some food, and just before nine I took him to bed and came home. Around midnight Pabitra called me: something had burst inside him; he was drenched in blood. Saroja and I rushed over, and doctors came. Gopal and I cleaned him and changed his clothes. By morning he was talking again and seemed improved. We went home, I had a shower, and Pabitra called me; she had hardly finished the sentence before Saroja and I were back in the car. He was bleeding heavily now. Our brother and sisters arrived, and Om Daju, whom my father acknowledged with a nod. At 10.30 I was massaging his chest and Om Daju his legs, with my other siblings all around. He asked for a painkiller, then fell asleep. I felt for his pulse and couldn't find it. Om Daju checked: he wasn't breathing. Apart from those bouts of bleeding, he had not suffered. He had lived to 94 – a good life and a good death. I bent down, took his hand and put it on my head. He was still wearing the ring I had put on his finger at Kathmandu airport before my departure for Australia.

Under Brahmin tradition, when a parent dies all sons and their wives, plus all daughters, must remain in his house for 13 days. Men and women cook and eat separately; they cannot touch. Under COVID rules, only ten people could attend the funeral and spend the 13 days in the house. One of our local priests, Tek Nath Nepal, husband of Om Daju's younger sister, presided over the funeral, with Om Daju as his assistant. While he is not trained as a pandit, he knows all the rituals and traditions. Once again, Om Daju, Big Om, my brother, was beside me at a vital moment in my life.

The saddest thing was that COVID rules prevented Puspa, Chandra's husband, who is a son to our parents, from being with us. In other ways, the rules were a relief. Otherwise, the house would have been packed with people, some of them holding forth about what was and wasn't allowed under Brahmin tradition, some disapproving of Saroja's presence, whispering to Mum that things weren't quite right. I would have got upset. For example, when a man dies, neither his wife nor children can take salt for 13 days. But Mum, whose health is fragile, needs salt. Many priests will say, 'Well, OK, but try for as long as possible not to take it.' That is a terrible pressure to impose on a 90-year-old woman who wants to live right and go to heaven.

After my father died, Mona moved downstairs and into my parents' room to be company for my mother. She would come home from school and start explaining to her what an amoeba was, or how this insect fertilised a flower. No one asked her to do these things; she just knew Mum needed company.

*

My mother and father taught me to take things as they come, to be grateful for everything I have. Since leaving Telstra I have made time to meditate and practise yoga every day. After I collapsed in the street that day in the Sydney CBD, I realised that if I let my mind run on autopilot my thoughts would drive me crazy. Yet I have also learnt that my strongest experiences do not come from outside but from within. I call it 'inner engineering': every day I try to simplify my life, to eat carefully and well, to sit in the morning and at night quietly feeling gratitude for all of creation: the friend I love, the apple I eat, the air I breathe.

The greatest gratitude I feel is to Saroja. She has committed her married life to looking after not only her 'two kids', as she calls Smriti and me, but my extended family as well. To repay her in a small way, I bring her tea every morning in bed. On the wall of our bedroom is a framed poster, 'Ten Rules for a Happy Marriage'.

The turmoil of our years in Bhutan and Nepal, plus the three years we spent apart, probably cost Saroja and me the chance to have more children, something we would have dearly loved. But a few years ago the old cliché came true for us: we did not lose a daughter, we gained a son.

Smriti met Sudeep Tuladhar at an Australia Day party at a friend's house. He offered to drive her to the train station; some months later, he texted her. We first met him at the airport, where he had come to see her off; she introduced him to us as a friend. His family was of Nepali heritage but lived in Darjeeling, north-east India, and he worked as a banker at ANZ after coming to Australia to study a master's in finance.

He was very polite, humble and respectful; he didn't say much, but clearly thought a lot.

In 2017, Smriti went on a retreat to Dharamsala in India. We had sensed for a while that she and Sudeep had grown close. Thinking he might be lonely, we invited him for lunch. He came with a beautiful orchid plant. That day, we knew he was right for our daughter.

After Smriti got home, she announced that Sudeep wanted to come and see us. In our culture a young man usually makes this visit accompanied by his father and a few male relatives, but in Australia Sudeep had no senior family member and he came alone. It must have been a tough night: he turned up at the door to find about 15 of my extended family all there to check him out. 'Oh, he is such a nice boy,' my father said after he left. The next day his parents called from Darjeeling, and formally asked us for our daughter's hand.

From late 2017, I closed shop and did no other work. Smriti created an online group for allocating people tasks. Life was about one thing only. Mum said, 'All this, because one girl is getting married?'

The wedding would be held on 3 March in Kalimpong, where Saroja's mother, Ama, lived and where Smriti had spent six years as a girl. In Nepali culture, there are only certain auspicious days on which a couple can marry. If they had not married in March, the next possible date was December. There would be a reception the next day in Darjeeling, three hours' drive away, and a second reception, a few weeks later, in Blacktown.

I had to battle to have it in Blacktown. Smriti had wanted it to be on the NSW south coast, where she had found a lovely venue. I said to her, 'Not in Blacktown?' Not all the old people would be able to come to the coast, and we needed their blessing. And if we held it in some commercial place, at the end of the night we'd wind up the party, pull down the decorations, stay in a hotel and come home the next day. Someone else would do everything for us. In Blacktown, everyone would pitch in, which would keep memories alive and allow people to say, 'Oh, I made the leaf plate for Smriti and Sudeep's wedding.' I doubt I could have changed her mind, but Sudeep was able to persuade her.

In Kalimpong Saroja and I met Sudeep's parents, Deepa and Jyoti, when they came for the engagement party. After the wedding, we would call them Samdini and Samdi, the relationship terms between the parents of children who marry. I liked them immediately. Sudeep and Smriti are different castes – he is Tuladhar – but no one cared. Sudeep's father Jyoti and I said, 'Let's bring elements of all three castes into the wedding.' What mattered was our children's happiness.

It rained lightly in Kalimpong the night before the wedding – an auspicious sign – and in the morning Sudeep walked shyly towards Ama's house, as people threw rice at him and others tried to shield him with umbrellas. I had made the same walk nearly 30 years before, although that time I didn't have a photographer's drone hovering overhead. I held Sudeep's hand and guided him to the mandap (a wedding pavilion), where he waited for Smriti. She arrived with a shy smile, radiant in a red sari, a red muslin veil half covering her face.

Traditionally, the reception the following day marks the moment when the bride enters the house of the groom's family, which is why the bride's parents don't go. We heard all about it: more food, more dancing, as the couple sat on a stage and 750 people walked up to them and gave the bridesmaids money in envelopes, some of them crying and saying they had waited for this day for so long. The newlyweds, who often did not know who these tearful people were, smiled 750 times.

Back in Australia, we had 20 or 30 people in our house every day. Every Bhutanese person in Sydney was invited to the wedding; nearly all of them played a role in it. We wanted to serve our sel roti on tapari, a plate made of leaves stitched together with fine bamboo sticks that is traditionally used at weddings. A man of my age, Khadga Bahadur Poudel, knew of two parks in Blacktown where you could find the right leaves. He and I went collecting, then dropped them off at the house of my 84-year-old aunt, Nar Maya Adhikari, and the houses of other elderly women who knew how to make leaf plates.

Saroja and Smriti and other close relatives and friends planned the menu: someone would do chicken, another goat, another dahl. Someone turned up at midnight, when I was in bed, and said I had to try their goat dish on the spot. At 11.30 one night, my sister Chandra asked Dad if it wasn't time to go to bed. He ostentatiously looked at his watch. 'It's my granddaughter's wedding. Why should I go to bed?'

As the day got close, Saroja's phone was buzzing, the kitchen was packed, people tramped in and out the front door with a hundred questions: 'Have the banana trunks for the wedding entrance been organised? Will the ten people sleeping in the house have blankets? Where is the hair dryer for Smriti? The photographer is here for the photo shoot – where is Uncle? Aunty, can you please taste, is it good?'. Through it all Saroja stayed supremely calm. I did not. On the Friday I almost collapsed, I was so tired. But I was excited too. Tomorrow was my daughter's wedding day.

*

At 4.30 am we open our garage, where we have installed four burners, and ten friends and family members come in, carrying pots, ready to cook. Smriti is getting made up as the sun comes up on a bright, warm Sydney day. The decoration team is panicking – they have to hang their decorations, go home and change, then race back to Bowman Hall, the Blacktown art deco landmark where Gough Whitlam launched his famous campaign in 1972 and where so many Blacktown families now hold weddings or attend citizen ceremonies and become Australian.

The day unrolls as two events: one for our friends and community in the morning, another for Smriti and Sudeep's friends in the evening. By 10.30 am, the MCs are standing at the front of Bowman Hall to greet 450 guests and usher them through the Nepali wedding gate festooned with banana leaves taken from our investment property in Blacktown. Ten people come from Saroja's work. I've invited plenty of old friends: Sarjoh Bah and Noël Zihabamwe; Susan Bannigan of the Westpac Foundation; Violet Roumeliotis of Settlement Services International; Serge Derkatch, my mentor on the MTC board; and Stephen Bali, the Blacktown MP. Everything is so well planned.

Or nearly everything. Mona, Dristi and Ashlyn, daughter of Saroja's niece Juliana Dahal, perform a lovely dance, but another does not go as planned. Saroja and I are supposed to join a dance by my niece Divyanka and Tika Bhandari, a cousin's granddaughter. We have practised our part at home. But with the MCs alternating, technical errors, things running behind schedule, commotion and confusion, it is totally missed. Divyanka and Tika are disappointed. I apologise to them.

Also, I have specifically asked for the cooking team to put on their suits after they finish, and come and eat with the other guests. But when the food is laid out so beautifully, no one is there to serve it. So one of the cooks, my cousin Dambaru Kafley, jumps up and serves and others follow. As I learnt from my African friends, no event goes wrong if it happens from the heart.

The evening crowd of about 300 is younger – a lot of people from different cultures and backgrounds, our extended family. A Pacific Islander troupe whom I know from SydWest perform a fire dance. The MCs this time are Smriti's high school friends Alison Tenoria and Crystal Pegg, who is four or five months pregnant. As people enter the main hall, Alison and Crystal announce: 'The grandparents of the bride, Mr and Mrs Dhungel!' Baa and Ama walk in together to great applause, Dad looking so tall and handsome and well-dressed, beaming at everyone, and Mum smiling and arranging her naugedi, the gold necklace worn by married women, for the photographers.

Saroja, Smriti, Sudeep and I give speeches. At the end of his speech, Sudeep turns to the cameras and surprises his mum, Deepa, who is in Darjeeling, by getting the whole crowd to sing her 'Happy Birthday'.

Near midnight things began to die down. Slowly guests walk out, thanking us. We clear the tables, collect the hired tablecloths and chair covers, mop the floor, load the car and leave.

But the night is not over. Back at our place, a big group gathers, including our nieces Kunta Koirala from Perth and Januka Sharma, with her husband Umesh, from Adelaide. For two hours we talk and laugh and drink wine and give lots of 'Cheers!' 'How good was the food? *Everyone* was talking about it.' As we sit there, my cousin Dambaru stands up, calls the room to attention, and points at me. 'What happened to the famous guidelines Daju insisted on? I had cooked all day and was just looking forward to sitting down to a lovely meal, and there was no one there to serve! The whole wedding was nearly ruined!' Everyone laughs so hard that a little while later, Dambaru stands up and tells the joke all over again.

I slump back on the couch, feeling a tide of relief. The wedding is over. Our daughter is married to a good man. I've kept my promises to my parents to always look after them, and to Ama, back in Kalimpong, to always look after Saroja. I'm sitting in my living room, drinking, laughing and telling stories with people I love. But what does 'my living room' mean? How can I call anything mine, without acknowledging all the other people who helped to make it mine?

In my early days in Australia I dreamt every day of bringing my family together under one roof. But I was in Sydney, Smriti was in India, Saroja in Nepal, my parents and youngest siblings in a refugee camp. Then one day we were all sitting together again in our living room, Bhakti Khatiwada and his musicians were singing songs that I remembered from Lamidara, and I was in tears. Not tears for what I had lost, but for all that I had gained. We had a home, a home for all of us.

At about 2 am, people leave. Others go upstairs to bed. There are five or six dirty pots and a pile of other utensils in the yard. 'Don't come over in the morning,' I tell people. 'I'll do it.'

The next day I get up early and bring Saroja tea. We sit on the bed and talk a little, but she is exhausted and wants more sleep. My mind is racing too much with thoughts of the night before, so I go into the yard and start cleaning the pots.

Shortly after, my nephew Bedanidhi turns up and joins me. Oh, here comes Gopal. Here's Puspa and Chandra; here's Uma and Paras.

I look up to see Naresh walking in, putting on rubber gloves, and grabbing the largest of the pots. We get them scrubbed in no time at all.

GRATITUDE

Human beings are interdependent – and that includes authors. This book has two authors, but ideas come from many. I want to express my gratitude to all those people who over many years have taught me and helped me to refine my ideas. Any errors or omissions of ideas or people in the book are mine.

The book wouldn't have been possible without the love, support and trust I have received from the Bhutanese community in Sydney and across Australia. I also warmly thank our countryfolk, spread across Bhutan, Nepal, India and seven other resettlement countries, whom I have had the privilege to meet. I particularly acknowledge the contribution of the teachers, doctors, nurses, health workers, volunteers and leaders who over nearly 20 years in refugee camps saved and started many lives. Our Bhutanese diaspora is strong today because of you.

This book began in a budding friendship. I met James Button, a writer and journalist, in 2020 when James was researching a long narrative on Blacktown for the Scanlon Foundation. We talked at length several times at the Two by Four café by the lake in Fairwater and created a beautiful multicultural Australia in our minds. Out of those conversations James agreed to co-write this book, which is based on many email exchanges, many long interviews via Zoom and a few late nights at our house, where James and his wife May Lam shared with us Saroja's momos and a good bottle of red.

James also drew on a draft manuscript I had written, especially in telling the story of my early life in Lamidara and the arrival of the Bhutanese in Sydney. My manuscript was at first largely a manual of refugee settlement; James pushed me to make the book much more personal. I thank James for his patience, perseverance and companionship, everything he has given to enable us to pull it together. Our task was made easier by May's valuable work to kickstart the book and provide ongoing feedback. Virginia Macleod and Louise Whelan had previously interviewed me for the Australian National Library and NSW State Library respectively, and generously allowed us to use material from those interviews in the book.

All quotations from Michael Hutt, apart from one on page 97 that comes from a conversation with me, come from his book, *Unbecoming Citizens: Culture, Nationhood, and the Flight of Refugees from Bhutan*, Oxford University Press, 2005. Michael is Emeritus Professor of Nepali and Himalayan Studies at the School of Oriental and African Studies, University of London.

Many people made this book possible. Merryn Jones (now Merryn Howell) was instrumental in my employment journey, as was Bhim Subba in my writing journey and Serge Derkatch in my board journey. Emeritus Professor Geoff Scott and Dr Debra Keenahan from Western Sydney University (WSU) provided the initial inspiration and guidance that enabled me to write my first draft manuscript, with Geoff always saying: 'Let me know if I can help'.

Other intellectual inspirations were Dr Paul Hodge from Newcastle University, Professor Jim Ife from WSU and Dr Louise Olliff from the Australian National University, and my asset-based community development colleagues Dee Brooks, Michelle Dunscombe and Fiona Miller. Jill Gillespie, then settlement services manager at ACL, showed great creativity and warmth in working with the Association of Bhutanese in Australia and her ideas about settlement have shaped mine.

For our long and deep conversations about refugee and migrant settlement over the years I thank settlement sector leaders Violet Roumeliotis, Elfa Moraitakis, Melissa Monterio, Jasmina Bajraktarevic, Esta Paschalidis-Chilas, Gail Kerr, Kamalle Dabboussy, Catherine Scarth, Shama Pande, Clement Meru, Sandra Wright, David Keegan, and Frances Rush; and community leaders Dr Bushra Al-Obaidi, Sarjoh Bah, Nalika Padmasena, Noël Zihabamwe, Assefa Bekele and Daniel Gobena. Susan Bannigan from the Westpac Foundation believed in me and helped me to probe deeper into refugee settlement in different countries.

I thank the many employers who gave me the opportunity to gain the life experience that forms the basis of this book while contributing to the wider community. I thank our fellow residents at Fairwater for all their love and support, and the smiles that we share every day.

Special thanks to Mika Tabata for her cover design, and Elspeth Menzies, Sophia Oravecz, Rosina Di Marzo, Tricia Dearborn, Joumana Awad and Josephine Pajor-Markus, NewSouth's most supportive and accommodating publishing team; the book was greatly enhanced by the suggestions and input that you all provided.

Henry Rosenbloom, Nathan Hollier, Duncan Fardon, Karen Middleton, Kit Carstairs and Catherine Moolenschot also offered guidance and advice about publishing and editing this book, as did many friends and well-wishers who always asked me: 'When will you write it?'

To Om Daju, my siblings and the extended Dhungel, Gurung and Kafley families, this is your book as much as mine. Thank you for your love and support, particularly during challenging times. I am deeply indebted to my parents Durga Prasad and Damanta Dhungel, along with Saroja's parents Ganga Prasad, Kamala and Hari Maya Gurung, who are my parents as well. Without the love and blessings of these people, I wouldn't be where I am today or have written this book.

Most importantly, to my wife Saroja and our most beautiful children – our daughter Smriti and son-in-law Sudeep – the unconditional love and support that flows through you has enabled me to see everyone as a human being first and has fuelled my passion to work for the good of humanity. I am ever grateful to you all.

Finally, to you the reader, thank you for reading this book!